"An ancient Talmudic adage warned: 'Those who are kind to the cruel will be cruel to the kind.' This law of life explains why fourteen high school students and three adults were murdered on Valentine's Day 2018 in Broward County, Florida. Max Eden and Andy Pollack, the father of one of the murdered students, have written one of the most important books on American life published in the last few years. *Why Meadow Died* is shocking, illuminating, and ultimately angering. If the media ignore this book, it will prove they put ideology above truth."

—DENNIS PRAGER, nationally syndicated radio talk show host, syndicated columnist, and *New York Times* bestselling author of, most recently, *The Rational Bible*

"This book could be titled: *Andrew Pollack vs. Broward County.* Mr. Pollack is the bold, striking colossus of Parkland politics. He deals justice with an iron fist and will likely be portrayed by Arnold Schwarzenegger when the movie version of this book is inevitably made."

—CAMERON KASKY, Co-Founder of March For Our Lives

"*Why Meadow Died* is a Shakespearean tragedy set in a public school system. The dark truths about our society and ourselves that shine through may be painful, but parents can't afford not to confront them. Moms: read this book like your child's life depends on it. It just might."

—NICOLE LANDERS, Mom, Nurse, Founder Parent2Parent Network

"Every teacher in America should read *Why Meadow Died,* because as Pollack and Eden show, the policies responsible for the Parkland tragedy have spread across America. School administrators across the country are rewarded for not enforcing the rules, which leads to a thousand tragedies a day that go unrecorded. Public education is headed down a dark path, and this book should be a wakeup call to teachers and parents across the country."

—JUDY KIDD, President, Classroom Teachers Association of North Carolina

"After the Parkland shooting, media attention devoted far more attention to the model of gun used than to the role the school may have played in making this tragedy possible. Max Eden and Andrew Pollack refused to leave it at that, calling out the troubling failures of the Broward County School District, which seems to have, at times, been more intent on buffing its public image than on giving the community answers and keeping children safe. Given that the disciplinary practices in question were hailed as a national model by many in public education, *Why Meadow Died* is a timely and bracing contribution."

—FREDERICK M. HESS, Director of Education Policy Studies, American Enterprise Institute

WHY
MEADOW
DIED

WHY MEADOW DIED

THE PEOPLE AND POLICIES THAT CREATED THE PARKLAND SHOOTER AND ENDANGER AMERICA'S STUDENTS

ANDREW POLLACK AND **MAX EDEN**

A POST HILL PRESS BOOK

Why Meadow Died:
The People and Policies That Created The Parkland Shooter
and Endanger America's Students
© 2019 by Andrew Pollack and Max Eden
All Rights Reserved

ISBN: 978-1-64293-219-5
ISBN (eBook): 978-1-64293-220-1

Cover art by Cody Corcoran
Interior design and composition, Greg Johnson, Textbook Perfect

This is a work of nonfiction. All people, locations, events, and
situations are portrayed to the best of the authors' memory.

Post Hill Press
New York • Nashville
posthillpress.com

Published in the United States of America

For Meadow

The victims and their families
and everyone we pray will never join us

Contents

Foreword

"My Sister"

I was sitting in class on February 14, 2018, when I got a call that there was a shooting at Marjory Stoneman Douglas High School, where my little sister, Meadow, was a senior. I called her, but she didn't answer. I ran to my car and drove six hours from Florida State University to Parkland. The whole way back home, I kept hoping that the next minute, the next mile, she would call me back.

How can I possibly tell you about Meadow? My sister was as close to perfect as someone can be. She was beautiful, ambitious, and smart. She was my best friend. She would always ask me to take her to the gym to teach her how to work out and train. She would text me before all my exams to make sure I was studying. She would ask me to spend time with her during the holidays, but a lot of the time I chose to work instead.

Meadow didn't have a selfish bone in her body. She was so caring. She was so kind. She loved our cats, Lola and Fiona, and took care of our puppies, Sonny and Bear. And she'd also take care of me. Whenever I needed comfort, she was there. Whenever I needed encouragement, she was there.

Now she is my screen saver.

I am not good with expressing emotion in writing. But I want to give you a sense of who she was. So, I will do something that she would kill me for if she were alive: show you her diary.

Here is what she wrote about me: "My brother is more than just a brother to me, he is my diary, my guidance of how family should be, and my best friend. If anyone is over protective over me, it's definitely him. Personally, I look up to him in a variety of ways."

Here is what she wrote about her boyfriend, Brandon: "I met my soulmate freshmen year and we instantly clicked. Currently I've never been happier and I couldn't ask for a better friend, shoulder to lean on, and therapist. I'm looking forward to our life together and I can't wait to see what's in store for the future."

Here is what she wrote about our mom: "My mom is everything to me and more. She is my light in a dark room, my sun on a stormy day, and most importantly she's my inspiration."

Here is what she was thinking about college: "Lucky me, I already applied and got accepted into the school I would really love to attend. Visiting Lynn University's campus impressed me beyond belief. I'm beyond excited to start this journey and new chapter in my life. Building my career at Lynn University is more than I could ever ask for. After college I'm thinking about starting a family, kids, a husband, my own car, and my own house... it's all so exciting."

And here is what she said about her future: "Thinking about the future can be very scary. I think about happiness, success, and simply living life to the fullest. What I'm most excited for isn't just the family I will make and the career I will have but the life I will live in terms of reaching for the stars."

What can you do when someone like that can't have that future? When your baby sister is ripped away from you? For my dad and me, the only thing we could do was try to find answers and get justice.

After my sister Meadow was murdered at Marjory Stoneman Douglas High School, the media obsessed for months about the type of rifle the killer used. It was all clickbait and politics, not answers or justice. That wasn't good enough for us. My dad is a real tough guy, but Meadow had him wrapped around her little finger. He would do anything she wanted, and she would want him to find every answer so that this never happens again.

My dad teamed up with one of America's leading education experts to launch his own investigation. We found the answers to the questions the media refused to ask. Questions about school safety that go far beyond the national gun debate. And the answers to those questions matter for parents, teachers, and schoolchildren nationwide.

If one single adult in the Broward County school district had made one responsible decision about the Parkland shooter, then my sister would still be alive. But every bad decision they made makes total sense once you understand the district's politically correct policies, which started here in Broward and have spread to thousands of schools across America.

—*Hunter Pollack*

Preface

"Daddy, Keep Going"

This book is in your hands because I don't want you—or anyone—to feel the way I feel. After my daughter Meadow was murdered on Valentine's Day 2018 at Marjory Stoneman Douglas High School, I wanted answers. At first, I thought getting those answers might help me come to terms with losing her. It didn't. But my hope is that what I've learned will at least help you keep your kids safe.

In ways I never could have imagined, what happened here matters far beyond the city limits of Parkland, Florida. That's because the Broward County school district was ground zero for a dangerous new approach to school safety that has taken root nationwide. I teamed up with my friend Max Eden, a nationally renowned education policy expert, to write this book in order to help parents understand what's really going on in our schools.

Before Meadow was murdered, I never paid much attention to what was happening at her school. Why should I have? Who really does?

I had a great life. I had provided a solid middle-class upbringing for my three kids, Huck, Hunter, and Meadow. I never went to college, but I did pretty well in business. Back in New York, where I grew up, I built a great scrap metal company. Then, when I moved down to Florida, I got into real estate. I raised my kids in Parkland and gave them everything I could.

I almost got wiped out when the housing bubble burst, and at the same time I went through a bad divorce. I thought that was the darkest time I'd ever go through. But I rebuilt my life. I remarried. My second wife, Julie, is a brilliant, kind, and wonderful woman. Business was good again. I hit the gym twice a day. My two boys were in college, and Meadow was a few months away from graduating high school and going to college herself. I was ready to ride off into the sunset. Literally. I was planning to sell my house and take my truck and RV across the country to be closer to Julie's family in Northern California. Maybe I'd buy a little ranch up there.

On February 14, 2018, Julie and I put our bikes on the back of our truck, packed a picnic, and drove out to the Everglades. There's a great bike loop out there, and you can see alligators and all sorts of wildlife. Halfway through the loop, I got a text from my son Huck saying there were shots fired at Meadow's school. At first, I thought maybe it was fireworks and someone just thought the sound was gunshots. But then I got more calls saying it was a shooting. Still, I tried to rationalize it: It can't be *my* daughter. What are the odds? It just *can't* be Meadow. But Julie and I blew through every red light to get back to Parkland.

When I got to Marjory Stoneman Douglas, Huck was already there with his mom. They couldn't find Meadow. Julie and I decided to check the trauma centers. She's an ER doctor, and we thought maybe Meadow was in surgery. We tailed an ambulance and police cars to the nearest hospital. When we got there, Julie went inside. I stayed outside talking to the police officers. They told me that Nikolas Cruz was in the ambulance that I had followed. I didn't realize at the time what that meant: I had seen my daughter's murderer get wheeled into the hospital on a stretcher.

Julie couldn't find Meadow, so we decided to try another hospital. We were about to leave when a reporter approached our truck. I showed him a picture of Meadow on my phone and he took a picture of us. That morning, I had thrown on the T-shirt on the top of the clean laundry pile for the bike ride. It happened to be a Donald Trump campaign T-shirt. The photo made the news, and in the next few days I got so much hatred on social media saying I deserved to have my daughter murdered because I support the president of the United States. Some people are really sick.

On our way to the second hospital, someone called Julie saying Meadow was in surgery. I remember wishing that she wasn't. Now I wish she had been. But she wasn't at that hospital or any others. Hours passed and it started to hit me that she was dead. Other families who couldn't find their children went to a Marriott hotel to wait for news. But I couldn't bear to go there. I knew that the police would find me when the time came. And at 2:15 a.m., they did. They told me what I already knew, but part of me still can't believe.

Meadow was my princess. So sweet, but so tough. She could be like a supermodel one day and then go off-roading with the boys the next. She was just an all-American girl. Family meant everything to her. She had been dating her boyfriend, Brandon, for three years. He's like another son to me now.

Meadow lit up every room. So many people told me after her death how kind she had been to them. If she saw a new kid at school, she would welcome them, show them around, and introduce them to people she thought they might like. She was sweet like that.

You know, Meadow's brothers always wanted to protect her. But a lot of the time, she was the one protecting them. Out of all my kids, she was the one who was most like me. I had to be careful around her because if she wanted something, she'd *always* get it. And ever since the shooting, she's been on my shoulder saying, "Daddy, keep going." She wants me to find all the answers, expose everything that led to her murder, and dedicate my life to ensuring that what happened to her doesn't happen to other kids.

One week after the shooting, I flew up to Washington, D.C. for a listening session at the White House. When I took the microphone to share my thoughts with President Trump, I spoke from the heart:

> *I'm here because my daughter has no voice. She was murdered last week. She was taken from us. Shot nine times on the third floor. We, as a country, failed our children.... Everyone has to come together as a country, not different parties, and figure out how we protect the schools. It's simple. It's not difficult. 9/11 happened once and they*

fixed everything. We protect airports, we protect concerts, stadiums, embassies....

How many schools, how many children have to get shot? There should have been one school shooting and we should have fixed it! And I'm pissed! Because my daughter—I'm never going to see again. It stops here with this administration and me. I'm not going to sleep until it's fixed. And, Mr. President, we're going to fix it.... We all work together and come up with the right idea, and it's school safety.

After that listening session, Trump asked to meet with my family and me. My son Hunter wore a Jewish yarmulke to the Oval Office to represent the strength of our people. I was so proud of him for that. We talked with the president about what happened and what we could do to make schools safe again.

I urged the president to form a national commission on school safety to study the problems and propose solutions. He nodded, then pointed his finger at Hope Hicks, the White House communications director, and said, "I like that. I want to do that." And he did.

The president also told me about some bills in Congress that could help. A few other dads and I went to Congress and lobbied hard for those bills to become law. We got Congress to pass the Fix NICS (National Instant Criminal Background Check System) Act to improve the background checks for gun purchases. (The background check system played no role in what happened at Parkland, for reasons that I'll explain later, but this law could help keep guns out of the hands of other criminals.) We also got Congress to pass the STOP School Violence Act to provide funding and training to improve school safety across the country. Maybe that act could have prevented this shooting. I believe it will prevent others.

Then I went to Tallahassee to lobby the Florida Legislature to pass the Marjory Stoneman Douglas High School Public Safety Act. You'd think that, after a tragedy like this, our politicians could come together for once. But it was hard for them. Republicans didn't like the bill because it had the strongest gun control provisions Florida had ever seen. Democrats didn't like it because of the Coach Aaron Feis Guardian Program. Coach Feis died that day rushing at the shooter with his bare hands. The Guardian Program provides funding for schools to have highly trained armed guards. Because if Aaron had been armed, Meadow would be alive.

I also wanted to do something sweet to honor Meadow, so I started raising money to build a playground in memory of her and the sixteen other victims. Somewhere I can go instead of the cemetery to feel like I'm with my daughter, a place where I can see kids laughing and playing like she used to laugh and play. I organized a motorcycle ride, the Ride for Meadow, and other fundraisers and ended up raising half a million dollars to build Princess Meadow's Playground.

But I wasn't going to stop fighting for school safety after getting a few laws passed. I founded a nonprofit: Americans for Children's Lives and School Safety (CLASS). I use it as a platform to influence legislators and school leaders to #Fixit by adopting policies that make our schools safer. I also went to the March For Our Lives gun control rally on March 24, 2018, in Washington, D.C. The organizers told my son Hunter that he could give a speech. It was such a beautiful speech. Here's part of it:

> The hatred and sickness that fuels a killer to kill innocent students is something most of us will never understand. But that doesn't mean it's something we can ignore. We need to be on a mission to stop these monsters before they take action inside our school. We must demand our leaders to help those who are sick. But we must also demand that they protect those of us that are not....
>
> To my sister who is up there in heaven, I promise you that my dad and I who are here along with millions of people at our side will do our part at making schools safe so that this never happens again. We vow to protect America's children. We will keep them safe from the killers and all the weapons they use. Until we meet again, Meadow. I miss you like crazy. I love you. We all love you. May you shine on us today and every day going forward.

But after the Hollywood producer running the event read Hunter's speech, she decided that they didn't have room for it in "the show." You see the problem they had with it, don't you? It was about more than just guns. You have no idea how painful it was for Hunter.

I don't blame the March For Our Lives student activists for that. That's on the adult organizers behind the scenes, the same people who weaponized the tragedy to stoke controversy and division and to advance their political agenda. If you tried to talk about anything other than gun control, anything that Americans might actually agree on, they'd attack you. When I tried saying, "Hey, the shooter walked through an unlocked gate. Maybe we can talk about making sure school gates are locked when they're supposed to be," people called me a shill for the National Rifle Association.

If the shooter had acquired his gun through a legal loophole, or if a background check had failed and there was some NRA connection to what happened, I would have gone after the NRA. Hard. But when 18-1958 (I don't like to say his name, so I usually call him by his prison number) bought his guns, he had a totally clean record. On paper, he was a model citizen. In reality, he was a psychopathic felon. Our laws already say that psychopaths and felons can't buy guns. But he was never institutionalized. He was never arrested. And maybe most important of all: he was never really *helped*.

I wanted to know everything about why the shooting happened, so I launched an investigation. The more I learned, the less I could believe how much incompetence there was.

I truly mean that. It didn't even make sense how everyone in Broward County could have been so incompetent. But eventually I figured out the explanation: political correctness.

You could write several books about the failures that enabled my daughter's murder. You could write a book about the police and how their politically correct policy to reduce juvenile arrests allowed 18-1958 to keep a clean record despite forty-five police visits to his home. You could write a book about the mental health authorities and how they refused to institutionalize him three different times—when he was suicidal, threatening to kill, and obsessed with buying a gun—in the name of "civil liberty."

This book is about the Broward County school district. It might sound strange to point a finger at the schools. After all, when people think of schools, they think about caring teachers who want to do right by kids. But teachers don't have much power anymore. They report to their principals, who report to district bureaucrats and superintendents. In theory, superintendents report to locally elected school boards that are accountable to citizens. But citizens don't have much power over our schools anymore either.

Instead, school superintendents follow orders and cues from federal bureaucrats and social justice activist groups. Those folks view students and schools as statistics on a spreadsheet. They slice every data set by students' race, income, and disability status, and then blame every inequality on teachers. They view schools as laboratories for social justice engineering and force politically correct policies into our schools based on the assumption that teachers are too prejudiced to be trusted do the right things.

One policy is known as "discipline reform" or "restorative justice." Activists and bureaucrats saw that minority students were being disciplined at higher rates than white students, and rather than recognize that misbehavior might reflect bigger problems and inequities outside of school, they blamed teachers for the disparity. They essentially accused teachers of racism and sought to prevent teachers from enforcing consequences for bad behavior. They thought that if students didn't get disciplined at school, if instead teachers did "healing circles" with them or something, then students wouldn't get in trouble in the real world. Superintendents then started pressuring principals to lower the number of suspensions, expulsions, and school-based arrests. All that actually happened was that everyone looked the other way or swept disturbing behavior under the rug, making our schools more dangerous.

Nationwide, this pressure to reduce discipline is especially strong when it comes to students with disabilities. The bureaucrats and activists think that teachers unfairly discipline them as well. In truth, most students with disabilities are disciplined less often than their peers. The exception is students with "emotional and behavioral" disabilities, which is a blanket label for students who frequently behave very badly. 18–1958 was one of those kids. The ridiculous thing is that principals are pressured to punish kids who behave badly at the same rate as students who behave well. Principals also face pressure to educate students with disabilities in the "least restrictive environment" possible. It sounds nice in theory. But it means pushing troubled kids into normal classrooms rather than giving them the specialized services they need to actually address their issues.

Kids with severe behavior problems are forced into classrooms where they don't belong, and principals have a strong reason to ignore their misbehavior. This is great for superintendents, who can advance their careers on manipulated statistics. It is fine for principals, who get rewarded for not documenting problems so that their school's data looks good.

It is bad for teachers, but they have little say. It's worse for regular students, but they have even less. And it's the worst for the troubled and disturbed students, who have the least say of all. This is what happened to 18–1958, and it is why the Parkland massacre happened.

His entire life, 18–1958 was practically screaming, "If you ignore me, I could become a mass murderer." At every critical point in his life, the adults in the school system had a choice: do the obviously responsible thing, or do the easy thing that's encouraged by these policies. They did the latter every time. Parkland was the most avoidable mass shooting in American history. 18–1958 was never going to be a model citizen, but it truly took a village to raise him into a school shooter. I can't even say *he* killed my daughter. *They* killed my daughter.

18–1958's story is so bad that, after I learned everything that I'll share with you in this book, I approached his defense attorney. I said, "Give me all of his education documents and I'll testify as a witness for the defense about how the system failed him." I understand that this might sound crazy. This psychopath murdered my daughter, and I firmly believe in the death penalty. But the most important thing is that America learns from what happened so that this never happens again.

Right after the tragedy, people started raising questions about the role that the Broward County school district's disciplinary leniency policies might have played. Broward had launched the PROMISE program to dramatically decrease student arrests. Students told the media after the tragedy that 18–1958 had committed all sorts of crimes in school without consequence. If he'd been arrested, he could have been prohibited from buying a gun. Or maybe an arrest would have made the FBI follow up on, rather than drop, tips that 18–1958 might shoot up the school. This seemed like an issue worth investigating.

But Broward County Public Schools superintendent Robert Runcie called me and others "reprehensible" for even asking it. First, he said there was no connection whatsoever between PROMISE and the shooter. Then, I guess after someone on his staff actually looked at 18–1958's school records, Runcie said that he "had never been referred to the PROMISE program nor committed a PROMISE-eligible offense *while in high school*." (Emphasis added.) Then he called the whole question "fake news."

Runcie went to Harvard, so I'm sure he thinks he's clever. Me, I barely graduated high school. But I knew that if he was saying "while in high school," it meant that 18–1958 was sent to PROMISE *while in middle school*. Months later, a reporter proved that. The reporter also revealed that 18–1958 never actually attended the program, but the district didn't follow up on his absence and couldn't explain what had happened. The media called this a "shocking revelation." But I knew it.

The fact that 18–1958 had been referred to PROMISE once isn't that important in itself. Runcie could have told the whole truth rather than telling a half-truth (or just not looking into it) and then labeling grieving families as "fake news" mongers. But the morning after the tragedy, he blamed the gun, maybe expecting that the media would be content to leave it at that. And they were.

But I wasn't about to let anyone off the hook. Now that I've investigated, I think I have a pretty good idea why the school district didn't tell the full truth. Part of it has to do with this culture of pathological unaccountability within the Broward County school district. For a bureaucrat like Runcie pushing a social justice policy, the very idea of accountability became politically incorrect.

But more of it, I think, is the fact that these discipline policies had made Runcie a national star and transformed American education. President Barack Obama's Secretary of Education, Arne Duncan, who was Runcie's boss back when they both worked in the Chicago Public Schools, forced hundreds of school districts serving millions of students to adopt Runcie's discipline policies. Thousands more districts serving millions more students adopted the policies because of pressure from other bureaucrats or because the policies were the new politically correct thing to do. And that's why what happened here matters far beyond Parkland: the policies and the culture that enabled my daughter's murder have probably come to your child's school.

I wrote this book with my good friend Max Eden, whom I met when he traveled to Parkland to investigate what went wrong in our schools. Max is a senior fellow in education policy at the Manhattan Institute, a think tank, and he originally thought maybe he'd just write an article. But when I met him, I told him that he should work with me on my investigation. After his second trip here, he told me the investigation had to become a book. I replied, "Let's do it together."

Max is a policy and ideas guy. I'm a business and people guy. I told him that if we were going to get readers to truly understand the policies and the ideas, we had to tell the story through people. A lot of this book is told through the team of total strangers that came together in the wake of the tragedy to uncover information that the school district was trying to hide. After your daughter is murdered at school, the last thing you might expect is a cover-up. But there was one in Broward County. I can't say the cover-up was worse than the crime, because nothing could have been worse than this crime. But it was bad.

This book has four parts. The first part, "Picking Up the Pieces," tells the stories of my new friends as they grappled with this tragedy and gravitated toward my mission to expose everything. You'll meet Kim, a Marjory Stoneman Douglas (MSD) teacher who kept all her students alive during the shooting and wants to speak out about what happened, even if it means losing her job. You'll meet Royer, who came to the United States from Venezuela to keep his kids safe, only for his son Anthony to be shot five times in school (and, incredibly, survive). Royer was one of the first people to point a finger at the school district. You'll meet Max and read about how his work in education policy brought him to Parkland. And you'll meet Kenny, the student journalist who managed to expose more of what went wrong in Broward than the entire American press corps.

The second part, "Cruz Control," is the only part of the book where I'll use the killer's name. Because his story needs to be told. It must be remembered and repeated as a cautionary tale of what can happen when everyone in a school system has an incentive to do the wrong thing. The reason he murdered my daughter and sixteen other people was that the system around him was even sicker than he was.

When you read the killer's story, you might find it almost unbelievable. But maybe the most unbelievable part is that every wrong decision actually makes sense given the school district's policies.

In the third part of the book, "The Politically Correct School District," we take a deeper dive into Broward schools. You'll read about the discipline policies and the PROMISE program. You'll learn about how school administrators responded to pressure from school district bureaucrats by sweeping problems under the rug to make themselves look good. Then, when anyone questioned them, these bureaucrats hid behind political correctness and accused critics of racism. Even though these policies are doing terrible damage to minority students. Even though we were asking those questions because our children were murdered.

And the fourth part is about our "Fight to #Fixit." We ran Richard Mendelson, a former teacher at MSD, as a school board candidate. We recruited over two hundred volunteers and knocked on over thirty thousand doors. We explained to voters how the school district had failed, covered up its failure, and was still not taking school safety seriously. We fought hard to elect someone who would fight for accountability and change. I don't think America has ever seen a school board race like it.

This book is about exposing what went wrong in the schools so that parents across the country can learn from the MSD tragedy, find out what's happening in their own kids' schools, and keep their kids safe. School safety shouldn't have to be political. But I will say this: If, after the most avoidable school shooting in American history, leaders aren't held accountable and lessons aren't learned; if the idea that leaders should be held accountable or lessons should be learned has become politically incorrect; and if a school shooting is only permitted to become a partisan issue that divides our country further, then society is basically over.

I want you to read this book, to learn, to think for yourself, and then to take action to make our schools safe again. Because whatever you think about me or my politics, this isn't really my book. It's the story of how a group of strangers came together to figure out why this tragedy happened and do something about it. And above all, this is Meadow's story. Because she'll never have her own story after high school. A sick psychopath, created by a sicker system, took her from us. But Meadow was smart. She was tough. She was always willing to call out bullshit, and she'd *always* get what she wanted. She's still on my shoulder saying, "Daddy, keep going."

Meadow wants me to expose everything. And she wants us to #Fixit.

—Andy Pollack

PART I

Picking Up the Pieces

In the first part of this book, I'll tell you the stories of a few members of my team in the wake of this tragedy. Max's chapter in this part is written in the first person, and I have a chapter in the first person in Part 4, but most of this book is written in the third person. Because it was a team effort and I want you to see their stories, their experiences, and their insights into the school system. I know I couldn't have understood it all without them.

—Andy

CHAPTER I

A Teacher Survivor

Today is Thursday, February 15. My name is Kimberly Krawczyk. I am a math teacher at Marjory Stoneman Douglas High School. I am at home. My son is at home. I am safe.

Today is Friday, February 16. My name is Kimberly Krawczyk. I am a math teacher at Marjory Stoneman Douglas High School. I am at home. My son is at home. I am safe.

Today is Saturday, February 17. My name is Kimberly Krawczyk. I am a math teacher at Marjory Stoneman Douglas High School. I am at home. My son is at home. I am safe.

Every morning after Valentine's Day, Kim recited these basic facts as she rose from her bed. Her son Matthew, a high school senior, had picked her up from school after the shooting. She had been teaching on the third floor of Building 12, the site of the massacre. The shooter stopped to reload right outside her classroom door. Kim kept all of her students in her room, behind cover, quiet, and alive. Then she walked them over six dead bodies on the way out of the school. In the days that followed, whenever she became disoriented from the trauma, she would recite who she was, where she was, and what she was doing.

She went to a funeral. She went home. She went to a funeral. She went home. She tried to go to every service. But she couldn't manage it.

Kim expected a call from the school district offering mental health counseling. After three days went by without a call, Kim's family urged her to seek care. Her brother drove her to the temporary trauma treatment center at the Parkland's Pine Trails Park. But there, she was told that the school district's Employee Assistance Program didn't have any available appointments. A staff member pointed her to a Fort Lauderdale provider, but that provider told her they didn't have evening appointments to fit her schedule. She went home, untreated. Three days later, someone from employee assistance called. They still had no appointments but wanted to ask whether she was "taking care" of herself.

"I'm trying," Kim said. "You know, Scott Beigel was across the hall and the first one I saw when I walked out of my classroom."

"Oh," the man said. "Should we have someone contact him? We don't have him on our list."

"He's dead."

The man fumbled an apology and told Kim they'd call when an appointment opened up. She didn't hear from employee assistance again for three months.

On Monday, February 19, Kim sent an email of gratitude to her former principal at Coral Glades High School, Mike Ramirez. Ramirez was now a "cadre director" overseeing several high schools, including Marjory Stoneman Douglas. Back in 2012, right after the Sandy Hook Elementary School shooting in Newtown, Connecticut, Ramirez granted a request from the Coral Springs Police Department to do an active shooter drill at Coral Glades High. Blanks were fired, the hallway was filled with smoke, the fire alarm went off, and recordings were played of students begging to be let into teachers' classrooms.

On Valentine's Day, Kim knew what was happening because she had *experienced* it in that drill. That's the reason why she, unlike some other third-floor teachers in Building 12, refused to let her students leave the classroom when the fire alarm went off. That's how she kept them all alive. She wrote:

4

I just wanted to say thank you for putting us through the live action drill at Glades. I'm room 1257 and for at least 3 minutes I thought it was the same drill and was able to be calm and think clearly. There are a lot of "B" words to describe me. Brave is not one of them.... Thank you again from the bottom of my heart and from my family. Be strong. I will continue to pray for all of us.[1]

Ramirez called her and they exchanged words of encouragement and support. He asked Kim if she needed anything. Kim told him she would be fine and that employee assistance would call her back soon. (She didn't realize yet that they wouldn't.)

Before hanging up, Kim said, "Mike, it's not going to happen right now. But when I get all of my marbles back, I am coming for the Broward County school district. I'm coming for everyone. Because I want answers."

Ramirez responded, "I'm sure you're going to do whatever you have to do. But just understand that there were a lot of things involved in this."

"Yeah, Mike. I bet."

She thanked him again and said goodbye.

Kim 1.0

The old Kim would not have put her foot down like that. The old Kim didn't truly believe that her opinions were worth listening to or that her questions deserved answers.

Kimberly Kehoe married another Polish Catholic Michigander, Tom Krawczyk, when she was a junior at the University of Michigan-Dearborn. Kim dreamed of being a middle school math teacher, but Tom told her that a pretty 5"1' blonde wouldn't be safe teaching in Detroit. She told him she'd be fine, but he insisted she wouldn't be. She reluctantly gave up teaching and switched majors to mechanical engineering.

Shortly before graduation in 1990, Kim was thrilled to receive an internship offer to do computer-aided design with a company that made tools for car factories. If she did well, she could be offered a full-time job. But Tom told her to reject the offer. After all, he asked, did she really think she got the internship because of her skills rather than her looks?

Kim's confidence, already shaky after giving up her first dream of becoming a teacher, was now shattered. She declined the internship and settled in as a housewife. Kim and Tom had two sons, and they both needed her. Tom needed her. Her extended family needed her. Her son's preschool loved having her as a volunteer. Her life was, in a word, nice.

But in 2003, Tom moved the family to Florida for a new job. Her sons were old enough to attend school full time. Her extended family was back in Michigan. She had no community. She was home alone every day and getting restless. She began volunteering at her older son Steven's elementary school. After a few weeks, Steven's teacher said, "You're great with kids. Have you thought about becoming a teacher?"

Yes, in fact, she had!

Kim sent her resume to the Florida Department of Education. She figured she could be a substitute teacher or a teacher's aide. But the Department of Education called and said they would give her a temporary teaching certification to teach math. A few months later, Kim received a call: Coral Glades High School had just opened, and would she be interested in interviewing to teach there? Yes!

She aced the interview and was hired on the spot. Being a teacher changed Kim. Students looked up to her. Colleagues told her that she was smart. They asked for her opinion on topics ranging from curriculum design to politics. She was thirty-six years old, but this respect and appreciation was totally new. And it was life-changing. She always took political cues from her conservative husband and his family, but new, more liberal arguments, especially about female empowerment, started making more sense to her.

Kim vowed to herself that she'd never again be anyone's doormat. She resolved to always speak up for what she thought was right and advocate for herself and others. She became a new woman: Kim 2.0 was bold, brash, and maybe (as she put it) some other B-words too. The change ended up breaking her unhappy marriage. But Kim had finally come into her own.

"I Told Them I Was Joking…"

Kim fell in love with teaching, but by 2015 she'd had it with the Broward County school district. Over the past ten years she had watched

6

standards, both behavioral and academic, steadily decline. Every new federal law, state mandate, and district policy seemed to presume that teachers didn't know what they were doing and needed to be micro-managed and second-guessed.

Kim's concerns were hardly uncommon. Her colleagues felt like their school administrators were becoming more condescending and controlling in order to produce better "outcome statistics" for central office bureaucrats. And the fastest way to produce better numbers was to lower standards. In the spring of 2012, Kim thought that Coral Glades had finally hit rock bottom when the valedictorian gave his commence-ment speech, walked off the podium, and tweeted, "Got caught drinking at school twice, spoke anyway!"

But, to Kim's dismay, the decline only accelerated.

In 2013, Broward County Public Schools superintendent Robert Runcie launched the PROMISE program, which made him a national education superstar. The PROMISE program was the cornerstone of Broward's new disciplinary leniency policies. Runcie sought to fight the so-called "schoolhouse-to-jailhouse pipeline" by lowering suspen-sions, expulsions, and arrests. He made it harder to suspend and expel and arrest students, and as those discipline statistics plummeted, Runcie's star rose.[2]

But Kim was becoming increasingly exasperated. Behavior hadn't magically improved. Administrators were just sweeping problems under the rug. The notion that not enforcing rules would keep students on the right path struck Kim as bonkers, and she saw the damage first-hand. Under the PROMISE program, the penalty for drug use decreased from a lengthy stint in an alternative school and the threat of expulsion to three days at an alternative school. Before PROMISE, the serious consequence for drug use helped get kids back on track. But now, facing only a slap on the wrist, many more students were sliding down the path toward addiction.

Kim saw bullying rise because teachers no longer had the authority to police it. Before, teachers could immediately send a student to the assistant principal's office for misbehavior. But now, they had to fill out extensive paperwork first. And if they still sent a student to the office, teachers found that administrators were more likely to blame rather than support them.

The last straw for Kim at Coral Glades came in the spring of 2015. She had called a student's parents about his behavior, and the next day the student said, "You try calling my dad again, Ms. K, and you just see what happens next." Kim would not stand for that kind of threat. She sent him to the office. But, five minutes later, he was back.

"What are you doing back here?" Kim demanded.

"I told them I was joking. They told me it was fine," he said with a smirk.

If that was how administrators would treat her, she was done. Kim mailed her letter of resignation to the school board and sent dozens of applications to companies that could put her math talent to good use. But with two kids to provide for, she couldn't risk being unemployed for very long. She applied to a couple of teaching jobs just in case—outside the Broward County school district.

The Astrologer

A week after Kim sent her letter of resignation, her friend Terry Sutton told her about a Hindu Vedic astrologer she'd just consulted. This wasn't fluff, Terry assured her. Shivanan, a professional astrophysicist who offers astrology readings as a hobby, was eerily spot-on. Kim didn't always take stuff like this seriously, but she is a firm believer that there is no such thing as a cosmic accident. If her friend recommended this astrologer at this crossroads in her life, she had to check him out. Kim emailed Shivanan her birth name, birthplace, and birth date. A week later, he sent Kim her reading. It *was* spot-on. But he wanted to talk on the phone, he said, because some of what he saw alarmed him.

"So, tell me," Kim asked. "Am I finally getting out of education?"

"No," he laughed. "Not for a while, at least."

Then he asked, "Have you ever gotten into a fight at work?"

"No, not really."

"Have you ever been shot?"

"No."

"Well, have you ever been shot *at*?"

"No."

"Have you ever lost a child?"

"No."

"Okay. Well, have you ever been attacked by a dog?"

"No."

"Have you ever been surrounded by a pack of dogs?"

"No."

"I'm seeing you surrounded by dogs. It's not a good situation. You should be very, very careful around animals. Especially dogs."

"Okay."

"I don't know exactly what I'm seeing, Kim. But it's not good."

"Okay..."

"Also, are you involved in politics?"

"No, not really."

"I see you working with politicians. You are going to make a very big difference."

"Okay..."

After the astrology reading, Kim felt let down by the conversation, which seemed to have no relevance to her life. But Shivanan's first assertion was soon proven true: She stayed in education. Kim received an offer to teach Advanced Placement math at nearby Pembroke Pines Charter School. She would be teaching the district's smartest kids at a school that actually enforced a code of conduct. She spent two happy years there, but in the spring of 2017, she got a call from Jeff Morford, a former colleague at Coral Glades who was now an assistant principal at Marjory Stoneman Douglas High School. He asked whether she would be interested in joining MSD's math department.

Kim had sworn that she was done with Broward schools. But MSD was the best high school in Broward, with three thousand students who were predominantly upper-middle-class and high-achieving. MSD's math department had won five national competitions! MSD also had the best marching band in the state, the best baseball team in the state, and sent a host of students to Ivy League colleges every year. What's more, MSD would pay substantially more than Pembroke Pines could. She accepted the job and started in August 2017, six months before the tragedy.

Five days after the massacre, Kim sent Shivanan a Facebook message.

I am not sure if you remember me…. When you did my reading you asked if I had ever been shot. Good news: I can still answer no, but I came much closer than I ever wanted to. I work at Stoneman Douglas on the 3rd floor. I wanted you to know that I am ok and I carry your words with me every day. Thank you for your warnings. They give me strength and guidance. God bless you and your family.

He replied, "I do remember you and I asked [Terry] about you. Then I read on Facebook that you were ok. God bless you."

"He asked about me after the shooting?" Kim thought. "I never even told him where I lived…"

Kim called Terry after her first day back at school. Terry said, "At least you don't have to worry about being shot anymore. Though I guess you should be even more afraid of dogs, right?"

"I don't think so!" Kim said. "I think he saw the comfort animals! When I went back to school today, I walked straight past a horse with '#MSD' painted on its ass, then past a pig in a stroller, and I was up to my ears in therapy dogs!"

"I Want Goddamn Answers!"

That same day, perhaps as Shivanan also foresaw, Kim got into a fight at work. Despite her efforts, Kim had not received any mental health treatment before returning to MSD, and she had barely slept in five days.

The first school administrator Kim saw that day was Assistant Principal Denise Reed, and Kim pounced. "I want answers, Denise! I want to know what the fuck happened! Who the fuck was this kid? You knew he was out there! And you did nothing to protect us! Do you have a plan to bring our students back from the edge? I don't know how to tell my students that they'll be safe!"

"Kim," Denise said, "why don't you come over here and pet a dog?"

"I don't need to pet a fucking dog, Denise. I want goddamn answers!"

A county social worker spotted trouble and tried to calm Kim down.

"I want to know what the fuck happened with this kid," Kim said, beginning her tirade anew. "This shit doesn't just happen. I bet he was shuffled through the whole fucking system without anyone ever really looking at him. I bet he was way behind grade level but got passed along anyway because principals wanted to keep their fucking promotion numbers up. I bet he was special ed and should never have even been in this school, but we take crazy kids and put them in normal classrooms and think, 'Aren't we so fucking *inclusive?*' I bet he was acting crazy the whole time he was here, but nothing ever happened because the administrators hid all his shit to make this fucking school look safe. That's what they do. They care more about their fucking numbers and their fucking careers than the kids. This shit doesn't *just happen!* I bet—"

"Hold on!" the social worker said. "I think maybe you should write this all down in a journal."

"You're a fucking therapist!" Kim exploded. "You can't even listen to me? You're telling me to fucking journal?"

The social worker laughed. "You know, you might not realize it right now because every third word coming out of your mouth is 'fuck.' But if you crossed all the 'fucks' out, you're making some very good points. You should collect your thoughts, write them down, and help make a policy or something to fix things."

Kim was momentarily mollified. But she still wanted answers. A few days later, she ran into Mike Ramirez in the hallway.

"I mean this from the bottom of my heart," Kim said. "PROMISE has to go away, Mike. PROMISE goes away."

"Kim, PROMISE has nothing to do with this."

"I don't know, Mike. This all just reeks."

MSD students were telling the media frightening stories about the shooter. He threatened to kill them; he brought knives and bullets to school; he brought dead animals to school and bragged about mutilating them. No one was surprised he had done it. Everyone knew he could. So, why was he never stopped or helped?

Kim was tempted to log into the student tracking software system to look at his disciplinary and academic records. But school district officials told teachers that they could track all activity in the system, and if information about the shooter leaked, teachers who accessed it could lose their jobs.

A few days later, Kim ran into Danny Tritto, who worked in the district's Office of School Counseling. She still only knew what she had seen on the news, but she had suspicions about what happened and later recalled the conversation to us.

"Danny, PROMISE has got to go," Kim told him. "It's got to end."

"This has nothing to do with PROMISE."

"Maybe. Maybe not. But the underreporting has got to end, Danny."

"The underreporting...yeah." That wasn't exactly an admission, Kim thought. Danny was too professional for that. Kim took his response as, "Oh, you teachers figured out that all this 'progress' we've been bragging about is really just us hiding the problems?"

"That's the Guy Who Will Get You Answers"

When Kim wasn't at work, she was watching coverage of the shooting on TV. On February 15, she saw Superintendent Runcie insist on CNN that the school district was as prepared as it could have been:

> We have single-point entry. We have all that.... But, again, there's no solution that's going to be 100 percent foolproof. It takes an entire community to ensure the safety of our kids. We rely on tips. We rely on information from students, parents, anyone in the community. We take every one of them seriously.... This incident that occurred, this outrageous tragedy that we have had to deal with, we really had no signs, no warning, no tips.[3]

At the time, Kim was too numb to do more than mumble her objections. But Runcie's claims stuck with her. The day of the shooting, people seemed to know who the shooter was before anyone told them. Students insisted they had said something, but that school administrators had done nothing. And MSD didn't have a single point of entry because administrators didn't actually enforce it! Students could come through any number of entrances, and that day the shooter had simply walked through an open gate and an unlocked door.

A few weeks later, with her mother in town to keep her company, Kim watched Lori Alhadeff, who lost her daughter, Alyssa, appear on *Megyn Kelly Today* and accuse the school district of having done too little to prepare for an active shooter.[4] Kelly read a statement from the school district saying that MSD teachers had received Code Red training weeks earlier.

"They better retract that!" Kim told her mother. "I've done active shooter training. Last month wasn't 'training.' That was a Power-Point! They didn't even get through the PowerPoint fast enough to run the drill!"

Kim's mother was familiar with her daughter's complaints about the Broward County school district. Kim had genuinely thought MSD would be different because it was the best school in the district. But after a few months, she realized that it just *looked* like the best. Students came to school late and roamed the halls freely, but rather than discipline them for loitering, administrators blamed and punished teachers. On the morning of the massacre, teachers were told that they would lose points for "collegiality" on their performance evaluations if they gave out too many hall passes.

Kim had been even more annoyed by the locked bathrooms. She thought Coral Glades had a drug problem, but that was nothing compared to MSD's. There were only ten reported incidents of drug use during the last school year, but everyone knew that there was so much more than that going on. The vaping problem was getting out of hand, especially in the bathrooms. But rather than crack down on it, Assistant Principal Winfred Porter decided to lock most of the bathrooms and have security staff periodically patrol the remaining ones to deter vaping without having to enforce the rules (or, if there was THC in an e-cigarette, enforce the law).

Kim had almost thought it was funny. But a few days after the shooting, she learned about what happened to Joaquin Oliver. As the senior fled down the third-floor hallway, he tried to enter the women's bathroom. Finding it locked, he ran toward the stairwell but was shot in the knee. He tried taking cover in the alcove of the men's bathroom, which was also locked. Almost a minute later, he was killed by a shot to the back of the head.[5]

Months later, Kim learned that Meadow had been right next to Joaquin in front of the women's bathroom. She tried to cross the hallway, but was shot four times. She crawled to a classroom, but the door was locked (as it was supposed to be). Next to her was freshman Cara Loughran, who had also been shot. Meadow draped her body over Cara's to protect her. Five more shots went through both of their bodies.

No, Kim raged, the locked bathrooms weren't funny anymore.

Kim's mother listened in horror as it became clearer and clearer that the insulting and annoying policies her daughter had long complained about had turned deadly. She didn't know what to do except be there for Kim and offer whatever comfort she could. When they watched Andy Pollack speak at the White House, Kim's mom said, "That's the guy who will get you answers and get people to listen to what you have to say."

Kim would have laughed if she could. The guy in the Trump T-shirt? Her heart broke for him, but he didn't seem like someone she would hit it off with. She could only barely tolerate her "Make America Great Again" hat-wearing brothers.

But Kim was starting to realize that she wasn't going to get answers from the school district by herself. And Andy clearly meant business. Seeing him with President Trump, she wondered if maybe this was what Shivanan meant about working with politicians.

A few weeks later, Kim's colleague Robyn Mickow, who also taught on the third floor of Building 12, asked if she would join her at Andy's Ride for Meadow. Robyn had seen Meadow on the third floor and was the first MSD teacher to join Andy's team.

"He's intense," Robyn told Kim. "Kind of hard to handle. But you need to meet him."

The first thing Andy asked Kim was her classroom number. When she told him, he knew that her classroom was right across the hall from Meadow's. Had Kim seen Meadow in the hallway after the fire alarm went off? What were her final moments like? Did Kim see her body?

Kim was taken aback. She knew everyone grieved differently. But she hadn't encountered anything like this before. And she had no useful information for him; she hadn't seen Meadow at all.

"I'm going to find out everything!" Andy told her. "Everything! All the incompetence. I'm going to expose everything." Kim said she would do anything she could to help.

#MSDStrong?

But getting answers had to take a backseat to helping her students get through each day. The March For Our Lives student gun control activists helped give the school a sense of purpose, a sense that something good could come out of the tragedy. Kim supported their mission. She had grown up around guns, but didn't think anyone needed to own an AR-15 semi-automatic rifle. Her brother told her that she didn't understand the adrenaline rush of firing one. She told him he didn't understand what it felt like to hear children screaming as they were shot by one. That was the end of that family conversation.

But as the weeks dragged on, Kim's feelings about the March For Our Lives became more mixed. The more the media homed in on a couple of students and created a "showdown" narrative between them and the NRA, the more the other students seemed to fade into the background. The media covered MSD student David Hogg's Twitter fights in detail, but they missed how horribly the school district was treating its students, its teachers, and the families of the victims in the wake of the tragedy.

Mental health counseling at MSD became its own trauma. The school district piled elementary school counselors with no trauma training into MSD's media center. There was no privacy. If students wanted to talk to someone, they would have to do it in front of their peers. When they broke down and wept, everyone could see and hear them. People kept telling Kim that "there's no how-to guide for this." Kim later learned that there were, in fact, best practices that the district apparently hadn't bothered to research or to implement. Privacy for counseling was a basic standard. But the district didn't even provide curtains.

What's more, the counselors cycled in and out every few days, preventing students from forming any bond of trust. "I keep telling the same story to different people who can't handle it," a student told Kim. "I don't want to talk to them again. They're stupid!"

"Don't say that," Kim said. "They're not stupid. They're trying. They're just not trained."

"I'm sorry, Ms. Krawczyk. They're not stupid. They're just shitty."

Kim couldn't argue with that. Employee assistance had never called her back. The teachers union had done nothing to provide support. But alumni were stepping up. They organized and funded an off-site, after-school counseling center. Two months after the shooting, they brought in a specialist to hold a group trauma therapy session with the Building 12 teachers.

"We usually do this a day after the event," the therapist explained. "It's absurd that we're only doing this now. But let's make the most of our time together."

America saw none of this. America saw the press conferences and the photo ops. It saw MSD Principal Ty Thompson offer to hug every MSD student and hold them for as long as they needed. It saw Thompson meet with Derek Jeter and other celebrities. But America didn't see what Kim and other teachers recounted to us: Thompson bragging to his staff that he was more popular than Mickey Mouse, even as he avoided eye contact with teachers from Building 12.

America saw the hashtag #MSDStrong. But as the hashtag grew more prominent, it also started to hurt. Teachers and students felt pressure to appear #MSDStrong. If you admitted that you weren't okay and needed help, or if you complained about how you were being treated, were you really being #MSDStrong? America focused on the inspiring hashtag and missed the true aftermath.

On April 10, almost two months after the shooting, an MSD parent, Lisa Olson, gave a speech at a school board meeting that captured everything Kim had been feeling.[6]

> *I am the mother of a Stoneman Douglas high school freshman, William Olson, who was in Classroom 1216 on the day of the attack. As a result of the shooting, my son will carry Nikolas Cruz's bullets inside both of his arms for the rest of his life.... How could the district fail to contact each of the students in the classrooms where murders and injuries occurred? This borders on negligence. The silence coming from the Broward school district speaks volumes. It seems to me and to my son that high-speed media events and politics have gotten in the way of helping those who have been hurt.*
>
> *The district's first concern should be MSD students and families that have been most affected and injured. Photo ops and press conferences seem to be the district's focus, rather than focusing on those who are suffering.... It wasn't easy for our family to see some of the people in this room being more impressed with posing with [basketball star] Dwyane Wade than [concerned with] checking on the children who couldn't even make it to school that day. And that includes my son.*

The complete lack of communication from the district is why I am here today.... If the school board and the district focused on actually governing, rather than politicking, after this tragedy, I would be here supporting you. Not being angry and critical. Is a meeting with the students and parents of some of the most affected survivors too much to ask? Is some guidance on how the students can return to their classes after seeing their classmates murdered too much to ask?...

This district really should be embarrassed by these failures. Even the president of the United States, the first lady, the governor, the attorney general, and a senator had the time to hug my son. But not my school district, and not my son's principal.

Meeting the Superintendent

By April, Kim's shock had turned to rage. No one from the school district had admitted any fault or accepted any responsibility. The national gun control debate had played out, and the media had moved on without investigating why this tragedy happened.

In late April, Superintendent Runcie met with the Building 12 teachers. Kim couldn't make it; she had already missed too many shifts at her second job as a math tutor and couldn't afford the time off. But she still wanted answers. How did a kid this troubled ever set foot in MSD? Why wasn't he transferred to a specialized school? Why did none of the administrators have any idea what to do during the massacre?

Kim wrote her questions down and gave them to a colleague. She then asked two colleagues to invite one school board member each to the meeting with Runcie. According to Florida's Sunshine Law, if two school board members are present for a meeting about school board business, minutes must be taken and made available to the public. Kim wanted the answers on the record.

Two board members, Robin Bartleman and Abby Freedman, attended. But teachers told us that they took turns walking in and out of the room. They were never in the room at the same time. By the end of the meeting, each was standing in the doorway with one foot in the room and one foot out. One teacher said it was the "weirdest fucking thing I ever saw." But it worked. No public record was made. Not that it particularly mattered, because Kim's questions weren't even asked.

"No one wants to come to MSD to get yelled at," her colleague explained.

"I didn't come to MSD to get shot at," Kim retorted. "But no one stopped that from happening."

Kim resolved not to miss the next meeting in May. The district clearly had no interest in oversight or accountability. She'd have to enforce it herself. Kim and two of her colleagues related to us what happened at that meeting.

Teachers asked when the portable classroom trailers would arrive to alleviate overcrowding from the permanent closure of Building 12. Runcie and his deputies couldn't say; there was so much red tape to cut through. Runcie asked for patience and explained he was doing the best he could, but this was just one of many problems he had to navigate. There was one dad, he sighed, who had lost his son and always wanted to talk to him about security upgrades that the district would never actually implement. Runcie also lamented that, after pulling strings to provide a check to the family of freshman Anthony Borges, Anthony's family still sued the district.

Kim was astonished that Runcie was surprised. Anthony had been shot five times by a killer who'd walked on campus with an AR-15 totally unchallenged. He had spent two months in the hospital. He would never fully recover. Of course his family would sue.

Kim said, "I want to know what you were doing on February 15."

When Runcie responded that he was very busy that day, Kim bristled. "Not busy talking to families. Not busy talking to students. Not busy talking to teachers."

Runcie's deputy Michaelle "Mickey" Pope insisted that the school district took the time to call each and every teacher.

That was the final straw for English teacher Debbie Jacobson. Debbie's colleagues describe her as a sweet lady, "grandma cute," who always listened first and talked second. But Debbie had heard enough. "No, you didn't!" she said. "I will pull my phone record. I have never gotten a call from you people. You need to stop lying about what you're doing for us." Other teachers, by their own characterization, "went apeshit." Ernie Rospierski, a social studies teacher who risked his life by using his body to barricade the stairwell door against 18-1958 to give his students time to flee, stood up and said, "I've had it. I'm fucking done." He walked out and three other teachers followed.

But not Kim, who said, "Employee assistance called me a week after to say that they didn't have any appointments but would get back to me. But they never did. Actually, they called me *today*, but when I picked up, they asked for someone else."

Mickey Pope reminded teachers that the school district offered students and teachers free therapy.

"Your therapy sucked," said Robyn Mickow. "Your family counselors weren't trained in trauma." (Robyn gave up on the counselors after one looked as though he would vomit when she started describing what she had seen.)

Pope insisted that all of the counselors were trained. Robyn retorted, "The high school guidance counselor I spoke to told me he had no trauma training. Why would he lie?"

Pope pleaded that there was no handbook for this. The district was doing its best to triage. It had even put a call out on Facebook for extra help.

"Did you vet the counselors you got from Facebook?" Kim asked.

They hadn't. Kim sat back. These people didn't have a clue.

A few minutes later, Kim pressed Pope, "We are about to go on summer break. What are you going to do for students who still need some structure and somewhere to go?"

Pope told the teachers that the counseling center at Pine Trails Park would remain open.

Kim replied, "Our school is twenty-five percent free and reduced-price lunch. There were eight hundred kids in the building that day. That means we're looking at two hundred kids who might really need services but whose parents are at work and who can't afford to Uber. How are they going to get there?"

Pope turned to a colleague and told her to write down "transportation." It apparently hadn't occurred to them.

"The School District Did Everything Right"

In her more detached moments, Kim was almost amused by the absurdity of it all. It seemed like everyone in America, from the hosts of the Grammy Awards to ESPN anchors, was celebrating #MSDStrong. But no one was looking under the hood.

What's more, Runcie's top staff were given huge pay raises. Shortly after Kim and her colleagues tore into Mickey Pope—and after a local NPR reporter revealed that, contra Runcie's categorical denial, 18–1958 had been referred to PROMISE, which Pope oversaw—the school board announced that Pope's salary would increase by $24,000, to almost $175,000.[7]

The *Sun Sentinel* ran an editorial rebuking the school board titled, "Big raise, bad optics."[8] The editors declared, "The Stoneman Douglas family and the public want answers and accountability about that terrible day, about what may have caused it and about what's being done to prevent it from happening again. The time has come for answers, not pay raises and promotions."

Four months later, *Sun Sentinel* education reporter Scott Travis discovered that Pope's raise was the tip of the iceberg. The district also gave large raises to other central office bureaucrats, including (most gallingly to the families of the victims) $12,000 to Mary Mucenic, who oversaw a threat assessment program that failed to identify 18–1958 as a significant threat.[9]

The school district explained that the raises were for the sake of "equity." Runcie, who makes almost half a million dollars a year, denied any responsibility. Asked to justify the secret raises his staff received, he said, "It's not some arbitrary thing the superintendent decides to do."[10] The school board professed ignorance and demanded an explanation.[11]

Kim, who was earning $46,000 with a master's degree and fifteen years of experience, couldn't help but laugh when the district proposed spending an additional $400,000 on new public relations staff even as Runcie insisted the district couldn't afford teacher raises and security upgrades.[12]

But her sense of detachment never lasted long. Kim received Facebook messages and texts from students at all hours telling her that they were worried about their friends slipping into drug addiction or potentially committing suicide.

However she felt inside, she had to look strong for the students. Kim felt she had no right to wallow because she had not lost a child. Kim had hoped that even though the school and the district had failed students and teachers, they were at least making a good-faith effort to support the families of the victims.

But on May 22, more than three months after the tragedy, Kim heard April and Philip Schentrup, who lost their daughter Carmen, speak at a school board meeting. April, a Broward elementary school principal, spoke first.[13]

> *My name is April Schentrup. I've worked for Broward schools for twenty years, the last seven as a principal. My daughter Carmen was one of the seventeen murdered at MSD. Since February 14, I have waited for our school leaders to do what they promised. To prioritize the well-being of students, staff, and families and lead the quest to understand the conditions that led up to the tragedy with both transparency and a sense of urgency. I stand here today to say that I've waited enough.*
>
> *Minutes after the FBI told us that Carmen was murdered, an MSD board member entered the room and offered to do everything in her power to help. I begged her to find out all that happened and ensure that this never happens again, as my only remaining daughter still attends MSD. I did not hear from her until the evening of May 8, the first phone call from any board member since Carmen's name was released to the media. And coincidentally, the day after I added my name to speak at this meeting.*
>
> *In addition, my family and other victims' families didn't get cards, letters, or even emails of condolences from any board members. The only email we received was one blasted to the entire district, stating that the school's mass shooting [victims] would be lumped together as one tragedy for insurance purposes [so one $300,000 sum would be divided among all of the families]. What happened to making the well-being of students, staff, and families a priority?*

A few days after Carmen's funeral, Mr. Runcie came to my home and said he would do anything he could for me and my family. Weeks later, I called him seeking help and advice. With deep concern for the stability of my school community, I requested a full-time interim principal and discussed my options for a leave [of absence]. Mr. Runcie was quick to say that being a principal was not a part-time job. Other options were not available, as reassigning me might appear as favoritism since MSD staff had to return to their school.

After that call, however, I came to find out that he did less for me than what was done for the MSD staff. On Easter Sunday, I discovered that MSD staff were given leave through spring break to cope and grieve. My time off to mourn my daughter's death was docked [from my pay]. It was only after I asked for the same treatment that my time was restored.

Her husband, Philip, spoke just as forcefully.

As a parent of a child murdered at MSD, I expected a transparent and swift investigation into this tragedy.... To date, however, the district has failed.... In fact, a week after my daughter's murder, Mr. Runcie came to my house, sat at my kitchen table, and told my wife and I that the school district and the school itself had done everything right. An outrage, given I was burying my sixteen-year-old daughter.

Additionally, school board employees require lawyers to talk to detectives, school board staff are delaying if not downright impeding the investigation, there has been no report issued to the community with findings and recommendations, and the school district has been less than forthcoming in public records requests.... I believe the district is dragging its feet, not because it did everything right, as stipulated by Mr. Runcie, but because it did so many things wrong.

Every time Kim thought nothing else could surprise her, something did. So, as her mother suggested, Kim stayed in Andy's orbit. Eventually, Andy connected her to a student journalist, Kenny Preston, who was writing a report about the school district's failures. Kenny introduced her to Max Eden, who was in town to investigate. Kim was a universal sounding board at MSD, a woman everyone trusted, and she became the key to Andy's investigation. But when the fuller picture emerged, she realized that she had identified what had gone wrong in her expletive-laden rant on her very first day back at school.

CHAPTER 2

An Immigrant Father

Royer Borges moved his family from Venezuela to America in 2014 to keep them safe.

He had tried living in the United States once before, more than a decade earlier. He met and married his wife, Emely, in Florida, and they had two sons, Anthony and Aquiles. However, Royer struggled to get a firm foothold on the economic ladder. In 2007, he returned to Venezuela and resumed his career as an accountant.

But Royer watched with dismay as Venezuela's totalitarian government dragged the country further and further into chaos. It didn't matter that Royer lived in a good community; nowhere in Venezuela was safe. The last straw was when, as he explained with his signature understatement, he "got into two fights in one week."

Royer had hired contractors to build a new room onto his house. Shortly after construction began, a thug from a local *colectivo* knocked on his front door. Aside from the military, only members of *colectivos*, government-sponsored gangs that are granted the right to extort and murder in exchange for their political support of the socialist regime, are allowed to own guns in Venezuela. The thug told Royer that he had to pay the *colectivo* if he wanted to continue his construction project. Royer refused, and that evening someone shot at the walls of his house.

The next day, Royer figured out where the thug lived, knocked on *his* door, punched him in the face, and told him that no one messes with his family.

To an American reader, this might sound reckless. But it was a calculated risk. The *colectivos'* demands were escalating across the country. Royer knew that if he gave in, they could put his family on the path to poverty and, eventually, force them to flee their home, as has happened to hundreds of thousands of others. But the gambit backfired. A few days after the confrontation, two men on a motorcycle shot at Royer and narrowly missed. That's when he knew that his family had to go back to America.

After settling in Broward County, Royer found a job as an air-conditioning repairman. He rode a beat-up bike to work for eight months until he saved enough money to buy a car, which he kept running with duct tape and elbow grease. His wife worked as an office assistant, and together they managed to make ends meet and even save a little. Royer was proud to be able to afford to send his son, Anthony, to a soccer academy in South Florida run by the world-class FC Barcelona team. He saw it as an investment, not a luxury. Royer thought Anthony could become good enough to get a college scholarship.

But then Aquiles was diagnosed with type 1 diabetes. Between the doctor visits and the insulin shots, there was no more money for Anthony to train. The family's savings soon ran dry and Royer started taking odd jobs to keep them afloat. Still, all in all, things were good. Royer found an apartment in Coral Springs so he could send his kids to the best schools in Broward County. Royer wasn't rich, but he had a happy home and his children were safe.

But on February 14, 2018, Royer's wife called to tell him there was a shooting at MSD, where Anthony was a freshman. Royer tried calling Anthony, but he didn't pick up. Then Royer got the second-worst call he could imagine: his son was in the hospital. When Royer arrived, the doctors told him Anthony had been shot five times and could be in surgery until the next day.

The following afternoon, the doctors finally let Royer see his son. Royer had seen people get shot in Venezuela. But he'd never seen anything like this. Three doctors had performed simultaneous surgeries because they feared there wasn't time to do them one by one. Anthony's femur was shattered. The doctors couldn't say whether he would ever walk again. They couldn't even assure Royer that his son would survive the night.

Royer did not leave the chair next to his son's bed for two days and did not leave the hospital for two weeks. He resisted going to the bathroom as long as he could when Anthony was unconscious. Anything could happen if he left. Anthony might wake up without his father by his side. Or he might die alone.

Two days after the shooting, two men from the Broward sheriff's office barged into Anthony's hospital room. Royer tried to tell them that Anthony couldn't speak yet and couldn't give a statement. But the words didn't come fast enough. An officer shook Anthony's hand, gave Royer a slap on the back, and left. Royer hadn't seen the other officer take a picture. But the next day, he saw that a photo of his son and Broward County Sheriff Scott Israel had gone viral. Royer was furious. He felt his son had been exploited by a police department that hadn't been able to protect him.

Anthony's friend Carlito told Royer that his son was a hero: he had taken those five shots while trying to barricade a door against the shooter. But the flash of pride couldn't temper Royer's feelings of despair and powerlessness. His son was fighting for his life, but Royer didn't know how to fight for his son. All he knew was that, in America, when bad things happen, you're supposed to get a lawyer.

The Lawyer

A friend introduced Royer to Alex Arreaza, a criminal defense attorney and fellow Venezuelan-American. Alex asked Royer where in Venezuela he was from. Royer told him he lived in Ciudad Ojeda, outside of Maracaibo. Alex smiled and said, "I wondered how your boy had managed to take five shots and pull through. That explains it—he's a *maracucho!*" *Maracuchos* are known for being tough as steel. For the first time in two weeks, Royer laughed. Shaking his head in awe of his son, Royer explained that Anthony survived by taking his shirt off, ripping it into two pieces, and using the pieces as tourniquets for his legs. Anthony had been a Boy Scout in Venezuela and had taken his survival training very seriously.[1]

Royer felt he could trust Alex. Royer told him, "I don't know how anything works. All I know is that my son is on death's door, and everybody is saying that the murderer was a crazy person. They're saying that he committed all these crimes but was never arrested. That everyone knew it was him the moment the shooting started. How does someone like that even get into a school? And why didn't anyone protect my son? I want answers. But I don't know how things work here. I trust you to find justice."

Alex had never felt a weight like that on his shoulders. He had taken some big cases before. But for Alex, big cases meant representing (allegedly) very bad men who had (allegedly) done very bad things. Representing a hero and his father in their quest for truth and justice? He didn't know where to start. That night, he Googled the shooting, searching for something, anything, he could bring to Royer to assure him that they would get to the bottom of it.

Alex continued searching until 3:00 a.m., when he came across a blog post from the right-wing Charles Carroll Society titled, "How the Polices [sic] of the Progressive Left Directly Caused the Florida Massacre."[2] The blog blamed the shooting on liberal billionaire George Soros. As a defense attorney, Alex always enjoyed reading fringe conspiracy theories. They kept his mind active, looking for new patterns in old facts. But this article presented Alex with something new: PROMISE.

The article included a link to the official "collaborative agreement" between the Broward school district and sheriff's office on how to handle crimes in schools. Reading the document, Alex figured that the agreement had to be a hoax. Students get three free misdemeanors a year before school administrators are even allowed to talk to law enforcement? What kind of weirdo, Alex wondered, would take the time to invent this as a way to blame George Soros for the Parkland shooting?

But at the bottom of the agreement, Alex saw names and signatures he recognized. Michael Satz, state attorney. Howard Finkelstein, public defender. Robert Runcie, school superintendent. Scott Israel, sheriff.

"This is a real document. This shit is real!" Alex marveled. He slumped back in his chair. A few minutes later, his worried wife came downstairs to find him staring at the ceiling, bathed in the blue light of his computer screen.

"Are you okay, honey?" she asked.

"I know why this happened," he replied.

Everyone was saying that the shooter had committed all sorts of crimes at school but was never arrested. The school district had a policy to do everything it could not to arrest students. Now it made sense.

What's Different About America

When Alex explained the PROMISE program to Royer, Royer was furious. He couldn't believe that public officials had decided that the law shouldn't apply in schools. And he couldn't believe that no one was going after Broward's leaders for rolling the dice with children's lives. It made no sense to Royer why instead of going after these local officials, everyone was marching on Washington, D.C. for gun control. Venezuela had total gun control. That's how the government and the *colectivos* were able to terrorize the citizens.

Alex explained that America would never ban guns like Venezuela. The debate here was around smaller measures, like closing loopholes and revising background check procedures. He explained that the fights over these smaller things become a big political football, with the National Rifle Association and Republicans on one side and Democrats and gun control groups on the other.

"Did any of these things contribute to what happened here?" Royer wanted to know.

Alex told Royer no, but everyone was focused on the fact that the shooter had used an AR-15. Royer shook his head. Anthony had regained the strength to speak and had told him that 18–1958 could hardly hold it straight during the shooting. It didn't matter whether the gun had been an AR-15, a handgun, or a shotgun; the murderer had a building full of eight hundred children all to himself for eleven minutes. The only man who could have stopped him, School Resource Officer Scot Peterson, refused to enter the building and actively prevented other officers from entering.

"This makes no sense," Royer said. "You're telling me that all these groups will pour money into a national political battle against a powerful organization over things that had no connection to what happened? And then what? Maybe the gun control people win some changes, but what about what actually happened? What about the people responsible in Broward? What about justice?"

Royer had always thought that what was different about America was that the people ruled. When something bad happened, the people would hold those responsible to account. Royer told Alex, "This is just like Venezuela. The local government does something awful, and then when people get angry, politicians point the finger at faraway enemies and consolidate power." Some of his friends told him that other parts of America were better, but Royer had already run away once and was not about to run again. Instead, he dug in his heels. "If you stand with me, Alex," he said, "I will go to the ends of the Earth with you to get justice."

Alex later reflected to us, "Here's the thing about *maracuchos*: They are known for being very tough people who don't take shit from anyone, especially the government. The government usually tries not to fight them because they are famous for not giving up. Eventually, Broward will learn that when these guys enter the fight, it's for the long haul."

Royer was sometimes a difficult client for Alex. Royer wanted to fight the school district head-on, as fast and as hard as possible, in the same way he had handled problems in Venezuela. But Alex counseled patience. Alex later reflected, "As a lawyer, I don't always have truth on my side. When I do, I make the absolute most of it. Here we have the truth, the full truth, and nothing but the truth."

Meeting the Superintendent

Several weeks after he was shot, Anthony's condition finally stabilized. The doctors told Royer that Anthony might need a few more weeks in the hospital, but he was out of the woods and would be able to walk again. Anthony didn't have the energy to talk very much, but he could smile, and that was enough for Royer. Anthony's progress made Royer feel steadier on his feet, and he told Alex to sue the school district. A week later, Superintendent Runcie visited Anthony at the hospital. When Royer noticed that Runcie had a check in his hand, he whispered to Alex in Spanish, "What is that? Does he think he can buy me off? I am not taking that."

Alex replied, "Take it. You will need it. You have no idea how expensive health care is here."

Royer shook the superintendent's hand and took his $25,000 check. "Alex," he whispered in Spanish, "it's not signed."

Alex inspected the check. He said, "Mr. Runcie, I couldn't help but notice that this check isn't signed. I'm sure this is just an oversight, but I imagine you must have signing authority, no?"

Flustered, the superintendent signed the check. Royer accepted it as an honest mistake.

Two weeks later, Royer received notice that the school board had another check for him but that he would have to pick it up at the district's central office. Royer still didn't want to leave Anthony's side, so his wife, Emely, went to pick up the check. She returned with one hundred dollars. "Twenty dollars," Emely later sighed, "for each bullet."

The Press Conference

Anthony was released from the hospital on April 4, nearly two months after the massacre. Royer told Alex that he wanted to use the occasion to draw attention to the Broward school district's and the sheriff's office's culpability in the tragedy. Alex arranged to provide NBC's *Today* an exclusive interview with Anthony. Alex made it very clear that he wanted the segment to focus on accountability, but it turned out to be mostly a puff piece about the student who took five bullets trying to save his classmates.[3] Anthony wanted the media to let go of their hero narrative. Royer was angry that they had missed the opportunity to expose the failures of the school district and police. Alex explained to Royer that the American media loves a hero, and once they have their script, they stick to it. The only way to get their point across would be to hold a press conference where Royer and Anthony could control the narrative.

On April 6, they held that press conference. Alex told the press point-blank, "The father wants this to be taken seriously, and he doesn't want any more bubblegum hero stuff."

Then Alex read Anthony's statement:

I don't know why I survived and others didn't. But I will tell you that my family and I will dedicate the rest of our lives to seeing that something like this never happens again.... Sheriff Israel, of the

Broward County Sheriff's Office, and Robert Runcie, superinten-
dent of schools, I want to thank you for visiting me in the hospital.
But I want to say that both of you failed us, students and parents
and teachers alike, on so many levels.

I want to ask you today to please end your policy agreement
that you will not arrest people committing crimes in our schools.... I
want all of us to move forward to end the environment that allowed
people like Nikolas Cruz to fall through the cracks. You knew he was
a problem years ago and you did nothing. He should have never been
in school with us.... People are tired of empty promises that allow
this environment to remain.

I know I have been called Iron Man. While I am honored to be
called this, I am not. I am a fifteen-year-old who was shot five times
while Broward sheriff deputies waited outside and decided that they
were not going to come into the building.... I would like to go back to
school, but I am afraid that this sort of thing might happen again. I
would like you, the press, to help me spread our message about safe
schools. I am not Iron Man. I am just a kid who wants to go back to
school without worrying about getting shot.

The press conference did the trick. The headlines were exactly
what Royer and his family had hoped for. ABC's story was titled, "Parkland Shooting Victim Criticizes Sheriff, School After Release from
Hospital."[4] Fox headlined its story, "Parkland Shooting Hero Blames
Sheriff and Superintendent for Failing to Prevent Massacre."[5] If the
media was going to play up the hero angle, Royer figured, at least now it
was put to good use.

A week later, when Alex went to the county courthouse on routine
business, several police officers pulled him aside to thank him for what
he had said and urge him to keep digging. They said he had his finger on
a big problem that all the cops knew needed to be changed but that no
politician would dare to question. Juveniles were being told there were
no consequences until they became adults and were incarcerated for
the same wrongdoing they had gotten away with as kids.

Ever since Anthony had been shot, the Borges family had received
hundreds of letters, calls, and emails from strangers offering love and

support. But after the press conference, a new wave of messages came in: parents telling them that their children, too, had faced problems under similar school leniency policies.

One email came from Nicole Landers, a mother and nurse from Baltimore County, Maryland, who explained that the problem had spread across the country because of a "Dear Colleague Letter" sent by Obama's secretary of education, Arne Duncan. She explained that her daughter had been sexually harassed, but school administrators told her that there was little they could do because the boy "had rights too." When Nicole's son told an assistant principal that another student brought a knife to school, that student threatened to kill him. She went to the school for help filing a police report, but administrators refused to help. When she went to the police, they told her that schools had become no-go zones for law enforcement. If her son had a problem, he should walk off campus and call the police. Then they could come.

Nicole ran a Facebook group for parents whose children had been bullied and beaten up in schools because administrators had decided to look the other way. She told Alex that their prayers were with the Borges family and that millions of parents across America were counting on Royer to expose what had really happened. When Alex told Royer this, Royer was overcome with emotion. But he didn't really understand. Neither, for that matter, did Alex. Nicole offered to connect Alex to Max Eden, whom she contacted after reading an article he wrote for the *New York Post* about the dangers of disciplinary leniency policies.

A couple of days after the press conference, Alex got a call from a number he didn't recognize.

"Alex, it's Andy Pollack. My daughter Meadow—"

"I know who you are, Mr. Pollack. I am so sorry for your loss. How can I help?"

"It's been two months and no one has been held accountable. I don't know what everyone else is doing. But I know when someone's making moves. You're making moves. Tell me what you're doing."

Alex explained everything he had learned to Andy. Up until that point, Andy had largely focused on promoting school safety laws and pursuing a civil case against School Resource Officer Scot Peterson. But what Alex was telling him about the PROMISE program and the culture of leniency it created was alarming. Andy told Alex that he wanted to answer the question that Royer was among the first to ask: What went wrong in the schools that allowed this to happen?

CHAPTER 3

An Education Expert

By Max Eden

Four days after the shooting, an article in the *Washington Post* exonerated the Broward school district: "Instead of slipping through the cracks, it appears Nikolas Cruz was the target of aggressive work to help put him on the right track."[1] The *Post* noted that Broward was "a leader in the national move toward a different kind of discipline—one that would not just punish students, but also would help them address the root causes of their misbehavior." The *Post* reporters wrote that the school district "might have hit the limit of what could be done" to help 18–1958.

However, when Alexander Russo, an education journalist for *Kappan* magazine, read the *Post* article, he drew a fundamentally different conclusion. He tweeted, "This piece makes Max Eden's argument."

As a senior fellow at the Manhattan Institute for Policy Research, I had regrettably determined that, in education, the truth is often the *opposite* of what gets reported. Shortly before the shooting, I had written a series of articles about the disastrous effects of "education reform" in Washington, D.C. schools. What I saw unfold there had convinced me that the leaders of a movement that purported to "put students first" were far more concerned about their reputations within an elite bubble than about what actually happens to students in schools.

Education's Social Justice Industrial Complex

In 2016, the *Washington Post* Editorial Board described the District of Columbia Public Schools (DCPS) as the "fastest improving urban school district in the country."[2] Philanthropic foundations had invested heavily in the district and deemed it the flagship of the education reform movement, which insisted that schools should be run more like businesses. The idea was that, if school administrators were given expertly designed management systems that stressed improving "bottom line" student outcomes such as test scores, suspensions, and graduation rates, struggling schools would see transformational improvement.[3]

This idea gained substantial bipartisan support but was derided by some progressive critics as the "corporate reform agenda."[4] These critics lamented that billionaires were propping up advocacy organizations to push an agenda that undercut teachers and sacrificed substantive education in favor of artificially inflated or deflated metrics. But according to the *Post* Editorial Board (and the activist groups), the numbers at DCPS were "unassailable."[5] Test scores had increased, suspensions had plummeted, and graduation rates had soared.

There was only one problem: the numbers were not real.

In 2017, I discovered that the test score gains were essentially a product of gentrification.[6] A local NPR reporter found that the graduation rate increase at one school was entirely attributable to fraud.[7] Following her explosive reporting, a third-party review concluded that principals across the district had dropped standards so low that students no longer needed to attend school in order to graduate. Two-thirds of DCPS students who missed more than half of their senior year graduated anyway.[8] One researcher calculated that if DCPS had followed its official policies, "last year's record 73 percent graduation rate would have been closer to 48 percent."[9]

And, as the *Post* eventually uncovered, the decrease in suspensions was also entirely fraudulent.[10] Principals had simply stopped reporting suspensions to the district office. Rather than following the formal process, they sent around e-mails to teachers telling them to not allow certain students into the building. The pressure to improve statistical "outcomes" did lead to better numbers, but at a tremendous cost to students. A survey of DCPS teachers found that principals used the district's nationally famous, "data-driven" evaluation system to coerce teachers to ignore bad behavior and pass students no matter what.[11] It was a systematic con job from the top down.

The most amazing thing was that, when these misdeeds came to light, no one who had promoted these policies seemed to care. After the news broke that DCPS's graduation rate increase was entirely fraudulent, the CEO of Teach Plus continued to laud the district's graduation rate as proof of the success of the movement. Months after it came out that DCPS had lowered suspensions by refusing to record them, the Center for American Progress invited DCPS's chief of equity to an event to highlight the district's success in lowering suspensions.[12]

Watching the flagship of the education reform movement sink, and no one seeming to care, made a profound impression on me. I realized that in this new era of "corporate" education policy, the only stakeholders who mattered were the outside activist groups. There were two ways to make a reputation within this billionaire-funded, progressive bubble: fake the numbers or compete for the status of most "woke" at education reform conferences.

At one such conference, held by the Standards Institute in 2018, the CEO of UnboundEd received applause for telling the audience, "If you are under the impression that there are good white people and bad white people, you're wrong." The speaker exhorted the audience to recognize that they were "part of a systematically racist system of education" and that the mission of education reform was to disrupt "patterns of implicit bias, privilege, and racism in ourselves and in the education field."[13]

A decade earlier, education reformers had viewed the racial achievement gap as evidence of serious societal problems that their policy ideas could ameliorate. But as their prescriptions failed, their diagnosis shifted: all racial gaps were now evidence of "institutional racism" in schools and "implicit bias" from teachers.

The education reform movement's new goal was to fix the problem of "biased" teachers. This was a fraught mission for education reformers, who believed that they were, according to a much-lauded internal review of the movement conducted by Promise54, tainted by a "white dominant culture" and its "systems, structures, stories, rituals, and behaviors."[14]

Yet somehow, they convinced themselves—and more importantly, their funders—that with they could fix the problem of racially biased teachers once and for all. And, naturally, anyone who questioned them or their policies must—whether that person realized it or not—be motivated by racial bias.

The term "corporate reformers" no longer seemed adequate to describe what this movement had become. A "social justice industrial complex" had taken hold of American education. Former Secretary of Education Arne Duncan, impressed by DCPS's apparent gains, used money from the 2009 stimulus bill to incentivize (some might say bribe) states to follow DCPS's policy lead on test-based teacher evaluations and the new (and much-hated) Common Core academic standards.[15] With those policy levers and incentives in place, and with ever more money flowing to "woke" conferences and training programs, school district leaders across the country have learned that the fastest path to career advancement is to fake statistical progress for minority students while passionately decrying privilege and institutional racism.

What Role Did Policy Play?

If Washington, D.C. was the flagship of the education reform movement writ large, Broward County was the standard-bearer for the new approach to school discipline: an aggressive push for leniency on the grounds that racially biased teachers were unfairly punishing minority students. This issue was personal for me because of my mom's experience at an inner-city school in Cleveland, Ohio.

My mom's first dozen years as a middle school teacher were great. Her students loved her, and the principal always had her back when one of them misbehaved. But in 2014, a new principal was hired as the school district was in the midst of a major shift in its approach to school discipline. Principals increasingly felt pressured to reduce not only the number of suspensions but also the number of times students were sent to the office. My mom's new principal told teachers that she didn't want students sent to her office unless they'd been violent.

The kids quickly realized that the rules had changed, that they could get away with almost anything, and that there was nothing Mrs. Eden could do about it. My mom lost control of her classroom, and she eventually decided to leave the Cleveland Metropolitan School District and become a substitute teacher in the suburbs. Today, she's doing just fine and enjoying her work. In the end, it was my mom's students who were hurt. They learned that they could be disrespectful and disruptive without consequence, and they were ultimately deprived of my mom and other great teachers who left for the same reason.

The more I researched, the more I found that my mom's story was far from unique. Shortly after Runcie launched the PROMISE program, Duncan issued a federal "Dear Colleague Letter" to pressure school districts to follow Runcie's lead. (More about that in chapter 9.) School administrators across the country were pressured to reduce their discipline numbers and generally reacted in one of two ways: by not enforcing the rules or not recording it when they did. After reading the *Post* article, I couldn't help but wonder whether this dynamic had played a role in the shooting. If the shooter had committed the crimes his classmates alleged, did school administrators forfeit opportunities to have him arrested, which could have prevented him from legally buying a gun?

I was not the first person to pose this question. CNN's Jake Tapper asked it almost two weeks after the shooting in a hard-hitting interview with Broward County Sheriff Scott Israel.[16] Days after the shooting, Israel declared that his officers had done incredible work and then pointed a finger at the National Rifle Association at a February 22 CNN "town hall." But three days later, after news broke that Broward deputy Scot Peterson had hidden outside the school during the shooting, Tapper invited Israel back on CNN for a scathing, one-on-one interview. Tapper listed all the red flags that Israel's department had missed, including the number of times the police were called to 18–1958's home. At that time, the official number from Israel's office was twenty-three; the press later determined that the true number was forty-five.[17]

Tapper asked Israel if he would, like any good leader, take responsibility for the failures of his organization. Israel responded, "I can only take responsibility for what I knew about. I exercised my due diligence. I have given amazing leadership to this agency."

"Amazing leadership?" Tapper was incredulous. "Maybe you [should] measure somebody's leadership by whether or not they protect the community.... I don't understand how you can sit there and claim amazing leadership."

Unfazed, Israel insisted, "In the five years I have been sheriff, we have taken the Broward Sheriff's Office to a new level."

That part of the interview went viral, but it was the next part that caught my attention.

TAPPER: *But let me ask you something else. A lot of people in the community have noted that the Broward County School Board entered into an agreement when you were sheriff in 2013 to pursue the "least punitive means of discipline" against students. This new policy encouraged warnings, consultations with parents and programs on conflict resolution instead of arresting students for crimes. Were there not incidents committed by the shooter as a student, had this new policy not been in place, that otherwise he would have been arrested for and not able to legally buy a gun?*

ISRAEL: *What you're referring to is the PROMISE program. And it's giving the school—the school has the ability under certain circumstances not to call the police, not to get the police involved on misdemeanor offenses and take care of it within the school. It's an excellent program. It's helping many, many people. What this program does is not put a person at fourteen, fifteen, sixteen years old into the criminal justice system.*

TAPPER: *What if he should be in the criminal justice system? What if he does something violent to a student? What if he takes bullets to school? What if he takes knives to schools? What if he threatens the lives of fellow students?*

ISRAEL: *Then he goes to jail. That's not applicable in the PROMISE program.*

TAPPER: *That's not what happened. But that's not what happened with the shooter.... I know that the agreement that you entered into with the school allowed the school to give this kid excuse after excuse after excuse, while, obviously—*

ISRAEL: *Not for bullets, not for guns, not for knives, not for felonies, not for anything like that. These are infractions within the school, small amounts of marijuana, some misdemeanors.*

TAPPER: *There are teachers at the school [who] had been told [by school administrators], "If you see Cruz come on campus with a backpack, let me know." Does that not indicate that there is something seriously awry with the PROMISE program if these teachers are being told, "Watch out for this kid," and you don't know about it?*

ISRAEL: *We don't know that that has anything to do with the PROMISE program. I didn't hear about this until after the fact. I [heard] this information about a week ago. I don't know about it. I don't know who the teacher was. It hasn't been corroborated, but that has nothing to do with the PROMISE program. I can't, nor can any other Broward sheriff's deputy, handle anything or act upon something if I don't know about it.*

Israel deflected blame by saying the shooter's crimes were never brought to the attention of police. But not referring criminal behavior to police was the whole point of the PROMISE program. Israel's defense that PROMISE only dealt with misdemeanors was technically true but practically dubious: If school leaders are pressured to lower arrests, they're likely to err on the side of leniency without consulting the fine print every time. Had the school willfully neglected opportunities to arrest 18–1958 for felonies that could have prevented him from buying a firearm? Or that could have made the FBI more likely to act on tips that he was planning to shoot up a school?

"The School-to-Mass-Murder Pipeline"

Besides Jake Tapper and me, everyone else was focused exclusively on gun control in the first two weeks after the shooting, and the debate was becoming (predictably) bitter and vitriolic. I wrote an op-ed for *City*

Journal headlined, "How Did the Parkland Shooter Slip Through the Cracks?"[18] After raising the question of whether the school district's initiative to not arrest students played a role in 18–1958 avoiding arrest, I concluded:

> *Reporters should dig deeper into the implementation of a policy that prevented school officials from contacting the police, even when common sense would call for it, as it surely did in Cruz's case. There remain more questions than answers at this point, but we owe the families of Cruz's 17 victims better than another scripted culture war, with each side voicing the usual talking points.*

It was an earnest sentiment, but also a naïve one. The piece sparked a brush fire in conservative media. *Breitbart*, Rush Limbaugh, and Fox News's Laura Ingraham all took up the argument, and two days after my piece was published, Ann Coulter penned a column headlined, "The School to Mass Murder Pipeline."[19] Coulter wrote:

> *Nikolas Cruz's psychosis ended in a bloody massacre not only because of the stunning incompetence of the Broward County Sheriff's Department. It was also the result of liberal insanity working exactly as it was intended to. School and law enforcement officials knew Cruz was a ticking time bomb. They did nothing because of a deliberate, willful, bragged-about policy to end the "school-to-prison pipeline." This is the feature part of the story, not the bug part.*

So much for moving beyond the culture war. As the issue I raised became a conservative counterargument to gun control, Superintendent Runcie held a press conference and declared, "[The shooter] was never a participant in the PROMISE program. He wasn't eligible for it. There's no connection between Cruz and the district's PROMISE program."[20]

If that were true, the situation seemed even worse. If the shooter committed felonies and wasn't even referred to the PROMISE program, then administrators must have been all the more negligent. But then Runcie's statement changed.

In late March, he penned an op-ed in the *Sun Sentinel* headlined, "Focusing on Safety and Security, and Toppling 'Fake News.'" He wrote:

As we focus on these issues and meeting the needs of our students and families during this difficult time, the rise in "fake news" related to this tragedy is reprehensible. To be clear...contrary to media reports, the district has no record of Nikolas Cruz committing a PROMISE eligible infraction or being assigned to PROMISE while in high school.[21] (Emphasis added.)

Why, I wondered, would Runcie include those last few words unless 18–1958 had been assigned to PROMISE in middle school?

What's more, the district claimed that PROMISE was for "13 *non-violent* misdemeanors" (emphasis in original).[22] That was a plain lie. Students could be sent to PROMISE for fighting, and footage had emerged of the shooter in a big fight at school a week before his eighteenth birthday. I figured that with all the media coverage, someone would eventually note these inconsistencies and dig deeper.

I was wrong. Asking about what went wrong at MSD became a "conservative" question. Mainstream reporters treated questions about the district's discipline policies as matters to be debunked rather than investigated. *Politico* reported that there was "no evidence" that the district's approach to discipline played any role in the shooting.[23] According to the *New York Times,* the question was a racially tinged red herring that Republicans were exploiting to distract from gun control:

After a gunman marauded through Marjory Stoneman Douglas High School last month, conservative commentators—looking for a culprit—seized on an unlikely target: an Obama-era guidance document that sought to rein in the suspensions and expulsions of minority students. Black students have never been the perpetrators of the mass shootings that have shocked the nation's conscience nor have minority schools been the targets. But the argument went that any relaxation of disciplinary efforts could let a killer slip through the cracks.[24]

It is true that the shooter was not black. He was, however, diagnosed with a disability. And the policies pioneered by Runcie, and spread across America by Arne Duncan, sought to reduce discipline for students with disabilities as well. When you hear that students with disabilities are "disproportionately" disciplined, it might conjure an image of students with physical impairments or learning disorders getting punished more frequently than their peers. But that doesn't happen.[25] Rather, students who habitually behave badly are often diagnosed with having an "Emotional and Behavioral Disability." And those badly behaved students are disciplined more frequently. This unremarkable fact is, however, bemoaned by education reformers as evidence of "ableist" discrimination.

Schools are pressured to discipline students who behave badly at the same rate as students who behave well, which creates predictably perverse incentives and consequences. Sometimes schools refuse to diagnose students in order to retain the flexibility to discipline them. Other times, schools decline to document misbehavior and troubled students get passed from one teacher to another with no paperwork trail to say, "This student needs help!"

What's more, federal and state policies pressure schools to push students with disabilities into the "least restrictive environment" possible. This pressure makes it harder for school districts to put students like 18–1958 into specialized schools that cater to their needs and encourages school administrators to keep troubled students in normal classrooms for the sake of "inclusion." The pressure to document fewer disciplinary incidents, especially for students with disabilities, makes administrators less willing to record behavioral problems, allowing issues to fester and leaving everyone worse off. Did these pressures, I wondered, contribute to the massacre?

To Superintendent Runcie, the only education policy problem was guns. He told the *Sun Sentinel*, "The biggest problem is, we could provide services perfectly, [but] if the individual is still able to go out and buy a semi-automatic weapon, that becomes a major hole in anything that we could possibly do."[26]

It seemed to me that if a school provides even adequate services, students don't become mass murderers.

Why I Traveled to Parkland

Many education journalists showed little interest in digging into what happened in the Broward County school district. Their attitude, like Runcie's, seemed to be that anything other than guns was a distraction.

By late May, after the revelation about the shooter's involvement in PROMISE, Alexander Russo included the coverage of Parkland on his list of the worst educational journalism of the 2017–2018 school year, noting:

Three months after the tragedy in Florida, initial national and local coverage of the Parkland school shooting...is proving to have been enormously sloppy and in ways misleading.... School systems and administrators shouldn't be treated with kid gloves in the aftermath of a shooting incident, as was the case for much too long here. As this case shows, they warrant as much scrutiny as anyone else.[27]

I never expected to do anything beyond writing that one op-ed in February posing a question. But in late April, I found myself in Andy Pollack's living room. A local student journalist, Kenny Preston, had read my *City Journal* column and contacted me on Facebook asking for help with a report he was writing on the school district's failures. I almost never accept Facebook friend requests from people I don't know, but for whatever reason, I accepted his. When I read his report, I was glad that I had. As I advised him, I became much more invested in trying to answer the question I had originally raised: how did the Parkland shooter slip through the cracks? And after I saw Runcie apparently orchestrate a smear campaign to discredit Kenny, I decided to go to Parkland myself to investigate further. I asked Kenny whether he could introduce me to any MSD teachers. He told me that I should meet Kim Krawczyk.

Separately, my new friend Nicole Landers encouraged Alex Arreaza to contact me. I decided I would meet with him while I was in Parkland. I had no plans to meet with Andy Pollack. But Alex told him that a guy from D.C. was digging for details about the school district, and Andy called me and asked me to come to his house.

At the time, Andy was a member of the state Marjory Stoneman Douglas High School Public Safety Commission investigating the causes of the tragedy and asked me if I had any questions he should bring up at its next meeting. I mentioned the lingering questions around the shooter's disciplinary history, and at the next meeting he asked about it.

Or rather, he tried to.

It had been nearly two months since the Florida Legislature provided the Commission with full authority to review all documents from all entities, from the school district, to the county's mental health provider, to the police. Andy asked the commission's lead investigator whether he had received all of the shooter's disciplinary records. The investigator replied that he wasn't sure whether the school district had handed everything over.

Andy asked, "Is that normal, two months after an investigation, not to have all his disciplinary records?"

The investigator replied, "I don't know if anything about this is normal."

Andy asked him whether the Broward school district was cooperating.

The investigator replied, "Some [entities] are probably being more cooperative than others."[28]

After that meeting, Andy texted me, "Max, thank you so much for helping. You will be such an asset in helping me find justice for my daughter's murder."

That's when it got real.

I couldn't find enough details in my first trip to write an article, and I had no plans to return. But after I got Andy's text, I felt I had no choice. I asked if he could spread the word that I was looking for answers about what happened at MSD.

Andy generated about a dozen leads for my second trip. By the end of that trip, I could hardly believe what we'd discovered. Discipline policy was only one part of a total system failure that was bigger than I could have imagined. As I pieced together the shooter's journey through the Broward County school district, it struck me that it was as though all the things that were going wrong in American public education had joined forces to let him slip through every crack.

I told Andy that it would take a book to expose it all and explain its full significance, and Andy said we should do it together. I felt a duty to do everything in my power to help Andy find justice for Meadow and help draft a book that did justice to his story. But this book would never have been written without Kenny Preston, the student journalist whose story we will tell next.

CHAPTER 4

A Student Journalist

When news of the massacre broke, it didn't mean too much to nineteen-year-old Kenny Preston. School shootings had become a fact of American life. Even though he had lived in Broward County all his life, Marjory Stoneman Douglas High School didn't ring a bell. Kenny didn't get out as much as most teenagers and was completing high school online.

Until sixth grade, Kenny had been a pretty typical student. But one morning, he woke up in pain all over. He and his parents figured it would pass, but the pain persisted and then a deep fatigue set in. As the days turned into weeks, Kenny began to have terrible headaches and memory loss, and he had a hard time thinking clearly. Finally, the diagnosis: Lyme disease. If treated quickly, patients can expect a speedy recovery. But if Lyme disease goes untreated long enough and breaks through the blood-brain barrier to affect cognition, as Kenny's had, the long-term consequences can be debilitating.

Kenny spent months shuttling between home and hospital. The treatments weren't helping, and his mother was getting desperate. She heard about a doctor in Connecticut who was pursuing experimental treatments. The doctor was also facing a multimillion-dollar malpractice lawsuit. But when he told Kenny's mother that his treatment was her son's only hope, she agreed to try it. Finally, Kenny's condition started to improve.

By eighth grade, Kenny decided to try attending a traditional school again. But he still got easily fatigued and couldn't shake the feeling that his mind used to be sharper. Kenny could focus on one thing at a time, but juggling seven classes a day was difficult. After tenth grade, Kenny and his family concluded that traditional high school wasn't the right fit. He would complete his last two years of high school from home. By his senior year, he was cruising through his coursework and had rebuilt a modest social life.

When the names of the victims were released, Kenny recognized two: Nicholas Dworet and Alyssa Alhadeff. He didn't know Nicholas well, but they had a mutual friend. Kenny recognized Alyssa from the district-wide debate program they both participated in. This was no longer just another school shooting to Kenny. His heart sank, his throat choked up, and he couldn't stop watching the coverage.

Politics and Corruption

The morning after the shooting, Kenny watched the first press conference at MSD. Superintendent Runcie said:

> *Students have been reaching out to me, reaching out to staff, probably board members and others saying that now, now is the time for this country to have a real conversation on sensible gun control laws in this country. So, our students are asking for that conversation. And I hope that we can get it done in this generation, but if we don't, they will.*[1]

Kenny yelled at the TV, "Can't you just fucking wait until the bodies are buried?"

Kenny didn't have strong opinions on gun control, and no one in his family owned a gun. But the morning after a mass murder seemed way too soon to make any kind of political argument. He only grew angrier when Runcie called on the Florida Legislature to allocate more funding to mental health.

Later in the press conference, Sheriff Israel admitted, "There are some bodies that are still in the school. It's a process."

That's when something inside of Kenny flipped. The bodies of children who had been murdered under Runcie's leadership were still lying on the schoolhouse floor directly behind him, and he had already started politicking.

"Who the hell is this guy?" Kenny wondered. He started to research. Robert Runcie had gone to Harvard for undergrad and Northwestern for business school. He got his start in education in 2003 when a college friend, Chicago Public Schools superintendent Arne Duncan, hired him to run his district's IT office. In 2009, President Obama tapped Duncan to be the U.S. secretary of education, and in 2011, the Broward County School Board, seeing that Duncan was one of Runcie's references, selected a man who had never been a teacher or a principal to lead the sixth-largest school district in America, with 270,000 students and 15,000 teachers in 234 schools and an annual operating budget of $3.8 billion.[2]

According to a Florida grand jury report published months before Runcie was hired, the school board's endemic corruption and incompetence should have disqualified it from having the authority to select a chief executive at all. Following allegations of bribery and corruption that landed some in jail, the grand jury reached the following conclusions:

> *The evidence we have been presented concerning the malfeasance, misfeasance and nonfeasance of the Broward County School Board (Board) and of the senior management of Broward County School District (District) and of the gross mismanagement and apparent ineptitude of so many individuals at so many levels is so overwhelming that we cannot imagine any level of incompetence that would explain what we have seen. Therefore, we are reluctantly compelled to conclude that at least some of this behavior can best be explained by corruption of our officials by contractors, vendors and their lobbyists. Moreover, many of the problems we identified in our inquiry are longstanding and have been pointed out by at least two previous Grand Juries. But for the Constitutional mandate that requires an elected School Board for each District, our first and foremost recommendation would have been to abolish the Broward County School Board altogether.[3]*

The grand jury identified three problems:

1. A culture of fear and intimidation: "We are aware of top-level managers who openly talk of targeting whistleblowers, boat-rockers, and other malcontents whose primary sin appears to be exposing flaws in the system and a lack of leadership among senior staff.... In short, we have a middle management staff that tolerates or is forced to tolerate incompetence, double-dealing, corruption, and laziness but which in turn is always fearful of being targeted by upper management."

2. The school board members themselves: "As serious as the problems are at the District, the problems with the Board are even worse. The Board has demonstrated an appalling lack of both leadership and awareness."

3. Incompetence if not corruption in construction contracts: "A great deal of money spent on this construction has been wasted as the direct result of the board's interference and self-dealing as well as a result of their failure to engage in any meaningful oversight of the District's building activities."

The 2011 grand jury report listed twenty-one recommendations, among them that the school board should establish an inspector general's office to guard against corruption; that it should not be allowed to vote on vendor contracts; and that it should not be allowed to hire superintendents. But the school board ignored these recommendations and hired Runcie from Chicago at the recommendation of his old boss, Secretary of Education Arne Duncan, who was then doling out billions of dollars in grants from the federal stimulus act.

Following the Sandy Hook school shooting in December 2012, the Florida Legislature proposed providing the Broward County school district with an additional $55 million for school safety.[4] But, according to the *Sun Sentinel,* Superintendent Runcie and the school board "hated the idea because control over the money would have gone to a separate taxing district board." School board member Ann Murray declared, "I'm not willing to give up any authority to anyone." Her colleague Robin Bartleman worried that the state money could interfere with the soon-to-be-launched PROMISE program. Superintendent Runcie wrote a letter to the legislature saying that he didn't want the additional money and explaining that he was already moving ahead on a host of school safety initiatives (which he never implemented).[5]

A few months later, Runcie and the school board persuaded Broward voters to fund an $800 million bond initiative called Safety, Music, Arts, Renovation, and Technology (SMART). After it passed, Runcie sought to further consolidate control over the bond money by limiting the power of the Qualification Selection Evaluation Committee (QSEC), an independent entity created to review vendor contracts.

"Anybody doing the math can see they're trying to control the outcome," said Nathalie Lynch-Walsh, chairwoman of the district's Facilities Task Force. "Why would you not put [contracts] through QSEC if you are not up to something?"[6]

School board member Robin Bartleman agreed with Lynch-Walsh that this move opened the door to corruption, noting, "It's going to be an issue. Stuff like this snowballs."

But board member Rosalind Osgood, Runcie's closest ally, backed his move: "I'm kind of fed up going back and forth with QSEC."

Runcie then nominated Leo Bobadilla, chief operating officer of the Houston Independent School District, to manage the $800 million bond. Shortly before the school board voted on his nomination, rumors began to swirl about a scathing audit of Bobadilla's management of Houston's $2 billion bond program. Runcie swore to the school board that there was no audit, and Bobadilla was confirmed by a five-to-three vote.

The day after Bobadilla was confirmed, news of the audit broke, and Runcie admitted he had known about it after all.[7] The Houston school district was more than $200 million over budget, and the audit found that the district repeatedly submitted multiple work orders for the same project to funnel more money than permitted to the contractors. Bobadilla's office failed to catch inaccurate and inappropriate charges and at times asked the school board to sign off on contracts *after* they were completed. Houston School Board member Anna Eastman concluded, "State law and district policies were at the very least ignored, but more likely knowingly circumvented."[8]

Kenny was astonished. He never imagined that a school district could reek this badly of corruption. And he was not surprised to find three years' worth of articles in the *Sun Sentinel* about how the projects funded by the bond initiative were running ever more over budget and behind schedule.[9]

With all this in mind, Kenny watched CNN's February 22 "town hall."[10] Runcie took the stage and declared, "Some of the dialogue that I've heard recently is about arming teachers. We don't need to put guns in the hands of teachers." The crowd gave him a standing ovation. He continued, "We need to arm our teachers with more money in their pocket." He paused for another standing ovation. "This country pays a lot of lip service to the importance of the teaching profession, but we never put our money behind it. Let teacher compensation, benefits, and working conditions be part of this national debate as well!"

"The taxpayers just gave you $800 million!" Kenny thought. "Safety was literally your first priority—it's the 'S' in SMART! What did you do with that money?"

Kenny read every *Sun Sentinel* article about the SMART bond and discovered that Florida TaxWatch, an independent nonprofit, had blasted the district for its poor management of the program.[11] But, Kenny wondered, how far behind was the district on its safety projects?

After scouring the school district's website, Kenny learned that there was a bond oversight committee. He visited the committee's website and printed out all of its reports as well as every relevant document he could find from Florida TaxWatch.

After over twenty hours wrestling with the documents, Kenny reached a conclusion he thought had to be a mistake: In the first four years of the SMART bond, the district had spent $5 million out of the $100 million allocated to safety projects. Only 5 percent of the money it had available to make the schools safer!

Kenny asked his accountant father to review the findings, and he confirmed that his son's calculations were correct. Kenny had no clue whether this had anything to do with the shooting. Sure, a new fire alarm system at MSD was delayed, but what difference would that have made? Still, his findings seemed worth bringing to the public's attention. Kenny decided to write a report, share it with the victims' families, present it to the school board, and demand answers.

Putting Together the Report

Kenny's report would be divided into two parts: one on school safety spending and the other on school discipline. Kenny also followed the media firestorm over the PROMISE program, and he became convinced that, whether or not PROMISE itself played a role, the culture of leniency it engendered could have affected the course of events.

He tried cold-calling and Facebook-messaging MSD students for details about the shooter's troubled history, but quickly abandoned that tactic. The first few students had no useful information but were so relieved that someone was looking into the shooting that they started contacting him at all hours to confide in or cry to him. Next, Kenny turned to teachers and administrators, also with limited success. All told, he emailed, cold-called, or Facebook-messaged about a hundred people. Barely a half-dozen responded.

One of the few people who did respond was Bob Sutton, a teacher at Broward's Piper High School. Bob had seen his colleagues reduced to tears after administrators blamed them for students' disruptive and violent behavior. Bob connected Kenny with Kim Krawczyk, who was friends with his wife, Terry (the same Terry who referred Kim to Shivanan the astrologer).

Bob also introduced Kenny to several other key sources, including Anna Fusco, president of the Broward Teachers Union (BTU). Fusco told Kenny that administrators were so eager to make their schools *look* safe and so reluctant to deal with disciplinary paperwork that they often refused to document problems.[12]

Fusco told Kenny that a lot of people were looking for the answers to the same questions: What if the shooter had been arrested? What if administrators hadn't decided to ignore his behavior? Could he have faced some sort of criminal charge that would have stopped him from legally buying a gun?

Fusco said she hadn't learned anything definitive yet, but an anonymous MSD teacher had given her a document alleging a cover-up by school administrators. Fusco promised to give Kenny the document, and a few days later Kenny received a call from a mutual friend. The friend directed Kenny, as though in a spy novel, to pick up the document from a cashier at a local gas station. All the secrecy seemed silly, and Kenny couldn't make heads or tails of the document, but he filed it away for future reference.

Kenny also talked to Robert Martinez, a recently retired school resource officer, who told him, "We all knew some sort of tragedy like this was going to happen in Broward. You can't just stop arresting kids without expecting something like this. As officers, our hands were tied." More alarming still, Martinez told Kenny that district officials had explicitly told school resource officers not to arrest students for felonies, in addition to the official PROMISE misdemeanors. (You'll hear more from Fusco and Martinez in chapter 11.)[13]

Kenny wrote his report but kept searching the Internet for additional information or insight. At about 4 a.m. on March 23, after a long night of researching and revising, Kenny saw that the U.S. House Judiciary Committee had held a hearing on the Parkland tragedy's policy implications. Kenny saw that Max Eden had testified about discipline policies, so he sent Max a Facebook message to ask if he would take a look at his report.

When Max read Kenny's three-thousand-word report, he was deeply impressed. It was better sourced and argued than he would have expected from a senior in college, let alone a senior in high school. They discussed some of the finer points of Kenny's analysis over the phone.

Eventually, Max asked, "Why don't you have anything in there about Runcie's brother?"

"Why should I?" Kenny asked.

Max mentioned to Kenny that Arne Duncan had appointed Robert Runcie's brother, James, to lead the U.S. Department of Education's Federal Student Aid (FSA) office. Judicial Watch, a nonprofit organization that files Freedom of Information Act lawsuits to expose government corruption and wrongdoing, found that "[u]nder Runcie's leadership there was pervasive fraud and corruption at the FSA...including skirting federal rules to hire friends and family and hefty off-the-books cash bonuses."[14] Under James Runcie's leadership, FSA's improper payments totaled $6 billion in 2016, and he gave himself $443,000 in bonuses.[15] In early 2017, when the House of Representatives asked Runcie to testify about what was happening under his leadership, he chose to resign instead, protesting that he had "been consistently on record and clear about not testifying at the upcoming hearing."[16]

"I know all that," Kenny said. "But why would I include it?"

"It's evidence of a pattern. Both James and Robert Runcie got jobs they weren't qualified for courtesy of Arne Duncan. Both totally financially mismanaged their organizations and faced persistent concerns about corruption."

"Yeah, I see that," Kenny said. "But it just seems like point-scoring. This report has to be focused. I'm doing it so the parents can get answers, so I can't go point-scoring."

Max was impressed by Kenny's maturity. "Do you want media coverage?" Max offered. "Mainstream media won't be interested. But conservative media is keyed in to discipline issues. I could send some emails."

"No," Kenny replied. "I don't want conservative coverage. There's been enough of that already. They're just repeating talking points, not investigating. I'm hoping that if I can get the families on board and they're the ones asking for answers, mainstream reporters will actually have to investigate."

Max told Kenny that he had to get clear answers regarding the school district's "discipline matrix," which prescribed consequences for behavioral infractions. "The way I read it," Max said, "everything is optional. I could be wrong, but I don't think school administrators are required to report felonies to law enforcement."

Kenny called school board chairwoman Nora Rupert, who was Runcie's most vocal critic. She had previously confirmed that Kenny's analysis regarding the district's bond initiative was on track. Now she confirmed that, in fact, the discipline matrix doesn't *require* administrators to refer students to law enforcement for felonies. Combine that discretion with the general push to reduce arrests, and it started to make sense to Kenny how a policy intended to decriminalize misdemeanors had also led to a 30 percent reduction in felony arrests.

Real Facts as "Fake News"

With that knowledge, Kenny was confident enough to approach the victims' families. Most didn't reply, and Kenny wasn't going to pester them. At first, Kenny had no intention of contacting Andy. Andy had such a large social media following that Kenny figured he would never read a message from a stranger. But Bob Sutton told Kenny that Andy responded to everyone because he did not want to risk missing anything. So Kenny messaged Andy, and within an hour Andy responded, "Very interested. Maybe we can meet at my house this week? Can we talk tomorrow?"

After they met, Andy introduced Kenny to other parents. Kenny explained what he had learned to them and asked if they'd sign on to a letter asking for answers. At one point, he had fourteen out of the seventeen victims' families on board.

Kenny found that a lot more people were willing to speak with him now that he was working with Meadow's dad. Sometimes people would just come to him. Maria Colavito, a retired special education support facilitator at MSD who dealt with the shooter during his junior year, told Kenny that he was on the right track. She told Kenny that she once asked School Resource Officer Scot Peterson why 18–1958 had not been arrested and Peterson replied, "It's this PROMISE program stuff. My hands are tied."

But not every chance encounter turned out well. Dennis Michael Lynch, a conservative blogger and the producer of several straight-to-DVD documentaries about illegal immigration, was working on a documentary about the shooting and advising Andy on how to navigate the media. When Andy told Dennis about Kenny's report, Dennis interviewed him.

A few days after that interview, on March 27, Dennis ran an article previewing Kenny's report.[17] But Kenny wasn't flattered; he freaked out. He had figured that the interview would be part of a documentary that would air a year later. Now a scoop on his report had been published on a conservative clickbait website that, he reflected, "looked like it could give you a computer virus."

Kenny had wanted to write a serious report that would attract meaningful media attention. But now anyone who Googled him might see him as a partisan teenage attention-seeker.

A day later, an MSD mom tweeted Dennis's article at Superintendent Runcie: "@RobertRuncie you've got some explaining to do!...

#changeforschoolsafety #unhappydouglasparent." Runcie replied, "There is no explaining to do for fake news. However, if you're interested in facts, you can find all the details you desire on status of the capital bond projects from the independent citizens Bond Oversight Committee & Florida Tax Watch."

"That's where I got my information from!" Kenny thought. "Could I have been wrong?" Kenny emailed Florida TaxWatch Vice President Bob Nave, who confirmed that his facts were accurate.

But Kenny's report had been labeled "fake news" before anyone had read it. Kenny was frustrated, but not surprised, when parents of the victims said that they no longer wanted to publicly support his project.

Would all his work be for nothing because of one dumb interview?

Kenny wasn't sure if he should, or could, move forward with the project without the support of the families. But Andy told him, "I don't give a fuck if it turns out you're wrong. So what if it blows up in my face? That wouldn't bother me. Nothing can bother me anymore. I want to know everything, and you're trying to find stuff out. So however it goes, I'll be standing by you."

Bolstered by Andy's support, Kenny decided to present his report alongside Andy and student survivors at the next school board meeting on April 10.

Two days after the Dennis Michael Lynch story ran, Kenny called Max to ask if he could get conservative media coverage. He was concerned that not even local press would cover his report anymore.

"People have been telling me that Runcie is very vindictive," Kenny explained. "I'm just really worried about what happens if this gets no traction at all."

"Worst case, it just fizzles out, right? What's the worry?" Max asked.

Kenny explained that, because he was nineteen years old and homeschooled, he was in an administratively precarious position. The school district was not under any legal obligation to keep him enrolled, and if they found some paperwork technicality they could un-enroll him and prevent him from getting a diploma that spring.

Max figured that Kenny had become a bit paranoid. But he was interested to see how this would all play out, so he tipped off some reporters.

On Friday, April 6, Kenny received a furious phone call from a victim's father. The man screamed at Kenny, telling him that he was working with the superintendent on life-saving security upgrades and Kenny's report could ruin everything. If the public lost confidence in the superintendent, the father explained, they wouldn't approve new taxes. Then, if there was another school shooting, the blood would be on Kenny's hands.

The father demanded, presumably on Runcie's behalf, that Kenny meet with Runcie on April 9, the day before the school board meeting. The superintendent would set Kenny straight, and Kenny would realize how wrong he was and how terrible his report would be for the district. The father's tone was so threatening that if it had been anyone who hadn't just lost a child yelling that way, Kenny would have called the police.

Instead, Kenny called Max. "What should I do? Everyone's been telling me to be careful with Runcie. I mean, Runcie just set a grieving father on me like an attack dog! This is all so fucking weird. Should I take this meeting?"

Max told Kenny that he had no choice. Kenny couldn't present his findings and allow Runcie to say that Kenny had refused an invitation to discuss them. But Max advised Kenny to "get backup," like a teacher or a lawyer.

Kenny called Kim Krawczyk, who told Kenny that she loved what he was doing but that she didn't see the direct connection to MSD. Kenny admitted that the only delayed safety project at MSD was an upgraded fire alarm system.

"Hold the phone," Kim said. "Tell me everything about that."

"I, uh—"

"Find out."

Kenny made a couple of calls and then called Kim back and told her that the former director of school safety had recommended that the new alarm include what's called an "active trigger" mechanism. When the alarm is activated, it doesn't go off instantly; it sends a signal to the office and gives staff time to decide whether the alarm should go off.

"Because what if, instead of a fire, it's a gunman?" Kim said, her voice flat.

For all his research and interviews, Kenny had never asked any of the survivors to recount the event. Kim explained that not all of the teachers on the third floor had recognized the sound of gunshots. When the fire alarm went off, several teachers sent their students into the hallway, thinking it was just a drill. Everyone who died on the third floor was shot in the hallway. If the new fire alarm had been installed, then maybe someone in the central office could have stopped the alarm from sounding, and everyone on the third floor—including Meadow—would have survived.

Kenny reeled. He called school board chairwoman Nora Rupert to run this by her. He recalled that she replied, "Chilling, isn't it?" She had heard about it too. Until that moment, Kenny figured he was just revealing general bureaucratic incompetence. But now it was a matter of life and death. Was this why Runcie had demanded a meeting?

Meeting the Superintendent

Kim wanted to join Kenny for the meeting with Runcie but couldn't miss any more shifts at her second job. Kenny got Royer Borges's lawyer, Alex Arreaza, to join instead, but when they arrived, Runcie's staff would not allow Alex into the meeting. Runcie didn't have any counsel present, they explained, so Kenny couldn't either. Alex objected furiously and told Kenny he was foolish to proceed.

Kenny went in anyway. He had expected a one-on-one meeting. But when he entered the room, he saw Runcie, ten of his staff, and three parents who had lost a child. The only not-unfriendly face was a reporter from the *Weekly Standard*, Alice Lloyd, who at Max's recommendation traveled from Washington, D.C. to Broward to profile a student journalist trying to speak truth to power.[18] The following account of the meeting was pieced together from Alice's notes and Kenny's recollection.

Runcie opened the two-hour meeting casually, saying, "I meet with students all the time." But then he chided Kenny, saying that if Kenny fancied himself an investigative journalist, he should have been the one requesting this meeting.

Kenny spent twenty minutes explaining his findings. When he finished, Runcie told Kenny that he didn't know who was giving him all this information, but it wasn't accurate. Kenny told him that he had spoken with Nora Rupert and BTU President Anna Fusco. Runcie told him that he had just gotten off the phone with both of them and that they would both go on record at the school board meeting about what they had actually said. Kenny knew what they had told him, so he didn't think much of it at the time.

Then Runcie explained the bond process and insisted that the safety projects had actually been expedited, not delayed. Kenny asked him how he could consider the project "expedited" when the fire alarms for MSD and other schools were pushed back from Year 1 to Year 5 priorities. Runcie explained that the delay was for "efficiency" and that he didn't understand why Kenny was harping on the fire alarm. "It's not like the building didn't have a working fire alarm," Runcie said. "Your assumption is that Building 12 didn't have any fire alarms working."

"I didn't say that," Kenny replied.

Kenny explained the active trigger mechanism and its implications. But the school district's recently hired fire chief, MaryAnn May, told him that she was unaware of any recommendation to upgrade the alarm and that it would have been impossible to do at that time because the technology hadn't even been invented yet. She told him that she had just recommended that the district pilot the new alarm system later this year.

Kenny would later learn that the technology had been around since the 1980s and was recommended by Florida state code. But he didn't know that at the time, so he shifted the conversation to school discipline. He told Runcie and his staff that he had talked to Nora Rupert and April Schentrup (whose passionate speech three months after the tragedy you read in chapter 1). They both told him that administrators have total discretion in reporting a crime to the police, no matter how serious.

The father who had demanded the meeting interrupted, "I talked with April too. But obviously if someone rapes somebody in school, it's not like they're not going to take it seriously."

"So," Kenny asked Runcie, "how can you not mandate it be reported?"

Runcie's deputy Mickey Pope explained that the U.S. Department of Education's "Dear Colleague Letter" on school discipline said that administrators should have total discretion to refer matters to law enforcement. Kenny would later learn that this wasn't strictly true, although it was clear that Pope thought it was.

Kenny kept pressing Runcie and Pope on how absurd it was to make reporting felonies optional. Runcie grew impatient and asked, "I'm trying to figure out what your point is. Are you suggesting that the discipline matrix contributed to this?"

"Yeah," Kenny said. "That's exactly—"

"So," Runcie interrupted, "if I look at Sandy Hook, if I look at Columbine, they had the same discipline matrix we have? If I look at the Pulse nightclub shooting, that would be the case? When we try to connect the discipline thing to some tragedy that occurs, it's just bizarre to me."

Kenny was flabbergasted. Was Runcie serious?

"One," Kenny said, "I don't understand how it's bizarre, considering the number of circumstances in which this student had committed arrestable offenses and was not arrested. And two, I don't understand how you can compare this to Pulse. Each individual circumstance requires an individual analysis of the system failures at play."

Kenny recalled that Runcie told him that he had been through every inch of the shooter's discipline record and did not know of any arrestable offenses. Kenny told him that if there was no official record of the behaviors that other students reported to the media after the shooting, then that would be even worse because it would mean that administrators had ignored the incidents. "Death threats, right?" Kenny said. "Those are very much arrestable offenses. If there's testimony from students that—"

Runcie interrupted and told him that every incident had to be weighed in context. "This is not an average student," Runcie said. "He's got a disability that's documented. And it's described by law—by law!—how you deal with his behavior." Runcie explained that Kenny was fundamentally mistaken for assuming that the shooter should have been handled in the same way as a general education student.

Kenny countered, "Are you alleging that death threats aren't arrestable offenses if they're made by special ed students?"

"No, I'm not saying they're not arrestable," Runcie replied. "Just that every case and situation is different."

The father joined in, "This is a larger conversation. It's not like the school district did something on its own here. These policies are coming from the U.S. Department of Education, right?"

Kenny wasn't going to argue with the father, so he brought up a new point. "This is a student who threatened to kill other students. Who brought knives to campus. Who wasn't allowed to bring a backpack to campus because he might be carrying weapons. Regardless of the nature of the disciplinary actions, I don't understand why a student like that would be at a traditional school at all."

Pope replied, "These decisions are not made whimsically. They are made according to the law. Where a student accesses their educational services is very much guided by law."

Kenny didn't know if the law actually required students who threaten to kill their peers to remain in traditional schools. He didn't know whether Pope honestly thought it did or whether she was using "the law" to shift blame away from decisions made by people under her watch.

Kenny held his own as best he could, but he had only started researching the policies a few weeks before. Eventually, the conversation petered out to no one's satisfaction. But what most concerned Kenny was that the victims' fathers were still on Runcie's side when the meeting concluded.

Kenny was certain that Runcie had been spinning and deflecting. He also felt certain that none of his points had been disproven. And he still had Nora Rupert in his corner. She had told him that he would have six minutes to speak at the school board meeting the next day rather than the standard three. There would also be seven speaking slots for student survivors, who could amplify his questions and ask their own.

The April 10 School Board Meeting

The morning of the school board meeting, Andy called Kenny and told him that he got called into a meeting with Florida Governor Rick Scott, but was sending his wife Julie in his place. "She'll have your back," Andy said.

One hour before he was scheduled to speak, Kenny received a call from Nora Rupert's assistant. The board would have to end the meeting early, so Kenny's speaking time would be cut to three minutes and there would be no time for the survivors to speak. Kenny knew he couldn't explain his findings in three minutes, so when he stepped forward, he abandoned his script.

> *I had intended to talk about the investigation today. The problem is that my remarks will be a little different than originally intended. You see, certain members of this board and the superintendent have tried by every means possible to subvert our message.*
>
> *For weeks, we have had additional speakers scheduled. Just an hour ago, I received word that all of our seven additional speakers would be cut and my time would be cut in half. A board and superintendent who insist on their commitment to transparency have decided to deny a voice to survivors and families of the victims who intended to speak tonight.*
>
> *This is no surprise after the fiasco I was involved in yesterday, though. It was requested that I meet with the superintendent and families of victims to discuss my report. When I arrived, I was denied the right to have an attorney present, I was refused the opportunity to record the meeting, and I was told that this was because the superintendent wouldn't have any representation of his own. The meeting was stacked with ten district officials in addition to the superintendent. We spoke for a total of two hours.*
>
> *You can call me a skeptic, but I have a hard time believing that a superintendent and ten district officials who represent two hundred thirty-four schools, fifteen thousand teachers, and two hundred seventy thousand students had the time to meet with a nineteen-year-old for two hours if they didn't believe that I was holding onto something crucial.... Something doesn't smell quite right in Broward, and this school district is the epicenter.*
>
> *Luckily, our report will be going live on* The Hill *and other national media outlets at around 6 p.m. today, and it will make clear the failures of the school system, and in particular the superintendent, in protecting our schools. Thank you.*[19]

The audience erupted in applause. Assuming that, as Rupert's assistant had told him, the meeting would end shortly, Kenny stepped into the hallway to field phone calls and texts from students, teachers, and a few journalists who were watching via livestream. But the meeting did not end early.

After the public speakers, board member Rosalind Osgood interjected, "Ms. Rupert, I just can't move away...I don't know where the fake news starts." Osgood insisted that PROMISE was totally irrelevant because the shooter was "never involved" in the program. Addressing Kenny's report, she turned to her colleagues and said, "I see your name mentioned, Ms. Rupert, as well as Ms. Bartleman's name.... It is disturbing to me, as a part of this team, to get this document and see [quotes from] leaders in the district."

Osgood continued, "I appreciate Ms. Fusco speaking here and addressing the fact that these are not comments that she made."

Earlier in the day, BTU President Anna Fusco disavowed the quote she gave to Kenny. She insisted that she totally supported the PROMISE program (Kenny never said otherwise) and that her comments had been misrepresented (in fact, Kenny had significantly understated her comments in an attempt to respect her political interests).

"I would like to give [Ms. Rupert] and Ms. Bartleman the same opportunity," Osgood prompted.

Bartleman fumbled, "Uh, my name is quoted in the document... regarding the bond. And I'm assuming that the quote was taken from a public meeting.... Uh, so anyone can quote me from a public meeting. It was not in reference to PROMISE." Bartleman insisted that the shooter had never been referred to PROMISE and that she totally supported it.

Rupert spoke next. "Mine is the same comment. [Any quotation] would be from a public meeting. And certainly, I have provided leadership over the last seven years that I have been a board member on moving towards commonsense safety measures as well as representing a very diverse district. My record stands on its own, and I usually don't comment on misinformation...it's very hurtful.... I really can't excuse people using quotes for political gain."

Watching the livestream, Max messaged Kenny, "You were just accused of misquoting Fusco and basically making up quotes from Rupert."

Kenny replied, "All of those quotes are accurate. Insane. Fusco forced me to rescind despite having confirmed the quote a week prior. Rupert stated on the call that I would be able to use her statement. I feel like I'm in the twilight zone."

Board member Patti Good acknowledged that it was unusual for the school board to respond to public speakers. But given comments that she called "not factual," she asked Runcie to address points that had been raised.

Runcie cleared his throat. "I guess I'll start with PROMISE, since we are on that piece. What I will tell the public is contrary to what people may actually believe or have heard. Nikolas Cruz was never part of the PROMISE program. Well, he didn't do any eligible infractions for the PROMISE program to be part of that program *while he was at Marjory Stoneman Douglas.*" (Emphasis added.)

He continued, "It is really ironic that folks are coming to lecture the district on our discipline piece when a couple of weeks ago I received a letter from the ACLU. I'm looking for it now. And I'll just read to the public exactly what they're saying."

He searched his desk for it. Five. Ten. Fifteen. Twenty seconds.

"What the hell?" thought Tim Sternberg (whom you'll get to know in chapter 11). Until the last school year, Tim had been an assistant principal helping to oversee the PROMISE program. A few minutes earlier, during the public comment period, he had begged the board to reply to his emails about how to make the program work better. "Did he just look at parents who lost their children," Tim thought, "and tell them that he finds it 'ironic' that they're 'lecturing' him? Because he got a letter from the ACLU?"[20]

Finally, Runcie found the letter on his desk and began to read it. "'Dear Superintendent Runcie and members of the Broward County School Board. We are troubled by the continued trend of removing at-risk students from regular public schools. Excluding students from their schools increases their risk of arrest and decreases their chance of graduation. This practice is generally known as expulsion...'"

Tim's mouth dropped open as Runcie continued to read the letter. Superintendent Runcie was, indeed, telling friends and families of the victims that their questions about the district's discipline policies were "ironic" because he had once received a letter from the ACLU saying that he hadn't gone far enough.

Circling back to PROMISE, Runcie declared, "The program, based on the data we have, has been very successful."

"You know that data is nonsense!" Tim thought.

"Again, uh," Runcie explained, "connecting PROMISE to this horrific tragedy, um, is truly unfortunate. I think it's reprehensible. And, you know, we're not going to dismantle a program in this district, um, that is serving and helping kids appropriately, uh, because of news that is not fact-based. And I'll leave it at that."

But he would not leave it at that. As he began to address Kenny's report directly, he started to stumble:

> Certainly, I want to commend, um, the, Mr. Preston, uh, the young man for his interest in the operations of the, um, public schools. Um, applaud him for his efforts, uh, to report on the information that he's been given. Uh, but that's where the concern comes in. It's with the information that he's been given and the narrative that has been spun, uh, with that. Um, you know, it's, it's my belief and what I've said to him that, uh, good investigative journalism...you know, without integrity in journalism you have, uh, what Shakespeare, uh, once said, a tale told with a lot of sound and fury yet saying nothing.

As Runcie continued, his speech found surer footing. "We are continuing to witness a significant amount of misinformation and fake news as a result of the MSD tragedy," he said. "It seems like everybody wants to use this for some type of agenda that's not focused on the interest of the students and the families that we're trying to support."

Then Runcie ran through the "fake news" he had dealt with. He had received calls from reporters asking whether the student activists were paid actors. "Last week," he said, shaking his head, "we continued to receive communication from sources that claim that the Parkland tragedy was a hoax.... Finally, emerging out of right-wing media, we saw stories trying to connect the district's PROMISE program to this shooter.... Today, we find ourselves with another narrative around the district's capital bond program. Somehow that was responsible for this tragedy."

"Um, so a couple of things with that I saw and heard, um, in, uh, the analysis done by this young man," Runcie began to stammer again. "I think first, um, there's a confusion with the, um, level of expenditures and budget, um, and the level of effort in terms of moving the project. Um, another one would be, uh, um, equating a delay in the start of a project with the actual timeline for completing a project." Runcie explained that the technology and arts components were going well. However, on the safety side, "it is absolutely true that we got off to a late start. Um, we had, a number of things that we had to, um, put in place."

Tim shook his head. Runcie could deliver prepared talking points with the best of them but always stumbled when he tried to spin. Nearly lost amid his "ums" and "uhs" was the fact that, after comparing Kenny to conspiracy theorists who declared the shooting a hoax, Runcie admitted that Kenny's report was correct: safety projects had been significantly delayed.

Kenny heard none of Runcie's monologue firsthand. But he got the gist of it from people texting him. "It's absolutely insane how much they're speaking about the document," he texted Max.

A few minutes later, a school district staffer came into the hallway to ask Kenny to come back to the room. Rosalind Osgood addressed Kenny:

> *Ms. Rupert articulated so well how hurtful it is when someone takes something, or adds your name to something, that you did not say. It's hurtful for Ms. Rupert, and it's hurtful for this board. So we encourage your research. We think it's great. But I'm just going to ask if, as you're quoting people, to be as precise as you can...so that we don't have this type of fake news....*
>
> *You being a very ambitious and bright young man, I just couldn't understand why adults would give you the misinformation that I saw in this document. And as we move forward on this, I'm just going to remind us that we lost seventeen people. Others were injured physically. More was impacted emotionally.... Whatever our ambitions are...let's be mindful of the blood that has been shed and not take this moment and exploit it for personal gain, or in a very mean and evil way.*

Kenny felt like he was on Mars. A school board member had just called him evil! Osgood continued, saying it was "appalling" that PROMISE had come up for debate.

> *Under no terms can we sit and allow erroneous information to come forward and a program like PROMISE to be drawn into this conversation in a very evil and mean-spirited way, when [the tragedy] has nothing to do with this program.... The board has constantly supported this program. It's so unfair to constantly have to defend something that you really support. It just makes no sense.*

What made no sense to Kenny was that an elected official thought it was "unfair" that she had to defend a policy position. What made no sense to Kenny was that a school board member had accused him of being evil. And what made the least sense of all was that Nora Rupert had publicly disavowed him. He had been told to expect the worst from Runcie, and he knew that Osgood was Runcie's closest ally. But Rupert? She had answered his questions, she had verified his claims, and it had seemed like she was proud of his efforts.

After the meeting, Kenny received a call from Rupert. Kenny recalled that she apologized and told him that she had been shaking when she said those things, but Runcie had told her to denounce his report and that she had been threatened by other school board members with an ethics investigation if she didn't recant her statements.

At least that made some strange sort of sense, Kenny thought.

At first, he figured that if the superintendent was willing to go to these lengths to discredit him, he must have really been onto something. But doubts quickly set in. Thinking back to the 2011 grand jury report's descriptions about how the district would aggressively silence any criticism, Kenny wondered, "Maybe this has nothing to do with anything I found. Maybe it's just about who they are as people."

Kenny's report received substantial press coverage from conservative media, which focused on the report's contents and how the district had tried to shut him down. But the families and survivors who watched the board meeting in person or on livestream focused on how Fusco and Rupert had accused Kenny of misrepresenting them.

Kenny's credibility was in tatters. Even his father no longer believed that he had reported accurately or fairly. One interview Kenny did with a SiriusXM reporter was picked up and run by NRATV, leading students to text him saying they felt betrayed and exploited by an NRA shill.

Rationally, Kenny knew that he had conducted himself with integrity and was the victim of an orchestrated smear campaign. But because no one else believed him, he started to doubt himself. A week later, Max called Kenny expecting to find him excited about the press coverage his report had generated. But Kenny was depressed.

"If these guys are really hiding things," Kenny groaned, "what I did only discredited the effort to find out what."

"The key," Max replied, "is asking the right people the right questions. If you can get me an MSD teacher or students to talk to, I'll fly down and see what I can find."

"Okay," Kenny said. "I can make some introductions."

PART II

Cruz Control

I couldn't make it to the school board meeting where Kenny presented his report, but my wife came home very upset. Almost nothing upsets Julie. She always wants to think the best of everyone, and it's nearly impossible for her to say an unkind word. But the way the superintendent and the school board treated Kenny left her feeling disgusted. I knew that if Julie was upset, there must really be something wrong with these people.

At that meeting they also voted to not allow money from the Marjory Stoneman Douglas High School Public Safety Act's Coach Aaron Feis Guardian Program to fund armed guards for Broward schools. The reason why, they said, was that they didn't want to arm teachers.

That was bullshit. The Guardian Program explicitly excluded teachers from participating. It was about allowing highly trained veterans or security staff to carry a gun to protect students. A new law was passed because of a failure on their watch, and then they used a politically correct talking point as an excuse to avoid complying with it.

Between that and the fact that Runcie was calling criticism of the PROMISE program "fake news," I knew I had to take a hard look at everything. All Runcie had to do was tell the truth. If he had, maybe Kenny and Max wouldn't have dug into it any further. But when Runcie started carefully crafting statements and crying, "fake news!" all of us knew he was hiding something. I made it my mission to figure out what, and together, Max, Kenny, Kim, Royer, and I started our own investigation.

I wanted to understand every single failure leading up to February 14, everything that went wrong, and every reason why it went wrong. And I wanted to expose it all so that America could learn from it. Once I started investigating, I realized that the biggest and most important failure was how the Broward County school district had handled Nikolas Cruz.

I hate using his name. Using a killer's name can spur copycats, sick people who want to become famous too. Before the tragedy, the shooter recorded a video saying, "By the power of my AR you will know my name." And the media made damn sure of that. That's why I almost always call him by his prison number, 18–1958, instead.

But Part II of this book is titled "Cruz Control" because the only reason this kid became a mass murderer was that the whole system in Broward was even sicker than he was. We'll take you step by step on his journey through the school system. We'll show you the decisions that the adults made and explain why they made them. Every step of the way, they had a choice: do the responsible thing and help him, or do the politically correct thing and ignore him. They made the wrong choice every single time.

Some people have said that the Parkland tragedy was a "total system failure." When you read Part II of this book, it will seem almost unbelievable. But when you take a deeper dive into the school district and its politically correct policies in Part III, every failure will make sense. In fact, in a fucked-up way, I'm not even sure you could call what happened a "failure" because everyone was doing exactly what these policies and this system encouraged them to do. Nikolas Cruz could not possibly have broadcast more clearly who and what he was.

That's why I only blame Cruz 50 percent for what happened. And that's why, in this part of the book, we use his name. Because his name should not be associated with the style of rifle he used, like he wants.

Rather, "Cruz Control" should become a thought that haunts educators, an answer to the rhetorical question, "What's the worst that can happen?" Because that's how we stop this from ever happening again: by studying what happened and learning from it. If our school leaders focus less on professional convenience and more on the students in front of them, America's schools will become safer at every level.

—Andy

CHAPTER 5

An Exceptional Student

There was something profoundly dark and disturbed at the core of Nikolas Cruz's soul. Even his mother, Lynda, described her son as "evil." But as a society, we build our institutions to contain our demons. There are hundreds if not thousands of students like Nikolas Cruz across the country. But they do not do what he did because we reach them. We help them or we stop them. Nothing in the next three chapters provides an excuse for what he did. But it does provide an explanation of how he was enabled to do it. Every institution around Cruz, especially the school system, failed. He did not have to become a mass murderer.

Early Life

Nikolas Cruz's birth mother, Brenda Woodard, was a career criminal and drug addict. She had been arrested twenty-eight times for crimes ranging from drugs and car theft to weapons possession, burglary, and domestic violence and was using crack while pregnant with her eldest child, Danielle. In middle school, Danielle was placed in her grandmother's care when her mother was sent to jail. Danielle, in turn, has been arrested seventeen times and is currently serving an eight-year prison sentence on charges including attempted murder of a police officer.[1]

Brenda was also arrested for possession of crack cocaine while pregnant with her second child, Nikolas.[2] He was born on September 24, 1998. Three days later, Jacob Cruz and Lynda Kumbatovich effectively bought him for $50,000. As an older (Jacob was sixty-two and Lynda forty-nine) and then-unmarried couple, they had difficulty adopting through the traditional system. So they paid Brenda's lawyer for the "expenses" associated with transferring custody of Nikolas. Brenda gave birth to Nikolas's half-brother Zachary in prison a year and a half later, and Lynda and Jacob adopted him as well.[3]

Elementary School

From the time he learned to walk, Cruz displayed deeply disturbing behavior. Former neighbor Trish Duvaney recalled, "My [four-month-old] son was crawling on the back patio and [Cruz] threw my son into the pool. And Cruz was only two then."[4] At age three, Cruz was kicked out of a private pre-K program because he wouldn't stop biting other students. Lynda brought him to specialists from the Broward school district and they determined that, at three years and five months old, Cruz had the mind of a child who had just turned two.[5] He was diagnosed at that time with a developmental delay; later, with a speech impairment, a language-processing deficiency, and attention deficit disorder. Specialists determined that because of his propensity to bite, pinch, and scratch, he required "maximum teacher assistance" to interact safely with peers in his public school pre-K class. For his two years of pre-K, he had to be placed in a restrictive harness in order to ride the school bus.

In June 2004, Cruz's kindergarten teachers met with Lynda to discuss his "aggression and animal fantasies." They explained that he "seems to identify as an animal. He often crawls on the floor or ground, pounces on another student, makes seemingly animal-like growling sounds, and grimaces while holding his hands in a paw-like manner." This was far beyond normal child's play. His teachers recorded that he was "impulsive with no sense of boundary; he acts out his fantasies, often explosively, in expressing his feelings of stress and anxiety. Transition times appear to be particularly threatening to him; [he] appears to react more aggressively." After the meeting, he was labeled as requiring

Exceptional Student Education (ESE), similar to special education in other states, due to his "emotional and behavioral" disability.

Two months after the meeting, Cruz walked into his kitchen in tears. "What's the matter?" Lynda asked. "Did Daddy punish you?" Cruz replied, "Nope. Daddy's dead."[6] Jacob had died of a heart attack in front of Cruz, a trauma that could do lasting and profound damage to even the most stable of children.

Later that month, Cruz entered kindergarten in a self-contained classroom for ESE students with behavioral disabilities. By the end of the year, Lynda decided that he should repeat kindergarten to "create a stronger foundation." By the end of his second year of kindergarten, he had transitioned successfully into a normal classroom and began first grade in 2006 as a normal student. But two months in, his teacher reported that she was unable to control his aggression. By the end of first grade, he had to be physically removed from the classroom on an almost daily basis, often several times a day. For second grade, Cruz returned to a self-contained classroom for ESE students with behavioral disabilities.

By third grade, Cruz was calmer but sadder. His ESE specialist wrote in her notes in May 2008 that Cruz "expressed feelings of sadness and not feeling as if he is in control of things. [Cruz] reported that nothing goes his way and he does not seem to be able to control what happens to him. He also reported that he almost always feels that his life is getting worse and worse and he used to be happier" and that he would physically lash out at other students.

In the middle of his fifth-grade year, Cruz's teachers had to make a choice that would define the future of his education. In an earlier era, a student like Cruz could continue to receive specialized attention in a self-contained classroom for students with similar disabilities for at least part of each day in middle school. However, between the pressure on schools to assess students using standardized tests under the federal No Child Left Behind Act and the pressure on schools to put students in the "least restrictive environment" possible under the federal Individuals with Disabilities Education Act, spending part of the day in a specialized classroom was no longer an option for a student like Cruz in a Broward middle school. It was either full "inclusion" at Westglades

Middle School or full "exclusion" at a specialized school for students with emotional and behavioral disabilities: Cross Creek.

His teachers decided to try to prepare him to attend Westglades. Halfway through his fifth-grade year, they placed him in a normal classroom for 40 percent of the day. By the end of the year, Lynda was pleased with her son's ability to sit in a normal classroom without being disruptive or violent. The educators on his Individualized Education Program (IEP) team, who create tailored plans for students with disabilities in consultation with their parents, decided to enroll him at Westglades as a sixth-grader for the 2011–2012 school year, where he would be treated essentially the same as any other student.

Westglades

Cruz struggled academically in sixth grade. His IQ was not substantially below average, but his teachers were not trained to address his language-processing impairment. One Westglades teacher noted that around the time Cruz enrolled, Broward teachers were receiving what she called "shotgun" ESE certifications via cursory online courses. She and other teachers felt unprepared to handle students like Cruz. But these certifications provided a way for the school district to comply with state law while also cutting costs by not providing students like Cruz with specialized support.

Cruz received occasional therapy and counseling services, and, according to his official records, he kept his aggression in check through most of sixth grade. But in April 2012, Lynda told her son's teachers that she intended to consult a doctor about his behavior, which had again become erratic and aggressive. His teachers noted that he frequently refused to complete assignments. By the end of sixth grade, his behavior had deteriorated further. He was suspended four times in the last three weeks of school, and his mother complained to teachers that he was "burnt out and sick of school."

In August 2012, during his first month as a seventh-grader, Cruz was disciplined for fighting. According to his official disciplinary records, he received no other disciplinary referrals until February 2013, after which he was suspended for nearly *half* of the next calendar year. The problem at Westglades certainly was not a refusal to suspend

Cruz. The problem was that Westglades school administrators kept a student who was displaying deeply disturbed and dangerous behavior on a daily basis for a full year before transferring him to Cross Creek, where everyone knew he needed to go.

Staff and Student Recollections

"I never had him as a student," one teacher recalled. "But everyone knew who he was because he wreaked havoc." What sticks out to her was his "screaming in the hall. And [me] trying to ignore it."

If something frustrated Cruz, he would curse and threaten anyone nearby. He would hide behind corners and doors, jump out and scream at people, and then cackle at their fear. Sometimes, for no apparent reason, he would burst into maniacal laughter.

One former Westglades student, Paige, met Cruz in eighth grade. As they both stood outside their classroom waiting for their teacher to open the door, Cruz offered her a hug, which Paige accepted. Paige loved hugs and was eager to make a new friend. Their teacher later pulled Paige aside and warned her, "Don't touch him. He just got caught jerking off."[7, 8]

Another student, Sarah, never learned Cruz's name but instinctively feared him. Whenever she saw him in the hallway, she would turn and walk the other way. She recalled a time when he threw his chair across the classroom. Later, Sarah recalled seeing him sitting outside the classroom with his desk tied down so he could not throw it again.

Sarah and other students recalled an incident where Cruz banged on a classroom door so violently that the glass shattered, striking students inside. His disciplinary records show that the teacher referred him to the principal for this action on September 4, 2013, which the teacher characterized as vandalism. (However, administrators do not appear to have recorded the incident in his formal disciplinary record.)

Cruz's torture and killing of animals became a source of pride for him as he interacted with other students. One student, Devin, recalled that, although he tried to avoid Cruz, Cruz would approach him almost every day and ask, "Would you like to see videos of me skinning animals?" Devin always declined, but Cruz kept asking.

One student—who spoke on condition of anonymity and whom we'll call Nicole—recalled being so frightened of him that she often wanted to stay home. One day, a rumor spread around school like wildfire: Cruz had killed his cat. Nicole and a friend worked up the nerve to ask him, "What happened to your cat?"

He replied, "I took it in the backyard. I have a lake. I put it in its cage and I drowned it."

"What do you mean?"

"I killed my cat."

Cruz showed them a series of pictures on his phone. His cat. His cat in the cage. The cage going into the water. The cage coming out of the water. The cat, wet and dead. Nicole was horrified. Cruz was transfixed, both by the pictures and by her horror.

"If Any Good Comes Out of All of This..."

Reflecting on Cruz, a Westglades teacher, who spoke to us on condition of anonymity for fear of professional retaliation and whom we'll call Mrs. Pangrace, said, "If any good comes out of [the Parkland shooting], I hope it's that the district finally gets rid of Response to Intervention."

Response to Intervention (RTI) is only one part of the alphabet soup of disciplinary reforms—which also includes Multi-Tiered System of Supports (MTSS), Positive Behavioral Intervention and Supports (PBIS), and restorative justice (RJ)—that thousands of schools serving millions of students now use. We explore these policies further in Chapter 9, but in short: the MTSS/RTI/PBIS approach to student behavior requires extensive documentation in the name of "data-driven decision-making." In practice, it deters teachers from reporting disciplinary problems and makes administrators less inclined to trust teachers' intuition and more inclined to make decisions that produce the disciplinary "data" that their district-level superiors want to see.

Mrs. Pangrace lamented, "A teacher can no longer just say, 'I have a bad feeling about this student. He needs serious help. Let's get him tested or into a different school,' and have the principal respond, 'I trust you. Let's do it.'" These days, she explained, "there's a lot of paperwork, a lot of wasted time, a lot of 'let's see what he does for the next three months.'"

In Broward, a school must document multiple parent conferences and mental health observations, conduct psychological and psychosocial evaluations, administer a Functional Behavioral Assessment (FBA) and then implement a Positive Behavioral Intervention Plan (PBIP) for at least six weeks before a student is eligible to transfer to a specialized school. The full process often takes four to six months.

Here is some of the "data" that was recorded at Westglades and would have been available to school administrators at Cross Creek and MSD.

Lynda's Perspective

As part of Cruz's FBA, Westglades's social worker interviewed Lynda Cruz.[9] Here is how Lynda answered the standard questions:

What is the child's problem behavior?
He can't control his temper, especially when faced with frustration. He has frequent anger outbursts.

How would you describe these behaviors?
He starts screaming, kicking, throwing things, and punching holes on the walls.

What are the most problematic for you?
"Destruction" when he throws a tantrum, things get broken, nothing is safe. I have polka dotted walls from all the Spackle I have to use to fill the holes in the walls.

How often do these behaviors occur?
Every day, especially while playing Xbox.

Are there situations in which the behaviors never or rarely occur?
No, if he is losing at Xbox there are no two ways about it.

What do you think needs to be done to help this child?
He needs to be properly diagnosed before he can be treated. I know ADD is not the cause of all of his problems. We need to know what is wrong with him.

Ms. Yon's Logs

Teachers are required to collect "data" for FBAs. The following excerpts are taken from notes kept by Cruz's eighth-grade language arts teacher Carrie Yon:

September 3: While reviewing [a] homophones worksheet, when another student mentioned the amendment that talks about 'the right to bear arms' Nick [sic] lit up when hearing the word that related to guns and shouted out "you mean like guns!" he was overly excited thinking that we were going to talk about guns. Nick later used his pencil as a gun...shooting around the classroom.

September 4: Nick drew naked stick figures (showing body parts, sexual) and drew pictures of people shooting each other with guns.

September 11: Nick returned from being out for [internal suspension]. After discussing and lecturing about the Civil War in America Nick became fixated on the death and the assassination of Abraham Lincoln. He asked inappropriate questions and was making shooting actions with his pencil. Some questions he asked were "What did it sound like when Lincoln was shot? Did it go pop pop or pop pop pop really fast? Was there blood everywhere? After the war what did they do with all the bodies? Did people eat them?"

September 16: When we began to read the Odyssey Nick paid partial attention (in-and-out) until we came up to the gruesome scene when the giant eats Odysseus' crew members, only then Nick was interested in the lesson and got my 100% attention.

September 18: Nick was very worked up and anxious and he was making obscene gestures with his pencil and his hands (sexual in content).

September 24: Nick then began making inappropriate hand gestures (pretending to masturbate) and looking at other kids and laughing.

September 27: Another student also informed me (once Nick was escorted out of class) that Nick asks him all of the time "How am I still at this school?"

October 1: When talking about figurative language and onomatopoeias, Nick shouted out "Like a gun shooting." Nick will find any excuse to bring up shooting guns or violence.... He got frustrated and said "I hate security, I hope they die." Then he stated to me, "Fuck you." I called security to pick him up immediately.

October 15: Spoke to his mother on the phone about the "F" in my class.[10]*... We discussed that he should not be playing violent video games and that he should be put in a different school that can help with his behavior and emotional issues. We also discussed his obsession with guns/violence. She stated that he is interested in buying a BB gun from Walmart and was asking his mom, repeatedly, if he could get the gun, promising that he would "just shoot at trees."*

October 17: Nick began reading the last couple of pages out to the students, intentionally trying to ruin the book for everyone else. I asked him to stop and he told me that he dislikes the book and then he stated, "I like guns" can we talk about that. Then he continued to read the book out loud again.

On October 21, Yon emailed assistant principal Antonio Lindsay: "I wanted to let you know about Nick's behavior today. He seems to be getting worse with each day. Following is what took place in the first ten minutes of class." Yon described how, when Cruz wouldn't stop screaming, she told him that she would have to ask him to leave if he kept up the disruption. When he stuck up his middle finger, she went over to the phone. Cruz ran over, took the phone from her, tried to dial 911, banged the phone on the receiver when that didn't work, and then ran out of the classroom.

On October 24, Lindsay came to class to observe Cruz. As soon as Lindsay left the room, Cruz yelled, "Yes, now I can talk!" He continued to be disruptive, and Yon said, "I know that you can behave, I have seen you. You're a good kid." Cruz shouted, "I'm a bad kid, I want to kill!"[11, 12]

Yon provided her opinion for the FBA:

I feel strongly that Nikolas is a danger to the students and faculty at this school. I do not feel that he understands the difference between his violent video games and reality. He is constantly showing aggressive behavior and poor judgment. His drawing in class show violent acts (people shooting at each other) or creepy sexual pictures (dogs with large penises). He has pretended to masturbate in class, he uses foul language and disregards everyone around him. Nikolas has been reprimanded on many occasions (verbally, referrals, IS, etc.) and continues to act in the same manner over and over again. I would like to see him sent to a facility that is more prepared and has the proper setting to deal with this type of child."

"I know that this issue is not conducive to you all doing your jobs..."

On September 13, 2013, Lindsay sent this email to Cruz's teachers and support staff:

This memo shall serve as notification from this day forth until otherwise notified. Nickolas [sic] Cruz will be on escort only status. If he needs to leave the class to use the restroom, go to the clinic, or any other reason please notify the front office and wait for a security escort. Under no circumstances should Nickolas [sic] be allowed to leave a supervised setting without an escort.

One month later, Lindsay sent a follow-up email:

As additional interventions, please be advised that N. Cruz will be "shadowed" by his mother when he chooses to run / walk out of class in "his attempts" of avoiding getting into trouble. His mother will be called immediately when it happens to come to school and "shadow" him for the rest of the day or she will "shadow" him the following day. As a result of today's incident of him running out of class, mom will come to "shadow" him tomorrow. Nick has been advised that if he feels as though he is having a bad day / period, that he is supposed to "ask" his teachers to be excused to go to Mr. Lindsay, Mrs. Watkins, or Mrs. Fondren. At that point, the teacher will need to call for an escort to take him to either location.

On another note, please do not alert him to when you are going to call security to have him removed as a result of his inappropriate behavior. Please call discreetly or send a student to the front office to alert security. When he hears a teacher say that they are calling for security, in his mind he needs to "escape" the situation to avoid getting in trouble.

I know that this issue is not conducive to you all doing your jobs to the best of your ability, but rest assured that we are working to ensure that N. Cruz is in the best situation possible to be academically and behaviorally successful. Please continue to work with us as we undergo this process of observation and decision-making. Thank you in advance!

Take a moment to put yourself in the position of any of Cruz's teachers. You have diligently documented this student's deranged behavior for months. You have related Cruz's many threatening statements to your assistant principal, as well as his troubling preoccupation with guns, killing, and cannibalism. All of your colleagues have had similar experiences with this student. You have expressed the opinion, supported by extensive "data," that Cruz is a danger to others and belongs at a specialized school. And after six weeks of diligent documentation, you get that e-mail from your assistant principal.

Then, imagine that three weeks later, on November 4, armed with all of the "data" from the Functional Behavior Assessment, your assistant principal sends you a new Positive Behavior Intervention Plan that provides these instructions for managing his behavior:

If Nikolas becomes disruptive,

1. *Try to assess what is causing it.*

2. *If he seems to be struggling with his work,*
   a. *DO NOT comment on his behavior or argue with him.*
   b. *Prompt him to request help appropriately. For example, "Nik, I can see you need help with that. The way to ask me is to raise your hand."*

3. *If he does not seem to need help, but wants to get others off task for attention or escape.*
   a. *DO NOT comment on his behavior or argue with him.*
   b. *If he escalates, prompt him to take a break/use a cool down pass. Remind him that this is not a reward break, but just a brief work break. For example, "I can see this is bothering you. Do you want to take a 5-minute break? Then you can get back on track and earn your reward.*

c. *If he continues to escalate, follow procedures for major disruption/property destruction.*

If Nikolas destroys property at a lower level,

1. *Calmly let him know he has not followed one of the expectations. Remind him what he is working for.*

2. *Prompt him to use a cool down pass and walk away to diffuse [sic] the situation*

3. *If he does not escalate, allow him to cool down until he has regained control*

4. *If he continues to escalate, follow procedures for major disruption/property destruction.*

If Nikolas engages in major disruption/property destruction,

1. *Let Nikolas know, "you're getting too loud. I need for you to get back into control by using a cool down pass or calming down at your desk. If you get back into control, you can stay in class. If you continue, I'll need for you leave [sic]."*

2. *Walk away and do not pay attention to his behavior.*

3. *If Nikolas regains control, praise him for being able to stay in class.*

4. *If Nikolas continues after a brief increase in behavior, call for support staff to remove Nikolas.*

5. *Send his work with him so that work is not avoided.*

6. *Do not argue with Nikolas or engage with him.*

7. *When class is over, Nikolas needs to go to his next class and behavior plan should re-set with able to [sic] earn reward breaks again.*

NOTE: For behaviors where others' safety is a concern (i.e. throwing objects at others which may injure them, such as books, etc.), immediately call for assistance and implement safety procedures. *

(*Document abridged; emphases in original.)

The "data-driven decision" regarding Cruz's behavior was that teachers should ignore it unless he commits sustained "major disruption/property destruction" or directly threatened the physical safety of other students.

District policy required that teachers implement this PBIP for at least six weeks before Cruz could transfer to Cross Creek. By this point, some teachers refused to allow him into their classrooms without the campus security monitor, Ms. Fondren, present. Several teachers, in exasperation and perhaps fear, tried to refuse to let him into their classroom. But they were informed by school administrators that this was not permitted.

Social Justice Child Abuse

Now imagine that you are a student at Westglades with Nikolas Cruz. In particular, imagine that you are a pre-teen girl named Isabelle Robinson. You have been deputized by school administrators to be Cruz's "peer counselor" as part of the Broward County Public Schools' new focus on restorative justice (RJ).

RJ comes to education from the world of criminal justice: after a criminal serves his prison sentence and is released, he is encouraged to make amends with his victims. But in K-12 education, rather than try to make amends *after* a punishment, RJ is done *instead of* punishment. It includes practices such as "reparative" dialogues to address the "root causes" of misbehavior, "healing circles," and peer counseling. In many school districts, RJ has become a catchall term that allows adults to ignore misbehavior by arguing that students are responsible for their peers' behavior. After the shooting, Isabelle described her peer counseling experience with Nikolas Cruz in the *New York Times*:

> *My first interaction with Nikolas Cruz happened when I was in seventh grade. I was eating lunch with my friends, most likely discussing One Direction or Ed Sheeran, when I felt a sudden pain in my lower back. The force of the blow knocked the wind out of my 90-pound body; tears stung my eyes. I turned around and saw him, smirking. I had never seen this boy before, but I would never forget his face. His eyes were lit up with a sick, twisted joy as he watched me cry.*

The apple that he had thrown at my back rolled slowly along the tiled floor. A cafeteria aide rushed over to ask me if I was O.K. I don't remember if Mr. Cruz was confronted over his actions, but in my 12-year-old naïveté, I trusted that the adults around me would take care of the situation....

A year after I was assaulted by Mr. Cruz, I was assigned to tutor him through my school's peer counseling program. Being a peer counselor was the first real responsibility I had ever had, my first glimpse of adulthood, and I took it very seriously. Despite my discomfort, I sat down with him, alone. I was forced to endure his cursing me out and ogling my chest until the hourlong session ended.

When I was done, I felt a surge of pride for having organized his binder and helped him with his homework. Looking back, I am horrified. I now understand that I was left, unassisted, with a student who had a known history of rage and brutality....

My little sister is now the age that I was when I was left alone with Mr. Cruz, anxious and defenseless. The thought of her being put in the same situation that I was fills me with rage.[13]

Some people might consider leaving a girl alone with a boy whom teachers considered profoundly dangerous, if not potentially murderous, to be child abuse. But in schools across the country, this is what passes for "social justice."

PROMISE

The RJ and the PBIP did not work. Cruz was suspended for nearly three quarters of the month of November. It was during this month that Cruz was referred to PROMISE for vandalizing a bathroom faucet. On its own, that may sound minor. But consider the broader context: the bathroom was literally the only place in school where a security escort was not watching Cruz's every move. He was referred to PROMISE instead of being arrested, but he did not attend for reasons the school district will not or cannot explain. If a student skips PROMISE, district policy requires that he be referred to the juvenile justice system.[14] But he was not for reasons the school district will not or cannot explain.[15]

Cruz's Suicide Attempt

On November 20, 2013, Cruz ran into the middle of a busy road during a fire drill. Former Westglades student Paige recalls being terrified because he could have died if an oncoming car had not stopped in time. Her teacher told her, "Don't worry, he's going to go somewhere where he can get the help that he needs now."

But Paige's teacher was being overly optimistic. Another teacher wrote a disciplinary referral for the incident, categorizing Cruz's suicide attempt as "Gross Insubordination" and "Aggressive and Dangerous Behavior." But school administrators rejected that categorization and categorized it instead as a minor act of disruption.

If Cruz had been involuntarily committed for psychiatric observation under Florida's Baker Act in response to his suicide attempt, it could have accelerated the process of sending him to Cross Creek. But he was not. It took until February 2014, five months after Westglades began the evaluation process and one year after his misbehavior became so severe that he was suspended essentially every other day, to send Cruz to Cross Creek. As Yon's records show, even Cruz couldn't understand why the school kept him there for so long.

Least Restrictive Environment

This may all sound like madness, but it was just a matter of following policy. An ESE expert with extensive experience in the Broward County school district spoke to us on condition of anonymity for fear of retaliation. This expert, whom we'll call Ms. Campbell, noted that the school clearly missed opportunities to commit Cruz for psychiatric observation. However, upon review of Cruz's middle school history, Ms. Campbell commented:

> It actually looks to me like the ESE specialist was sticking to the process. Surely everyone knew that he did not belong at that school. But to send a kid to a school like Cross Creek, you have to go through the checklist process established by the district. Ultimately, the school facilitates the process set by the district. It takes many, many months. It looks like the people at Westglades for the most part did what they could with the resources and constraints that they had.

You may recall from chapter 4 that, when student journalist Kenny Preston asked Superintendent Runcie's deputy Mickey Pope how a student like Cruz could even be allowed into a normal school, Pope replied, "Where a student accesses their educational services is very much guided by law." But Ms. Campbell rejects that excuse:

> *Nothing in federal law requires the full checklist that Broward uses. When it comes to students with physical disabilities, children who are medically fragile, non-verbal, who have nurses with them and g-tubes and trachs and all these incredible medical needs and they're sitting in a regular school in front of a computer screen because to get these kids into the [special education] center is so much work that school administrators don't even bother doing it. That's not federal law. That's just a local policy.*

School administrators often go through the months-long process of evaluating a student for placement in a specialized school for naught. Tim Sternberg, whom you'll hear from in chapter 11, once worked at Whispering Pines, a specialized school in Broward County similar to Cross Creek. He told us that eight or nine out of every ten recommendations to transfer a student to his school were rejected.

But it was not always this difficult. Joe Parsons, a recently retired art teacher who taught at Cross Creek for twenty-nine years, lamented that the impetus for making transfers more difficult was a desire to save money. It is far more expensive for a school district to serve a student like Cruz in a specialized school than in a traditional school.

It should sound awful that school districts systematically underserve emotionally disturbed students in order to save money, but it actually provides a strong public relations benefit to superintendents like Robert Runcie. That's because social justice activist groups frame this issue as a black-and-white question of "civil rights." Putting students like Cruz in schools like Cross Creek is alleged to be "ableist," (i.e., discrimination against the disabled) and keeping them in schools like Westglades is the self-evidently virtuous practice of "inclusion."

Shortly after Cruz transferred to Cross Creek, a scathing third-party review of Broward's ESE program was published.[16] The report noted that Broward's ratio of ESE students to staff was nineteen to one, almost twice that of neighboring Miami-Dade County, and that Broward's ESE program suffered from poor training and high turnover. Some of these problems could be attributed to administrative incompetence; in the previous year, Broward had cut nineteen positions even as it left over $5 million unspent. But if budgets reflect values, then Broward's special education spending reflects a perverse and immoral alignment between bureaucratic self-interest and social justice self-righteousness, wherein school districts shortchange ESE students and pat themselves on the back for it.

"How Is That Possible?"

When Westglades staff heard that Cruz had committed the massacre at MSD, some couldn't believe it. The fact that he became a mass murderer wasn't what surprised them. They were surprised that he attacked MSD. "How is that possible?" one Westglades educator recalled thinking. "We did our jobs. It took forever, but we got him where he needed to go. We couldn't believe they ever let him into MSD."

Cross Creek

Cross Creek is one of three specialized schools in Broward County for students with extreme behavioral disabilities. It serves about 150 students in grades K-12, most of whom have been diagnosed with mental illnesses and take psychotropic medications. It has a two-to-one student-to-adult ratio, including eleven counselors, fifteen behavior technicians, and three therapists.[17] There was no question that this was where Nikolas Cruz needed to be. The question that must be answered: How was he sent back to a normal school?

His First Semester

In his first semester at Cross Creek, Cruz's troubling behavior was much the same as it had been at Westglades. Dr. Nyrma Ortiz, a psychiatrist who consults with Cross Creek, noted, "He goes to YouTube to research wars, military material, and terrorist topics. Wears military related items before he goes to school. Parent stated that all of these ideas are related to his excessive gaming." Cruz told his school therapist Rona Kelly about a dream he had of killing people and being covered in their blood. By May, Cruz's consistently disturbing comments made staff fear that he would harm others, so they developed a safety plan for him and recommended that his mother remove all sharp objects from his home. When prompted to describe a perfect summer, Cruz wrote, "Buying some type of gun and shooting at targets that I set up with large amounts of ammo just for fun for hours."

Shortly before summer break, Kelly and Ortiz took the extremely unusual step of writing to his private psychiatrist, apparently with trepidation about what would happen over the summer when they were not monitoring him daily. They wrote:

> *Dear Dr. Negin,*
>
> *We are witting [sic] you with his mother's consent, to inform you of some of the behavioral problems he continues to display at home and school. Nikolas continues to present with extreme mood lability. He is usually very irritable and reactive. In school he displays oppositional and defiant behaviors and has become verbally aggressive in the classroom. He seems to be paranoid and places the blame on others for his behavioral problems. He has a preoccupation with guns and the military and perseverates on this topic inappropriately.*
>
> *At home, he continues to be aggressive and destructive with minimal provocation. For instance, he destroyed his television after loosing [sic] a video game that he was playing. Nikolas has a hatchet that he uses to chop up a dead tree in his backyard. Mom has not been able to locate that hatchet as of lately [sic]. When upset he punches holes in the walls and has used sharp tools to cut up the upholstery on the furniture and carve holes in the walls of the bathroom. Per recent information shared in school he dreams of killing others and [being] covered in blood. He has been assessed for the need of hospitalization in school and by the YES team from Henderson Behavioral Health....*
>
> *We would like you to be aware of the current concerns since you will see him for medication management during the summer and may need to re-assess his respond [sic] to the current medications. In our opinion his response to medications has been limited at best.*

The next fall got off to a rocky start. In late September, Kelly called Lynda and, according to her notes, "shared concerns with parent about obsession with guns/military and his poor anger control. He continues to deploy aggressive behaviors at home. Parent was advised against getting him a gun (pellet) or [shooting] classes for his birthday. Parent advised to restrict access to any weapons."[18] When asked what he was interested in or enjoyed, almost every single one of his teachers mentioned guns, the military, or war.

From October onward, however, Cruz appears to have calmed down. His therapist's notes reflect that his disruptive behavior and destructive tendencies had decreased, and he expressed the desire to attend a traditional school again. On May 21, his Cross Creek teachers recommended that he be mainstreamed to attend MSD.

Back in April, when Cruz told Dr. Ortiz that he wanted to attend a normal school and join a high school Junior Reserve Officers' Training Corps (JROTC) program in preparation for a military career, she noted, "interested in [J]ROTC?—not advised.... Discussed the safety of others/himself." But every member of his "Child Study Team" recommended that he be mainstreamed for two class periods a day at the beginning of the 2015-2016 school year: for JROTC and another class to be determined.

According to Ms. Campbell, before Robert Runcie became superintendent, she had never seen a student mainstreamed from a school like Cross Creek in less than three years. The process typically took several semesters, with the student's IEP team gradually adding class periods at the traditional school and carefully monitoring any changes in the student's behavior. Cruz spent his first semester at MSD taking two classes, largely unsupervised, and then began attending MSD full time the following semester. Ms. Campbell said that she had never heard of anything like it.

This all bears reiterating to emphasize the insanity of it: Cross Creek staff were well aware of Cruz's profoundly disturbing behavior at Westglades. They knew about his obsession with guns and dreams about killing people. They were so frightened that they took the extremely rare step of contacting his private psychiatrist. Yet not only did they return him to a traditional high school at an unprecedented speed, they also enrolled him in JROTC, a course in which he would learn to shoot using an air gun that resembled an AR-15.

Unfortunately, we do not believe that this was a random act of reckless negligence. Rather, we believe that the explanation is rooted in another policy-caused tragedy.

Why Cruz Was Mainstreamed

When Nikolas Cruz arrived at Cross Creek in the spring of 2014, the school was in upheaval as it struggled to accommodate an influx of students and staff from the recently shuttered Sunset School. The previous year, Superintendent Runcie had announced that the district would close that specialized school for students with behavioral disabilities because it was "under-enrolled."

Some teachers cried when they learned the news, and parents were even more distraught. For many of Sunset's disabled and disturbed students, it had taken years to build trust with adults other than their parents. Now those bonds were being broken. Melissa Smith explained that her autistic and nonverbal thirteen-year-old son had finally been successfully potty-trained at Sunset and had even started making friends. "He's going to go back to the 'throwing poo' days because all of this is being taken from him," Smith said. "He has *friends*...I never thought he would have friends.... Stuff like that, it matters big."[19]

Another mother, Jane Lauren, said, "It was a life-saving ordeal for Justin to get here. The school knew how to handle him." The fact that it was an ordeal to enroll students like Justin in a specialized school contributed to Sunset's "under-enrollment," and its "under-enrollment" was the justification for its closure in the name of administrative efficiency.

David Martinez, whose daughter is fed through a tube, complained, "It's not right, it's not right. On the backs of our children, they want to save money."

But the full story is even worse. Katherine Francis, head of the district's ESE department, allegedly pushed to close Sunset in part from a desire to use the building as office space for her and her staff. A few days after the closure was announced, she emailed other district administrators to inform them, "Should the current proposal be approved, my Division staff will move into the facility."[20]

When that e-mail became public, parents were even more outraged. "This is selfish," said one parent. "They are only thinking of themselves."[21] Runcie publicly backtracked, insisting that "there was never any official approved plan to do that."

Although Sunset ultimately did not become office space, it still closed at the end of the 2012–2013 school year. One mother lamented, "This decision is going to literally destroy the lives of hundreds of children."[22] However many lives were figuratively destroyed as children were uprooted from Sunset, we believe that the decision sparked a chain reaction that literally ended seventeen.

Even before the merger, Cross Creek staff were already facing pressures stemming from changes in federal, state, and district policy. The ever-growing emphasis on standardized testing disconcerted students and teachers alike. Broward eliminated teacher tenure, shifting teachers to one-year contracts and evaluating them by test scores, which, given Cross Creek's student population, made absolutely no sense. Former Cross Creek teacher Joe Parsons said, "Imagine how we teachers felt, let alone the students, about testing. It was highly toxic. Do you want to test a psychotic, schizophrenic, manic depressive, or otherwise emotionally and behaviorally disabled student, or a class of them? What is a fair test? What is a fair score?"[23]

Parsons also lamented that, just as the school district tried to reduce suspensions in traditional schools, the district also tried to reduce "the use of physical 'hands' on a student" at specialized schools. He explained:

> There was a significant movement to reduce the ability of security staff at our school to physically touch students. Training was given in "verbal de-escalation." This unfortunately gave license to the students to run around campus at will, and disrupt other classrooms, etc. ALL doors on campus were required to be locked at all times. The only "justified" hands-on practice was if the student was causing imminent physical harm to themselves or to others (banging their head on a wall/throwing a chair directly at a person).

Once hands-on was employed, a pile of district paperwork, parental notification, and other requirements had to be met.[24]

Add to all of these pressures the challenge of absorbing seventy percent of Sunset's staff and emotionally and behaviorally disturbed students, and it's no wonder that Cross Creek principal Ken Fulop decided to retire rather than oversee the merger.

The district selected as Fulop's replacement Colleen Stearn, who had until that point served as an assistant principal at traditional high schools. Things did not go smoothly. Parsons explained:

This merger was a disaster from the beginning. The district made NO apparent effort to assist in this merging of staff members. They provided no paid extra time, no "meet and greet," no staff development, no time for staff members to learn and share together (team building). The district appeared NOT to have helped the new principal in orchestrating a smooth merger. The Cross Creek [principal and assistant principal] appeared to make NO effort [either.] The merged staff members were just thrust together and expected to function....

There became issues between the "Cross Creek Way" and the "Sunset Way."... Both schools [believed] that they had the better/best way.... The climate was tense, beyond the usual tension of working in a center where a student can go ballistic in a heartbeat, or begin to cry uncontrollably or curse you or [their] peers at the top of their lungs, or throw a chair, or begin a physical fight. There were new staff members you did not know, [and you] did not know if they "had your back."[25]

Parsons believes that, despite the strife among the staff, Cross Creek maintained its full integrity when it came to serving students. But there is strong reason to suspect otherwise in the case of Nikolas Cruz.

The explanation as to why Cruz was mainstreamed lies in how two contradictory acts can be reconciled. According to MSD's ESE support facilitator Tara Bone, Cruz's therapist, Rona Kelly, called her mental health counterpart at MSD to say that she disagreed with the decision to mainstream him. But the therapist is usually the one steering those decisions. What's more, Kelly wrote in Cruz's IEP update when the decision was made that Cruz had proved that he could be "a model student."

Taken together, these acts suggest that Kelly, to whom Cruz had confided dreams of murder and gore, acted against her better judgment or was overruled. Kelly was from Sunset, and those who followed the "Cross Creek Way" did not trust the "Sunset Way." One ESE specialist on "Team Cross Creek" had taught Cruz in elementary school and was, along with Cruz's mother, pushing for him to be mainstreamed.

For her part, Principal Stearn appears to have been eager to demonstrate leadership over a school whose dysfunction had become fodder for gossip across the district. (Tim Sternberg recalled his former principal at Whispering Pines telling stories about shouting matches over office space between the factions at Cross Creek.) On an official "school improvement plan" Stearn was required to submit to the district in September 2016, she justified her leadership as follows:

> During the year of the initial merger of the two schools, trust and relationships had to be established with both staff and students. It was a struggle and we saw an increase in our suspension rates as inappropriate behaviors increased. We also did not see the learning gains in our students that we know they are capable of making.
>
> In the two years since the merger, we have established stability that has resulted in a 67% reduction in our suspension rates and a substantial increase in the number of our students who participate in the general education setting in their neighborhood schools on either a part time or full time basis....
>
> The number of students who participate in a general education setting has increased by 50%.[26]

Principals of traditional schools often point to (at times artificially) decreased suspension rates as proof of successful leadership. Stearn pointed both to decreased suspension rates and to increased mainstreaming rates. Historically, Cross Creek had never used mainstreaming numbers as a metric of success. Decisions about student placement were always made based on the needs of the individual student.

It is difficult to believe that Cross Creek's decision to not only mainstream a student with a history of disturbing behavior and murderous ideations and an obsession with guns, but also let him practice shooting with air guns as soon as he stepped foot on a traditional school was simply an instance of negligence. Instead, we believe it was either a conscious or subconscious response to explicit or implicit pressure to make Cross Creek appear orderly and successful.

CHAPTER 6

Going to MSD

Nikolas Cruz entered Marjory Stoneman Douglas High School as a sophomore in the fall of 2015. He was not quite the same screaming terror that he'd been at Westglades. But you didn't have to look very hard to see that he was a ticking time bomb.

"Stay in Your Lane"

During the fall semester, Cruz was scheduled to spend his first five class periods at Cross Creek and his last two at MSD. The ESE specialist responsible for him at MSD was Jessica DeCarlo. In mid-October, DeCarlo went on maternity leave. Assistant Principal Denise Reed tasked ESE support facilitator Tara Bone to cover for DeCarlo, but according to Bone, neither DeCarlo nor Reed told her about Cruz. Bone told us that Reed told her not to contact DeCarlo while she was on leave, to complete all paperwork without question, and to only bring to Reed's attention high-profile concerns raised by ESE parents.

In the last week of October, DeCarlo emailed Bone asking her to speak to teachers who taught "Nicholas" in anticipation of a December 14 meeting to decide whether to mainstream him full time.

Bone forwarded the email to a district ESE official and asked, "Do you know anything about this? This student is not on my support list nor do I have an IEP for him. This is the first time I am hearing about him." The district official replied, "No.... I am sure it was just an oversight." But then Bone received a call from the district office informing her that the email was not a mistake, and an administrator later forwarded her Cruz's IEP. Bone told us that she "read it, highlighted it, and ran to every [MSD] administrator saying this was bad. Bad, bad, bad."

The IEP suggested that Cruz had shown some signs of progress. For example, Cruz hadn't stolen anything while attending Cross Creek. The IEP also declared that Cruz had been "very focused on making appropriate choices in both the school and his neighborhood community."

But there were also warning flags. For example: "He continues to lack impulse control, [so] he needs to be monitored while in both the school and neighborhood communities.... He also has poor judgment in social situations. Recently he was punched numerous times by a peer for using racial slurs towards that peer. Cruz...refused to accept that the comments made by him caused the peer's reaction."

Bone knew that misbehavior had to be extreme to warrant sending a student to Cross Creek. In a special education system focused on putting students in the "least restrictive environment," the warning signs listed above were not necessarily enough to prove that Cruz wasn't ready to attend a normal school.

What truly alarmed Bone were the entries by three different educators about Cruz's fixation with guns and killing. When more than one educator writes the same thing on an IEP, it signals that it's very important. At the high school level, students are allowed to read their own IEPs, forcing educators to walk a fine line of communicating the truth to other educators while trying to be encouraging to the student.

One teacher wrote, "He can be distracted by his peers when he is interested in the topic, like military and weapons." Another wrote, "Nikolas, at times, will be distracted by inappropriate conversations of his peers if the topic is about guns, people being killed or the armed forces. He will also engage in the conversation." Rona Kelly wrote, "He becomes pre-occupied with things such as current events regarding wars and terrorists. He is fascinated by the use of guns and often speaks of weapons and the importance of 'having weapons to remain safe in this world.'"

Bone could not believe they had put him in JROTC. She wondered: Had anyone on his IEP team read what they'd written before they agreed to send him to MSD? Had anyone at MSD read his IEP? Later, Bone learned that the answer to both of her questions was no: When Jessica DeCarlo attended the meeting where Cross Creek staff decided to mainstream him for English and ROTC, the decision was presented to DeCarlo as a fait accompli. According to Bone, Cross Creek's ESE specialist did not guide the committee through Cruz's unusually long IEP, and DeCarlo left the meeting without reading it.

Bone voiced her concerns to MSD's assistant principal for ESE, Denise Reed, on November 6, 2015. Bone told us that she does not believe that Reed had read Cruz's IEP. Bone told Reed that Cruz was dangerous and it would be a grave mistake to mainstream him full time. Bone recalled that Reed told her to "stay in your lane" because these decisions were not hers to make.

Bone recalled that after raising her concerns about Cruz, Reed's attitude toward her changed. Bone started to hear that Reed was speaking ill of her to colleagues, and she felt that her workplace environment had been transformed. Until she first saw the name "Nicholas Cruz" in her email inbox, Bone had enjoyed her job at MSD. But between the hostility she felt from Reed and her fear of Cruz, Bone started looking for a new job six days after she was told to stay in her lane.

We made many attempts to interview Denise Reed, all of which were rebuffed. It is possible that, as Bone suspects, Reed never read Cruz's IEP and refused to have her authority questioned. But even if Reed had reviewed his disciplinary history from Westglades, she would not have seen sexually lewd acts, stealing, a suicide attempt, or weapons possession. Reed would only have seen a couple of instances of vandalism, a couple of fights, and a lot of profanity and disruption. Profanity and disruption could be tolerated, to a point. And, according to his teachers that first semester, Cruz was a quiet boy.

On December 14, 2015, Cruz's IEP team decided to allow him to attend MSD full time. Cruz had made progress in the intensive therapeutic setting of Cross Creek, where well-trained professionals could watch him like a hawk. But when he transitioned to MSD, his old "behavior management" plan was discontinued and no new plan was created. Teachers were left uninformed about who this student was, what to watch for, and how to support him.

Looking back on the transition, Bone lamented, "They just threw him to the wolves."

Ignoring Death Threats

Cruz's first day as a full-time MSD student was January 11, 2016. On February 5, 2016, a woman called the Broward sheriff's office to report an Instagram post in which Cruz showed off a gun and wrote, "I am going to get this gun and shoot up the school."

The officer who responded to the call, Edward Eason, informed the woman that Cruz's Instagram post "was protected by the First Amendment right of free speech."[1] When the woman asked Eason whether there would be any way to prevent Cruz from buying a gun when he turned eighteen, the officer told her that his right to purchase a firearm was protected by the Second Amendment and nothing could be done.

Eason was wrong on both counts. Threatening to shoot up a school is a felony that, if successfully prosecuted, could have prohibited Cruz from buying a firearm. (And even if Cruz was not convicted, an arrest could have gone a long way toward law enforcement taking future reports about Cruz seriously.) But Eason declined even to write a police report about the call, a decision for which he later received a three-day suspension. He did, however, according to his logs, notify MSD's school resource officer, Scot Peterson.

It is not known whether Peterson informed MSD administrators of Cruz's Instagram threat. There is, however, cause to believe that Principal Ty Thompson and other administrators were aware. Five days after the woman called police, Thompson emailed staff and parents: "Please be advised that we received a report of a potential threat through the school district's tip hotline today. School administrative and security staff followed all district safety protocols. The school district police and local law enforcement were immediately notified." Bone recalled that this e-mail related to a threat from Cruz.

If so, school administrators did not do anything about it.

Although it would have involved some paperwork, sending Cruz back to Cross Creek would not have been nearly as burdensome as sending him there in the first place. When a student with a deeply disturbed behavioral history threatens to shoot up a school, that is generally—to put it mildly—a sign that he is not well suited for that environment. But no action was taken. The incident was not even added to Cruz's official records. On paper, Cruz appeared to have been a model student in the spring semester of 2016.

But Cruz's official file bore little relationship to reality. MSD teacher Sandra Rennie later told the police that security staff "would always call [Cruz] over...and just, like, keep in contact with him all the time and [were] always calling him up to the office." Campus security monitor Andrew Medina told the police, "We always was [*sic*] watching [Cruz]. You know, he was one of those kids we always kept an eye on. You see him in the hallways, you see him out, call us up. Let's get him to the office."

That is what you would want security staff to do with a student like Cruz. Cruz often came to school dressed in full camouflage gear, mask included, and jumped out from behind poles to scare other students. He brought dead animals to school. Sometimes he'd fondle them under his desk. Other times he'd put a dead bird in a lunch box and give it to another student, telling her there was a treat inside. Occasionally he'd throw food at students. He brought knives to school and offered to sell them to other students. He wrote "I Hate Niggers" on his backpack and carved swastikas onto lunchroom tables. MSD staff recalled that he was sent to the office all the time, and students recalled that the impression that he was frequently suspended. This troubling pattern of behavior ought to have earned him a ticket back to Cross Creek. But his misbehavior was only officially documented once that semester.

As an ESE student, when Cruz was brought to MSD's office, he would have been brought to Denise Reed. Bone believes that Reed consistently refused to document Cruz's behavior. If true, this would not be an MSD-specific phenomenon. As you'll read about in chapter 10, school administrators frequently decline to administer discipline to ESE students. But at MSD, where well-resourced parents could easily avail themselves of legal assistance if they disagreed with a decision made by the school, ESE students became practically untouchable.

Reflecting on it, one longtime MSD teacher said, "As long as I have been here, whatever an ESE parent wants, they get. No one ever challenges an ESE parent or kid because it's not worth the risk of litigation." Regarding discipline, the teacher added, "Why bother? The parent will just say it wasn't the kid's fault."

Cruz was only officially disciplined once that semester, on February 22, 2016. What made that day different from all others? According to Bone, Denise Reed was off campus, allowing his behavior to be reported to Assistant Principal Winfred Porter. In a sworn statement to the police after the shooting, Porter confirmed that Cruz came to him that day because Cruz's usual assistant principal was absent. Porter gave Cruz a two-day internal suspension for drawing swastikas on lunchroom tables, labeling it "profanity."

In March, Cruz started dating another student, Emily. When Emily confided to her friend Dana Craig that Cruz was emotionally abusive, Dana urged her to end the relationship. In April, Emily took Dana's advice. But that did not put her out of danger. Emily's friend Connor Dietrich explained that, after the breakup, "[Cruz] stalked her and threatened her. He was like, 'I'm going to kill you,' and he would say awful things to her and harass her to the point I would walk her to the bus just to make sure she was okay. We all made sure she was never alone."[2]

Shortly after the breakup, Cruz accessed Emily's Instagram account and found the messages Dana had sent encouraging Emily to break up with him. Cruz started sending Dana messages that said, "I'm going to get you and I'm going to kill you because you took this person away from me. I'm going to kill your family."[3]

MSD students are told to report problems like this in writing rather than verbally, so Dana submitted a written report to Kelvin Greenleaf, MSD's head of school security. She told us that she wrote about the death threats and offered to show screenshots as evidence. She heard nothing further from Greenleaf or any administrator but assumed that school staff were handling it.

They weren't. Dana recalled that about six weeks after she'd reported Cruz's threats to Greenleaf, she was sitting in class when the door opened and Cruz entered. He wasn't supposed to be in that class.

He walked straight toward her and stood over her, staring and breathing loudly, as a hush fell across the classroom. After what seemed like an interminably long time, security monitor Anna Ramos entered the room and said, "Someone here isn't where he's supposed to be." She took him out of the classroom, but if she brought Cruz to the office that day it was not officially recorded.

In April, Bone was tasked with updating Cruz's IEP. She had heard plenty about his behavior, but she could only include in the document what had been officially recorded. While students, campus security, and administrators were aware of Cruz's alarming behavior, he did conduct himself quietly and unremarkably in many of his classes. Students and teachers insisted that, in his own way, he was *trying*. One math teacher wrote to Bone, "He tries very hard and works with the only high level student in my class on a regular basis. He can be quite disorganized but he seems very committed and his work as [sic] always complete just not usually correct."

On paper, Cruz's first semester at MSD was a great success. Although she knew it wasn't true, with only one disciplinary incident officially recorded, Bone could not write anything to the contrary on his IEP update at the end of the year. She did not return to MSD the next school year. She moved out of Broward County altogether.

"We Measure Our Success by the Kids We Keep Out of Jail"

Although this book primarily focuses on the school system, we cannot ignore the failures of the Broward sheriff's office. Sheriff Scott Israel signed the PROMISE agreement and ended up applying that same philosophy to the streets, declaring that "we measure our success by the kids we keep out of jail, not by the kids we put in jail." Crime statistics for adults in Broward County have stayed relatively stable over the past decade. But just as school-based arrests in Broward County plummeted from 1,056 to 392 from 2012 to 2016, juvenile arrests plummeted from 6,853 to 3,644.[4]

In the days following the shooting, the sheriff's office admitted that it had received twenty-three calls to Nikolas Cruz's home since 2008, none of which resulted in Cruz's arrest. Rumors swirled that the police had received even more calls than that, but the Broward sheriff's office issued a press release insisting, "Since 2008, [the sheriff's office] responded to 23 incidents where previous contact was made with the killer or his family. STOP REPORTING 39; IT'S SIMPLY NOT TRUE."[5]

Indeed, it was not. The final tally, which the sheriff's office eventually acknowledged, was forty-five. Some of those forty-five calls were made regarding Nikolas's brother Zachary, and others were made to his house without specific reference to either Zachary or Nikolas. The sheriff's office indicated in its defense that many of the calls were regarding matters too minor for the officer even to have filled out an incident report. However, given that deputy Edward Eason didn't see fit to fill out a report when he received word that Cruz had threatened to shoot up a school, we are not convinced that this is a compelling defense.

One of Cruz's former neighbors told us that Cruz shot his son with a BB gun but that the sheriff's office didn't do anything. (There is also no record of anything matching this description in the documents released by the sheriff's office.) Other neighbors told the media that Cruz routinely shot squirrels and stabbed rabbits, and he once ordered his dog to attack a neighbor's piglets. (There are no records matching this description, either.) Officers from other departments told us that, if they received this many calls about the same juvenile, they would watch him like a hawk and not be shy about making an arrest.

But if Sheriff Israel judged his success by how well he kept juveniles out of jail, then up until February 14, 2018, Nikolas Cruz was perhaps his most striking success.[6, 7]

Fall 2016

At the beginning of the 2016–2017 school year, MSD math teacher Suzanne Giorgione found out that she would be teaching Cruz, whom she had taught at Westglades a few years before. According to her colleague Kim Krawczyk, Giorgione went to school administrators and told them that she refused to set foot in the same classroom as a student who had previously threatened to kill her. As a result, administrators rearranged Cruz's schedule. Several students told us that they had friends whose parents had complained about having Cruz in their child's classroom, and the school responded by changing *their* schedules.

Cruz was not over his breakup with Emily when the school year began. When another student, Enea Sabidini, befriended Emily, he started receiving threats from Cruz through Emily's Instagram account, just as Dana had.[8] At first, these threats appeared idle, and after a few weeks, Cruz even approached Enea to shake his hand and call a "truce," telling him that he "could have her." Shortly after that, Enea and Emily began to date.

However, one day in early September, Cruz trailed Enea as he was leaving school. Cruz shouted, "Stop talking to her!" Enea told Cruz that he would not, and Cruz took a pen, held it like a knife, and started running at the half-black, half-Italian Enea, shouting, "Nigger! Nigger! Nigger!"

Enea had no intention of fighting Cruz; they were off campus, and he could face serious consequences for fighting. So Enea ran. He ran so fast that his friends nicknamed him "Gazelle." Enea and Dana both submitted reports to Greenleaf about Cruz's threatening messages and behavior. But, again, school staff did not follow up.

The Fight

On September 20, 2016, Enea, Dana, and several others were eating lunch in the school courtyard. All of a sudden, they heard Cruz scream, "Hey, nigger! Fuck you!" and saw a water bottle—intended to hit Enea—bounce on the ground nearby.

The next thing Dana heard was the sound of shuffling feet, and before anyone knew it, Cruz was practically on top of Enea, punching him. Much bigger than Cruz, Enea stood up to try to throw him to the ground. But Cruz held on tenaciously, at one point attempting to bite Enea's face, only to catch Enea's hair in his teeth and hold on that way.

"It was a bad fight," recalled a girl who asked not to be named and whom we'll call Arielle. "They were on the floor, punching each other. I think one smashed the other against the wall. No one wanted to help because everyone was taking videos." Eventually, a handful of students stepped forward to help Enea. Videos of the last few seconds of the fight would circulate widely in the days following the shooting.

Immediately after the fight, Dana, Arielle, and three other friends decided that enough was enough. Some of them had already warned school administrators about Cruz, but the administrators hadn't done anything. Cruz was capable of doing something really bad, and they felt obligated to report what they had heard, had seen, and knew.

The students went, as a group, to the school office and told Assistant Principal Winfred Porter that they wanted to make statements—not just about the fight, but about Cruz's behavior in general. Dana and Arielle told us that Porter separated them so they could not coordinate their written statements, but they all had the same things to say: Cruz had threatened to kill them and/or their families; he had threatened to rape people; he brought dead animals, knives, and bullets to school (one student urged administrators to check his backpack); and he stared at other students through binoculars at lunch. They were all worried that next time Cruz had a problem with somebody, he—in Arielle's words—"might pull a knife on someone or something worse."

That week, Arielle had nightmares about Cruz "shooting me or stabbing me...every single night. I couldn't go to school because I was afraid."

According to Dana and Arielle, Porter took the statements but did not follow up with any of the students. Arielle later lamented to us that school administrators "would freak out if somebody called me a dyke or something, but they didn't care when he threatened to kill my friends."

Joshua Charo, an MSD student, told us that Cruz told him that after the fight, administrators searched his backpack and found bullet casings, and that he thought that it was ridiculous that they were still alarmed even after he explained to them that he used that backpack when he went hunting. According to a document compiled by MSD staff and provided to us by Kim Krawczyk, when asked why he liked to hunt, Cruz replied that he liked to hunt to get food, then asked, "Isn't that what normal people would say?"

Before he attacked Enea, Cruz had told the students at his table what he was about to do, and they recorded the fight from the beginning. According to Dana, students who took these videos were called down to the office and, Dana told us, told to delete them. One student sent Dana's boyfriend Matthew the video. According to Dana, Matthew offered to show school administrators the video in order to prove that Cruz threw the first punch without provocation, but he was told to delete the video.

Those videos would have provided clear evidence of a hate crime. Enea's parents could easily have pressed charges against the disturbed young man who repeatedly threatened their son, called him a "nigger," and had now attacked him. But the videos would also have been embarrassing for the school if they were posted on YouTube. After administrators allegedly made students delete the videos, the genesis of the fight became a matter of hearsay. Enea was punished more severely than Cruz for the fight, receiving a one-day out-of-school suspension while Cruz got a two-day in-school suspension.

Dana recalled that later that day or the next, Greenleaf approached her and apologized. He told her that he knew that Cruz did not belong at MSD and that he was always taking Cruz to the office for one reason or another. Greenleaf also followed up with Dana's boyfriend Matthew a week later. Matthew told Greenleaf that Cruz whispered things to him in engineering class, "like 'I hate you,' and 'I'll kill you.'"[9] But again, MSD staff took no action. MSD student Ariana Lopez reflected, "Ignoring issues and listening to the bare minimum is exactly what Greenleaf did to us about Cruz."[10]

However, Greenleaf had no direct authority over Nikolas Cruz. All he could do was bring Cruz to the office and pass information up to assistant principals Winfred Porter, Denise Reed, and Jeff Morford. We do not know for certain whether Greenleaf passed along the death threats provided to him by students.

To recap: a deeply disturbed student with a history of threatening to shoot up the school and kill his peers called another student "a nigger" (not for the first time) and attacked him (not for the first time). At that point, five students provided statements to Assistant Principal Porter that Cruz had threatened to kill people and brought weapons to school. They also expressed concerns that Cruz might be carrying weapons and could kill someone the next time he became angry. At the students' urging, administrators allegedly searched Cruz's backpack and found bullets (or bullet casings).

It is difficult to imagine a set of circumstances that would more strongly argue for an arrest. But Scot Peterson's police logs from that month show no evidence that he was even consulted. Instead, administrators gave Cruz a two-day internal suspension and developed a "safety plan" that banned him from bringing a backpack on campus. The obvious rationale: if he has a backpack, he could bring a deadly weapon to school and kill people.

They decided that Nikolas Cruz was too dangerous to be allowed on campus with a backpack *but* he should not be arrested.

This may seem astonishing, but it is actually entirely faithful to philosophy of the Broward school district, as expressed by Superintendent Runcie: "We are not going to continue to arrest our kids" and give them a criminal record.[11] The fight with Enea was four days before Cruz turned eighteen, the age at which anyone without a criminal record can purchase firearms.

CHAPTER 7

Leaving MSD

C ruz appeared to be a law-abiding citizen on his eighteenth birthday, giving him the right to buy a gun. But there was another way for the authorities to prohibit him from doing so.

If Cruz had been involuntarily institutionalized under Florida's Baker Act, then he would have undergone intensive psychiatric evaluation. If a psychiatrist had deemed Cruz to be a danger to himself or others, that doctor could have recommended that a judge adjudicate Cruz as mentally defective and unfit to own a firearm.

The Broward school district's and the county's mental health services provider was Henderson Behavioral Health, which had treated Cruz for years. The week of Cruz's eighteenth birthday, Henderson received three calls asking them to examine Nikolas Cruz and determine whether he ought to be "Baker Acted."

The "No" Team

After the September 20 fight, Cruz felt humiliated and became even more unstable. On September 23, the day before his eighteenth birthday, Cruz's behavior at home was so erratic and threatening that Lynda Cruz called Henderson's Youth Emergency Services (YES) team to evaluate whether he should be institutionalized.

However, Tim Sternberg told us about a sad running joke in Broward schools: The YES team is actually the NO team because they will find any excuse to refuse to invoke the Baker Act. Tim told us about a student who smashed his own head into a wall hard enough to create a huge dent (not to mention a streak of blood). Tim demanded that Henderson invoke the Baker Act. But by the time the YES team arrived, the student had calmed down, so they deemed him not a threat to himself or others.

One mother told us about her daughter, who has bipolar disorder and had attempted suicide multiple times. But Henderson's YES team never Baker Acted the girl because she always denied to them that she wanted to die. Once, the mother recorded her daughter threatening to kill herself and played the recording for the Henderson clinician, but her daughter denied having any concrete plan, so no action was taken. Eventually, the mother realized that she would have to call the police—who also have the authority to invoke the Baker Act—to get her daughter immediate mental health treatment.

When Henderson's YES team arrived at Cruz's home on September 23, they asked him a series of standard questions: Did he have a history of violence? Had he been physically or sexually abused? Had he set fires in the past? Was he a smoker? Cruz was not stupid. He knew the answers he was supposed to give, and he gave them. The counselor recorded that he denied everything.[1] So the YES team said no.

On September 28, Cruz confided to a peer at MSD that he had been cutting himself and had attempted suicide by drinking gasoline. What's more, he revealed that he'd just had a big fight with his mom, who was reluctant to allow him to acquire a state ID so he could buy guns.

The student told a guidance counselor all of this, and she relayed the information to the Henderson clinic. When the YES team clinician came to MSD, she must have understood that her evaluation could play a decisive role in whether this deeply unstable young man would be allowed to buy a gun. Again, Cruz simply denied everything. He could not deny the cuts on his arms, but he insisted that they were not self-inflicted with suicidal intent. The records indicate that the Henderson clinician suspected that Cruz was being dishonest. However, she explained to school administrators that she could not invoke the Baker

Act if he denied an intent and plan. (This is not technically true; she had the discretion to do so if she believed that the person being evaluated was lying.) So, again, the YES team said no.[2]

Deputy Scot Peterson and MSD guidance counselors believed that Henderson's decision was wrong. Peterson had the authority to invoke the Baker Act, but despite expressing his belief that Cruz should have been committed, he did not do so himself.[3] Peterson told his colleagues that he would search Cruz's home for guns and weapons; however, his official logs suggest that he did not do so.

The Henderson clinician recommended to Lynda Cruz that she create another "safety plan" for her home, including monitoring sharp objects so her son couldn't cut himself again. The Henderson clinician also recommended that when Cruz's mood deteriorated, he engage "in coping skills such as reading magazines, watching TV, fishing and spending time with pets."

The next day, on September 29, a guidance counselor at MSD called Henderson again about Cruz. He had written "Kill" in a notebook and, when asked why, explained that his mother had decided not to allow him to get an ID, so he couldn't buy a gun. This prompted a third visit from Henderson's YES team. And yet again, the YES team said no.

The decision to invoke the Baker Act would not necessarily have prohibited Cruz from buying a gun. It merely would have provided a psychiatrist the opportunity to conduct a thorough analysis, which could conclude with Cruz being legally adjudicated as mentally defective.

It is difficult to imagine a stronger case for a mental health professional to declare, "This individual must not own a gun!" Cruz had required a constant security escort in middle school, had recently threatened to kill his peers, had evinced an obsession with guns, and had allegedly attempted suicide only a few days prior. But despite being called three times in one week and being told that he was on the verge of arming himself, Henderson, which had a long history treating Cruz, decided that Cruz did not even merit observation.[4]

Florida Department of Children and Families

After the second time that Henderson failed to invoke the Baker Act for Cruz, MSD guidance counselors called the Florida Department of

Children and Families (DCF) in the hope that maybe *they* would do something. On September 28, DCF opened an investigation into Nikolas Cruz and his mother, writing the following:

> Mr. Cruz is a vulnerable adult due to mental illness. He has Depression. In the past, he was taking medicine but it is unknown if he is taking any medicine now. Yesterday, Mr. Cruz and his Mom were arguing over paperwork he needs to get an identification card. Mr. Cruz said he needed the identification card to get a game. Mr. Cruz was on Snapchat cutting both of his arms. Mr. Cruz has fresh cuts on both his arms. Mr. Cruz stated he plans to go out and buy a gun. It is unknown what he is buying the gun for. A year ago, Mr. Cruz had hate signs on a book bag, stating "I hate niggers." In the past, Henderson Mental Health was called out to for [sic] Mr. Cruz to be Baker Acted but he denies everything. In the past, he was taking medicine for his Depression but it is unknown if he is taking any medicine now.[5]

The principal investigator for DCF was Beatrice Thomas. She was charged with looking into medical neglect, but never got an answer from Cruz about whether he was taking his medication. He simply "declined to discuss" the matter with her because "he [had] talked about the situation enough." Despite receiving the report that he had cut himself, Thomas did not even examine his arms, noting that she "was not able to see any scars or cuts on [Cruz's] arms because he was wearing long sleeves."

Thomas was also charged with investigating parental neglect, but she accepted and recorded statements from Lynda that were obviously untrue. Regarding the swastikas Cruz had carved into a lunchroom table at MSD, Lynda insisted that her son didn't know what the symbol meant. MSD guidance counselors had recorded that Cruz and his mother argued about getting an ID to buy a gun, but Cruz insisted to Thomas that the argument was about a video game. Lynda claimed that there had been no argument at all. Thomas reported that she called MSD to inquire about Cruz's behavioral history, but Deputy Peterson "refused to share any information."

Thomas concluded that Cruz's "level of risk was low as [he] resides with his mother, attends school and receives counseling through

Henderson." In most other circumstances, these would indeed be mitigating factors. But in this case, Cruz's mom was an overwhelmed enabler. Henderson's treatment had been scattershot, and it had refused to even formally observe him when it received calls that he was suicidal and about to arm himself. And the school's most negligent actions still lay ahead. Noting that Cruz did not own a gun, Thomas officially closed the investigation on November 12, 2016.

Less than one month later, on December 3, 2016 Lynda allowed her son to buy his first of many guns. Perhaps she did not believe her son was capable of pulling the trigger.

The Threat Assessment

Unlike Cruz's mother, the security staff at MSD thought that Cruz could pull the trigger. Campus security monitors Andrew Medina and David Taylor told the police, in sworn statements following the shooting, that security staff once had a meeting at which they decided that if anyone would become a school shooter, it would be Cruz. Taylor said that they joked with Assistant Principal Jeff Morford that Cruz would probably come for him first, because of all the problems that Morford had with Cruz.

In late September, Assistant Principals Morford and Reed conducted a threat assessment of Cruz. The final report of the MSD Public Safety Commission raised almost as many questions about the assessment as it answered. According to the commission, Reed started the paperwork because Morford told her that he didn't even know where to find a threat assessment, much less how to do one. Morford claimed that he had never done a threat assessment before despite the fact that he had been employed by the school district for thirty-one years and was responsible for security at MSD. According to the MSD Commission's report, MSD Principal Ty Thompson admitted to commission investigators that he has very little idea about threat assessments in general. MSDHS Principal Thompson stated that he does not review [threat assessment] results, and:

> When asked if he expects his administrators to inform him if
> "someone threatens to shoot up the school," Thompson replied,

"Usually it's not. Very rarely does that come up. Threat assessments don't always—it's not part of the protocol to bring it to me." Thompson further stated, "To be honest with you, no, I'm not made aware of all threat assessments that come in." Thompson could only guess at the number of threat assessments initiated at MSDHS annually and really had no idea of the process.[6]

According to the paperwork, the Level 1 threat assessment transitioned to a more in-depth Level 2 assessment. But the MSD Public Safety Commission noted that "no one interviewed by the Commission knows how or why the Level 2 was initiated, but there is evidence that it happened based on forms in the file." The commission noted:

Despite this being the only threat assessment that he has participated in during his 31-year career, it occurring in 2016, and it involving someone now known to him to be a mass shooter, Morford claims he has no recollection of the threat assessment process and can offer no explanation how it was handled. Morford also has no explanation how the Level 1 assessment became a Level 2 assessment.... Investigators found Morford to be remarkably absent-minded in remembering details about various events and/or being intentionally deceptive.

The commission could not determine whether Henderson or the Broward Sheriff's Office ever had access to the information within the threat assessment file.

Stripped of His ESE Protections

MSD should have reached out to Cross Creek to try to send Cruz back. But in October, it was Cross Creek that reached out to MSD after hearing of Cruz's deterioration. MSD staff should have initiated a discussion about sending Cruz back to Cross Creek eight months earlier, when allegedly informed of Cruz's threat to shoot up MSD, or any time after that based on his erratic actions and death threats throughout 2016. Now that Cruz had turned eighteen, school staff faced a major hurdle to returning him to Cross Creek: he now had a say in the decision, and he'd previously insisted that he didn't want to attend an ESE school.

MSD and Cross Creek staff met to discuss sending Cruz back to Cross Creek on November 4, 2016. Fearing that Cruz would instantly say no, they held the first part of the meeting with just his mother. Lynda indicated that she understood that her son should be at Cross Creek and would support the move, but that he would almost certainly not want to go. A third-party review of Cruz's educational history conducted by the Collaborative Educational Network (CEN) noted that "Given his history of explosive behavior and destruction of property within the home, staff believed that his mother would try to tell him what he should do, but would not force the issue and ultimately would support whatever final decision he made."

By protocol, Cruz should have been informed in advance of the meeting's purpose, but he was not. When he entered the meeting, he quickly realized what it was about and became upset and verbally aggressive, refusing to sit down and insisting that he would not go back to Cross Creek. Staff had expected him to take it poorly, but they were nonetheless disturbed at the vehemence of his reaction. The Cross Creek ESE specialist took him aside and laid out three options: he could agree to go back to Cross Creek; he could file a complaint against the district if he didn't want to go and let an administrative judge decide; or he could revoke his ESE protections, in which case no one could send him back to Cross Creek.

This was not a complete set of options. Cruz also could have asked MSD staff to develop a more robust plan to support him. And, as CEN noted, he could have simply "refused to consent to the placement," in which case he would stay at MSD and put the onus on them to try to move him.

Under these circumstances, the incomplete set of options presented to Cruz amounted to an ultimatum: if you don't want to go back to Cross Creek, you have to revoke your ESE protections. Naturally, Cruz said he wanted to revoke his ESE protections. This verbal declaration was not sufficient for anyone to act upon, but the meeting had proven so emotionally taxing for staff that it ended without any formal action.

Administrators could have met with Cruz to try to set up another plan to help him succeed. But this was, perhaps, unlikely to work, and they did not go this route either. They could have asked Cruz to provide written notice that he wanted to revoke his ESE protections. However, he appeared incapable—perhaps due to his language-processing impairment—of preparing the paperwork himself. His inability to express this decision in writing should have sent a strong signal to the school that it would be unwise for him to revoke his protections.

The most responsible decision would have been to send Cruz to Cross Creek and accept that he would challenge that decision. But, as noted in the previous chapter, MSD administrators allegedly rarely took any action regarding an ESE student if they expected the student or parent to challenge it. What's more, if administrators were, as students believe, suspending Cruz frequently but not recording it, then that likely would have been revealed during an administrative hearing. So instead of making the responsible but inconvenient decision to try to send him back to Cross Creek, MSD staff prepared the paperwork for him to revoke his ESE protections and provided it to him for his signature.

Kicked Out the Back Door

Now for all intents and purposes a normal student, Cruz was failing his classes, and his attendance was spotty. There was always some rumor about something he said or did, followed by his absence from school. Campus security staff often brought him to the office. Ray Feis recalled to us that his brother, campus security monitor Aaron Feis, "wasn't scared of anyone, but he would talk about 'that crazy motherfucker who threatens everyone' and shouldn't be at this school."

Yet only two additional infractions were officially recorded while Cruz remained at MSD: one in December stemming from an incident involving a former teacher, Laurel Holland (who declined comment), and one in January for an unspecified threat, the nature of which was not officially documented and no one we spoke with could recall.

But again, the official record bears little relationship to reality. Consider this story, not reflected in his official records, that was told to us by his classmate Hunter Dubois. Even though he had been in engineering class with Cruz for over a semester, Hunter still did not know his name. Cruz was frequently absent—either informally suspended or skipping school—and Hunter only knew him as the creepy kid who was always looking up guns and threatening to kill people. Hunter recalled, "Anyone that pissed him off or crossed him, he'd threaten how he was going to kill them."

One day in January, Cruz exploded, without any apparent provocation, and went around the classroom destroying his peers' model bridges. Hunter confronted him about it and Cruz told him, "I am not mentally stable! I am fucking crazy, yo! I love to see people in pain and I have two shotguns at my house." Hunter was alarmed and felt like it was his duty to inform an administrator. He talked to his friend Andrew, who "was always saying, 'That kid is going to do something someday,'" and Andrew advised him against coming forward.

If Hunter went to someone that day, Andrew told him, Cruz would know it had been him and might retaliate. If he waited a few days, then it could be another student reporting another incident and Hunter wouldn't have to worry. Hunter considered this advice but decided he had to report the incident immediately.

Hunter went to Assistant Principal Morford, who had full responsibility over Cruz now that he was no longer an ESE student. Hunter explained what had happened and also told Morford that he'd frequently seen Cruz looking at guns on his computer and walking around the courtyard at lunch making "bang" motions with his fingers as though he were shooting at birds. Because Hunter didn't know Cruz's name, Morford pulled out a yearbook. He pointed to a picture of Cruz and Hunter nodded. Hunter recalled Morford saying, "Oh yeah, we know all about him. This isn't the first time. You don't need to worry. He doesn't have any guns. And his mom is going to take him to a different school soon. Also, we're really not supposed to say anything about other students, but when you get back to a computer, try Googling 'autism.'" (Hunter also told this story to the MSD Commission. Morford denied to the commission that this encounter occurred.)

Hearing about this, a mother of one of Hunter's close friends went to the school the next day to register a strong objection to how Morford had dismissed the threat posed by Nikolas Cruz. She spoke to Principal Ty Thompson, whom she said told her that if she didn't like the way he ran the school, she could take her son out of it.[7] (Thompson denied to the commission that this encounter occurred.)

It is possible that, as Morford allegedly told Dubois, Lynda Cruz voluntarily withdrew her son from Stoneman Douglas. But that would have been entirely out of character. Cruz's brother Zachary confirmed to us that there was "no way" she did this of her own volition. Lynda later claimed that Cruz had been expelled for making threats.

Immediately after the shooting, several newspapers reported that Cruz had been expelled from MSD. However, subsequent reporting noted that he had never technically been expelled. Still, MSD teachers later suggested that it was wrong to criticize their school administrators because they "expelled" Cruz from their school. We're not sure whether they would have taken this stance if they had understood the answer to the riddle of how Cruz was expelled without being expelled.

Superintendent Runcie's policies had substantially decreased the number of expulsions in Broward, but, as we showed in chapter 4, he felt pressure from outside interest groups like the ACLU to decrease them even further. In addition to raising the threshold for what misbehavior warranted expulsion, district bureaucrats also erected subtler paperwork hurdles to expulsion.

However, because it was obviously necessary to protect students from criminal misbehavior, Broward relied on a shadow expulsion system known as the Behavior Intervention Committee. Through this system, a student who had a history of severe misbehavior could be forcibly transferred to an alternative school. This still involved some paperwork, but it allowed administrators to remove especially troublesome students without having an expulsion on the school's record. Cruz was no longer ESE, but through this process he could have been forced to attend an alternative school for non-ESE behaviorally troubled students, Cypress Run Education Center.

But Jeff Morford did not take Cruz's case to the Behavior Intervention Committee. Unless Lynda came up with the idea on her own, it seems all but certain that Morford advised—if not directed—Cruz to enroll in a "credit recovery" school, Riverside Off Campus Learning Center (OCLC). Credit recovery schools are centers where students work through online courses to earn enough credits to graduate. These schools have been at the center of several scandals in school districts across the country, when administrators enforce no academic standards and simply use these institutions as diploma mills to boost their official graduation rate.

Lynda would not have wanted her son to go to a school where he would not be in a traditional classroom. And, by all accounts, Cruz wanted to remain at MSD. We believe this decision was not made in accordance with their wishes but as a means for MSD administrators to remove him from their campus with as little hassle as possible.

On February 8, 2017, Cruz was "withdrawn" from MSD and placed at OCLC. The date is important for two reasons.

The first is that February 8, 2017, fell in the middle of "Full-Time Equivalent" week, which is when schools submit their official attendance numbers for the year to the state for the purpose of receiving their per-pupil funding. MSD kept him enrolled just long enough to collect the money they received for educating him.

The second is that February 8, 2017, was three days before Cruz bought the AR-15 that he would bring to MSD one year later.

And Stay Out

Cruz was miserable at OCLC. It wasn't a normal school with classrooms and teachers. There were just students sitting in front of computers, loosely supervised by adults. Although credit recovery programs are designed to give students as many academic credits as possible for as little work as possible, Cruz made little academic progress.

He told one girl that he wanted to "kill niggers," but she brushed it off. He showed one boy a lunch box full of bullets that he brought to school, but the student didn't report it.[8]

Yet, in his own way, Cruz still wanted to *try*. He did not want to be a loser who could not even graduate from high school. He finally realized that Cross Creek was his only real chance to graduate. In April, with her son's permission, Lynda called the ESE specialist at Cross Creek to ask how she could get him back into the school. But the CEN report noted that Cross Creek's ESE specialist did not know how he could regain his ESE status and transfer back to the school, so she called the district's ESE office for advice.

The district bureaucrat did not know the district's own policy or procedure. But she pretended to know and told Cross Creek's ESE specialist that Cruz would have to go through the standard six-week Response to Intervention evaluation like any other student, including a psychological evaluation and an extensive documentation of Cruz's response to a number of attempted interventions, before he could regain his ESE status and return to Cross Creek.

This was not true. Given his history, Cruz could have regained his ESE status and reenrolled in Cross Creek with a single meeting. But with that false requirement in mind, Cross Creek's ESE specialist emailed OCLC's ESE specialist to ask if she would conduct the exhaustive evaluation. The OCLC specialist did not respond to the email. A month later, Cross Creek's ESE specialist followed up and the two specialists talked on the phone. They appear to have provided inconsistent accounts of that conversation to CEN. After the conversation, Cross Creek's ESE specialist decided that the best course of action would be to reenroll Cruz at MSD so that the (unnecessary) six-week process could be done there. Cross Creek's ESE specialist contacted Jessica DeCarlo, who agreed to this course of action.

But when DeCarlo took this plan to Assistant Principals Reed and Morford, they vetoed it. They did not want Cruz back on campus under any circumstances, and (according to Tara Bone) they told DeCarlo so. DeCarlo called Lynda to explain the situation, after which point Lynda gave up. The CEN report notes, "When a parent (or adult student) requests an evaluation, the district must respond within 30 days by either requesting consent to conduct it or providing written notice of refusal that describes the reasons the district is denying the request.... This did not occur." Both Cruz and his mother had asked for his ESE services to be reinstated, but the school district—through a chain of incompetence—failed to follow up.

On the first day of the 2017–2018 school year, MSD teacher Sandra Rennie spotted Cruz trespassing on campus.[9] School administrators could have had School Resource Officer Scot Peterson arrest him, but did not. That would have been overkill for most former students, but not for one whom they suspected could shoot up their school. An arrest for trespassing would not have affected his gun rights, but it could have proven a decisive detail when the FBI received a tip that he'd become a school shooter.

Administrators also could have tried to talk to Cruz about how he was doing. This could have been the first step in sending him back to Cross Creek, where he could get the support he needed. But Cruz was simply asked to leave.

Things continued to go poorly for Cruz at OCLC. If he had regained his ESE status, he would have been a senior at Cross Creek at this point. But because the nineteen-year-old Cruz was no longer labeled ESE, he had to pass state tests just like any other student in order to graduate, and he had failed the tenth-grade Florida Standards Assessments at the end of the 2016–2017 school year. He tried retaking it in late September, but at the end of the test, his teacher noticed that he had his phone out, which was not permitted. The teacher's description of what happened next was published in CEN's report:

> I told the student his test would be invalidated due to the phone in his possession. He became upset and said "NO, this can't be." I said you will be able to retest the next time the test is offered. He said NO, I HATE THIS SCHOOL, kicked my desk. During this time I called Ms. Irons, the phone went straight to her voicemail. I then radioed her. The student during this time push [sic] the chair then went back to it, picked it up, and threw it across the classroom and walked out.

At this point it may have become clear to Cruz that he would never graduate high school. And this realization may have sent him into a tailspin.

Every Warning Missed

That same month, Cruz commented on a YouTube video under the username "nikolas cruz" that he wanted to become a "professional school shooter." The video's creator, Mississippi bail bondsman Ben Bennight, alerted the FBI. The FBI interviewed Bennight, but he knew nothing beyond what he had already told them: a "nikolas cruz" said that he wanted to become a school shooter. An agent searched FBI databases but found nothing (because Cruz had no criminal record) and closed the case.

Cruz also messaged Enea Sabidini: "you mother fucker. After a whole yeae. Iam still not dpne with you. Figth me fagget. Fucking fight me!!! Iam going to destroy you again. Iam going to rip your fucking hair again fagget. Fuck you !!!!" In another message, Cruz, apparently unable to keep track of which epithet he was supposed to use against the half-black, half-Italian Enea, wrote, "you underground hispanic wall jumper ill will fucking destroy you !!!!!"[10] Enea brushed off the messages and did not report them to the authorities. But we cannot blame him for this; Cruz was no longer enrolled at MSD, and Enea knew from past experience that no one would take his warnings seriously.

That month, Cruz also threatened to kill his brother and his mother. Zachary had always bullied him, and a friend of Lynda's later recalled that Lynda seemed to consider Zachary the real problem child. In middle school, Cruz slept with scissors under his pillow for fear that his brother would attack him.[11] But now that Cruz had guns, the power dynamic shifted. One day, after Zachary snatched a jar of Nutella away from his brother, Cruz went upstairs, grabbed a gun, came back down, pointed it at Zachary and demanded the Nutella back. That was the last time Zachary messed with his brother.[12]

Cruz also became violent and threatening toward his mother. At one point, he asked Lynda to drive him to Walmart so that he could buy a video game. When she refused, he punched her in the face so hard that she required dental work. Zachary recalls that when Lynda refused to take Cruz to a hunting cabin, Cruz "got his AR-15 and put it to my mom's head.... He yelled at her and said, 'I'm gonna blow your fucking brains out.'" Lynda ran to her car and fled. Cruz had cooled down by the time she returned.

Despite these incidents, Lynda let Cruz buy more guns. It is difficult to fathom the combination of fear, desperation, resignation, and perhaps even hope-against-all-hope naïveté of Lynda Cruz. Lynda had no friends, family, or community around her. She was reluctant even to leave her house for fear that Nikolas or Zachary would do major damage to it. A bank teller who had several phone conversations with Lynda during this time recalls that Cruz repeatedly told her to kill herself and threatened to burn down the house if she refused. When the bank teller asked her why she didn't kick him out, she replied, "Because I don't know what he's going to do." She described her son as "evil" and said, "If something happens to me, you'll know it was Nik."[13] At nearly seventy years old, Lynda's health was starting to fail from the never-ending terror of living with her son.

After the shooting, Zachary told the *Miami Herald* about a conversation with his brother about a year before the shooting that still haunts him. They were walking home from the community pool and Zachary asked Nikolas, "What would you do if mom died?"

Nikolas replied nonchalantly, "I would just kill people."[14]

On November 1, 2017, Lynda Cruz died from the flu.

That day, Lynda's cousin Katherine Blaine called the Broward sheriff's office to warn them about Nikolas and, according to police records, ask them to seize his firearms. According to the sheriff's call log, a "close family friend" agreed to take possession of Nikolas's guns at the time, and the officer did not write a formal report.

Nikolas and Zachary moved in with another family friend, Rocxanne Deschamps, in Lake Worth, Florida. The Deschamps family's hospitality came with one strict condition: Cruz was not allowed to have a gun at the house. At night, he made "demon noises" so loud that, according to Rocxanne, "Me and my mom were so afraid that we slept together, blocked the door with the dresser, machete in hand."[15]

During this time period, Cruz began publishing increasingly threatening posts on Instagram in which he posed with guns and expressed affinity for ISIS. Mary Hamel, a childhood friend of Lynda Cruz, saw the posts and reached out to him. Cruz expressed anger at the Deschamps family for not letting him own guns and not buying him whatever he asked for. Hamel insisted that they were being very good to him and Cruz stopped responding.[16]

At some point, Cruz also stopped respecting the Deschamps' rule about not having guns in the house. In late November, Rocxanne's son Rock called the police because Cruz was digging in their backyard and Rock believed Cruz had hidden a gun there. On November 29, Rocxanne called the cops after Rock and Cruz got into a fight and Cruz threatened to "get his gun and come back."[17] However, after Cruz had calmed down, Rocxanne and Rock told law enforcement they did not want him arrested. They did, however, tell him to move out, and he moved in with the Snead family, whose son J.T. had been a friend of Cruz at MSD.

While living with the Sneads, Cruz worked at a Dollar Tree store close to MSD. When students came into the store, recognized Cruz, and asked him how he'd been since leaving the school, he said that he planned to come back and shoot it up. But none of them took Cruz's statements seriously.

On November 30, Mary Hamel called the Broward sheriff's office to warn them about Cruz. She told the police that she had seen pictures of him with guns and knives on Instagram, that he was unstable, that his mother, Lynda, had recently died, and that "this might be Columbine in the making." She also said that Cruz no longer lived at his listed address in Parkland, that he had caused a disturbance two days ago, and that she believed he was now staying with a friend but she did not know where. She gave the officer Cruz's Instagram username and specifically mentioned that there were pictures of him posing like an ISIS jihadist, showing off weapons and making threats. The sheriff's office thanked her for her tip and told her than an officer would call her back.

When officer Guntis Treijs, called Hamel back, he asked, "Lynda's dead?" as though he knew her personally. It turns out that he did: he had been to her home on several occasions, most recently four months earlier in response to a call about Zachary.[18] Hamel was relieved that she had reached someone who had personal experience with Cruz. "All you have to do is look at him and you know the lights are on but no one is home," she told Treijs.

When Hamel hung up, she thought, "Wow, this guy knows what's going on and he's going to do something." But then, she recalled, "nothing happened. Nothing happened."

She saw more threatening Instagram posts in the days that followed and called Treijs back. She said, "This has to be stopped." Treijs thanked her and told her that if they had any questions, they would call her back, but that she couldn't talk to anybody from the sheriff's office again until they called her back. They never did.

Justifying his inaction, Treijs later told the sheriff's internal investigators that, when he entered "Nikolas Cruz" into the system, he "found so many of them" that he "couldn't pinpoint a location." (This was not true. Investigators found only seven entries for "Cruz" with varying spellings of "Nikolas.") Treijs closed the matter without writing an incident report.

Hamel discovered that Cruz was now staying with the Sneads and told us that she called the family to warn them that Cruz was dangerous and should not be allowed to possess guns. Her concerns were rebuffed.

She hadn't heard anything more from the Broward sheriff's office, so she decided to call the FBI. She told them all the same things she had told the local police and more: She'd seen Instagram posts of Cruz posing as a member of ISIS and threatening to kill himself and others and that Cruz mutilated small animals and threatened his now-deceased mother with a gun. She told them that Cruz was nineteen but had the mental capacity of a twelve-year-old and that he was going to explode, and that this was going to be another Columbine. The agent searched the FBI databases again, but the only thing the agent found was the closed lead from the September call regarding the YouTube post. The agent closed the case and did not forward any information to the local office.[19, 20]

This was the last call made to the authorities before the shooting. But there was one other call that, if handled appropriately, could have averted the massacre. According to a source familiar with Cruz's educational history, Cruz called Cross Creek after Lynda died and told them, "Before my mom died, I promised her I would graduate high school. I get that Cross Creek is the only place where I can do that. How do I get back in?"

Cruz was essentially alone. He had no family, few friends, and no future. Just his guns, his latent potential for murder, and profound resentment. If Cruz had been attending Cross Creek, as he would have been if not for a series of self-interested and incompetent decisions, then he would have had intensive therapeutic support and some hope of graduating high school. But when he called Cross Creek to ask how to reenroll, he was told that first he had to go to MSD, but that MSD hadn't been willing to cooperate.

On December 4, J.T.'s father, James Snead, emailed Assistant Principal Jeff Morford: "Nikolas Cruz just lost his mother and now resides with me and my family in Parkland. Nikolas is 19 yrs old. He is a senior at the moment. He was attending Dave Thomas Education Center.

He did attend MSD. I'm not sure why he left.... is it possible for him to return to MSD? If so, what will he need? I understand he is nineteen and an adult. I am just trying to see if it's possible. Nikolas is prepared to do what is necessary to return to MSD. Thank you for your time."

Morford replied, "I am sorry but Nikolas will have to continue his schooling at an adult school if he wants to finish his high school diploma."[21]

The e-mail from James Snead was sent from a Broward school district e-mail because, by strange coincidence, he was serving as a cost estimator for the SMART bond project (which had run hundreds of millions of dollars over budget). According to Jeff Morford's lawyer, the fact that Snead had a district e-mail address made Morford suspect that this was yet another instance where the district office was trying to put a dangerous student into his school, and he believed he was standing up to the district on behalf of his students by saying no.

In an open letter to the MSD Commission, the lawyer for Morford, Reed, and Porter said that Morford was deeply frustrated with Runcie's discipline policy and philosophy. "It was not enough," wrote Morford's attorney, "at the District to disqualify Cruz as a student after publicly proclaiming he wanted to murder a certain ethnic group," and that given the district's policy "to protect dangerous students" his other efforts "to have Cruz removed was [sic] frustrated by a policy and practice by the district to essentially look the other way."[22]

To the extent that MSD administrators looked the other way, there is a strong argument that they were essentially "just following orders." However irresponsible their decisions, by the time you've read Part III you will see that they were unfortunately not remarkable or unusual given the policies and culture of the Broward County school district. Their lawyer suggested that they were operating within a deeply flawed system and did what they could to get Cruz out and make sure he never came back.

CHAPTER 8

Returning to MSD

On February 14, 2018, at 2:19 p.m., 18–1958 stepped out of an Uber carrying a black canvas rifle bag and walked through an open gate at Marjory Stoneman Douglas High School.[1]

According to district policy, that gate should have been locked until 2:30 p.m. But, according to MSD teachers, a few months prior to the shooting, an assistant principal had ordered campus security monitors to start opening the gates earlier to expedite the process of getting ESE students onto school buses.

Campus security monitor Andrew Medina was riding around the perimeter in his golf cart unlocking the gates. He spotted 18–1958 as soon as he stepped out of the Uber, about a two-minute walk from Building 12. Medina later told the police, "I saw him with a bag, with like a rifle bag."[2] 18–1958 was "bee-lining" to Building 12, with his head down, "on a mission...walking with a purpose."[3] Medina started riding toward him.

18–1958 looked back and made eye contact with Medina. Medina realized who it was. "That's Crazy Boy!" he thought.

"I'm telling you I knew who that kid was," Medina told the police, "because we had a meeting about him last year and we said if there's going to be anybody who will come to this school and shoot this school up, it's going to be that kid." Then 18–1958 started running. Medina was close enough to intercept 18–1958, but he said that "something told me, 'don't approach him.' You know? Like, I don't know if he had a handgun. He could have had a handgun in a pocket."

At that point, Medina could have called a Code Red. If someone in the office relayed that call over the intercom, students in Building 12 would have taken cover in areas of their classrooms not visible from the hallway. But according to a security consultant, principal Ty Thompson had made it clear that only he was allowed call a Code Red, and Thompson was off-campus that day traveling to Paris with his girlfriend. [4]

Instead, Medina radioed fellow campus security monitor and baseball coach David Taylor to tell him that a suspicious intruder with a bag was heading into his building from the east side. Taylor was posted on the west side of the second floor, monitoring the only unlocked bathrooms in that building. (Assistant Principal Winfred Porter had decided to lock most bathrooms and patrol the remaining ones in order to deter vaping and drug use.)

Taylor ran down the west stairwell. As he walked across the first floor, he saw 18–1958 coming out of the east stairwell. 18–1958 saw him and retreated into the stairwell. Taylor figured that 18–1958 was heading up the east stairwell, so he ran back to the west stairwell to see if he could spot him on the second floor.

But 18–1958 did not go upstairs. He took out his AR-15 and began to load the magazine. Just then, a freshman, Chris McKenna, walked into the stairwell on his way to the second-floor bathroom. 18–1958, gun in hand, told him, "You better get out of here. Things are going to get messy." McKenna ran outside to find somebody to tell.

The first shots were fired down the first-floor hallway. A young girl who had left band class in a different building to use Building 12's bathrooms was hit. Forgetting that the first-floor bathroom was locked, she tried to enter and then pressed herself against the doorway. She saw that a classroom door across the hallway was open. She made a run for it, entered the room, and finally feeling the pain from the gunshot wound, collapsed on the floor. She lived.

The three students in the hallway behind her did not.

Martin Duque Anguiano, 14

Luke Hoyer, 15
Gina Montalto, 14

Students inside the classrooms on the first floor did not instantly comprehend that the loud noises were gunshots. One girl in Room 1216 said that she thought that the noise was balloons popping. But then a bullet burst through the window of the classroom door and hit the top of her laptop screen. Another went through her sleeve, barely missing her arm.

Here and throughout the rest of the chapter, we provide you with accounts given by students to the police on the day of the massacre:

That's when everyone started freaking out. And the teacher started screaming, saying to take cover and we all stood up and ran to her desk and she said that we couldn't all sit there 'cause it wasn't large enough to protect us all. We were all...she was all scared like something else was going to happen. So I stood up and ran back to my desk, grabbed my phone and then ran to the other side of the room where I wasn't in view of the door, and I stood against the wall, and I called 911 as fast as I could and I said, "Help Stoneman Douglas High School, there's a shooter active and shooting at us all. There are some people that are now injured," and she asked how many and I said, "By the looks of it was about five." And she said, "Stand up and see if there's any more," and I'd seen after I had gotten shot there were two more shots and one had hit one of the girls that had sat next to me, um...at some part of her chest up I don't really know exactly where it was. She slid against the wall and went down and that's what freaked me out the most and so I said, "There are about five people." And she asked me—the woman on the 911 call asked me to stand up and see if I saw any more, and I said that there was a boy hanging over the desk with blood dripping out of his head and he was like hyperventilating and trying to catch his breath and then all of a sudden he just stopped and like went limp. And I said, "I think he's dead. Like, you need to get here as fast as you can." I saw the bullet hole in his chest where the hole...where the shirt was so I knew he had gotten shot. I didn't know what had happened, though.... Later we heard shots upstairs and we're guessing that he had gone upstairs so the woman on the 911 called and said that if I felt comfortable I could stand up and try to do CPR and I said I would be OK with that. She said she'd talk me through it. So, I went to stand up and my teacher said no. That she didn't think it was safe if I made too much noise. Like, he could come back down and I said okay. I sat back down. I was screaming on the phone, everyone is telling me to be quiet.... [Later] the cops finally came in and they broke the rest of the window open and they unlocked the door and they asked if we were all okay and we said yes and I had no shoes on at the time because they're very uncomfortable and I'd taken them off and I walked over and I put them back on and I saw my best friend Alaina Petty and the original girl, Alyssa, down on the floor dead and I didn't realize it was Alaina until I'd gotten home, and then I realized that I didn't see her walk out.

Alyssa Alhadeff, 14
Alaina Petty, 14
Alex Schachter, 14

David Taylor heard the shots as he was heading up the stairwell and jumped into a closet to take cover. He did not call a Code Red.

Andrew Medina heard the shots from outside the building. He recalled:

I heard the first bang, like "POW!" and I'm like, uh-oh. [Then I heard] POP! POP! POP! POP! POP! POP! POP!... Three sets of five shots. And it was loud. You could kind of feel the percussion coming out of that building, the echo coming out of the doors of the building. It was loud. It was kind of surreal, because to hear that noise, it ain't a firecracker noise. It wasn't like somebody banging. It was something different. [I got on my radio and] I go "suspicious noises coming out of the 1200 Building," 'cause I don't know yet. I'm not gonna say "gunshots." You never know man, it could be, be, be, you know? That's crazy, you know? So, I'm like "suspicious noises coming out of the 1200 Building, we got a suspicious guy in there."

Later, in his conversation with the police, Medina explained why he did not call a Code Red.

I wasn't gonna yell a Code Black or a Code Red because I didn't actually visualize a gun, and I didn't really see the shots. So, I'm not...you know. We've been doing this training at the school, you know, "Don't yell it unless you actually get a good visual." Because you go Code Black they shut the whole—you get the cops out there for nothing and I don't want to be the guy who calls that, you know?

Medina turned around in his golf cart and started driving to the building where the only man on campus with a gun, Deputy Scot Peterson, was stationed.

When the students in Room 1214 heard the shots that were killing their classmates in Room 1216, they knew what was happening but not what to do. One student explained:

So the door is facing all the desks and then the teacher's desk is over here and there's a little...the desk is kind of in a cubby. It's a cutout, then the door is in front of it so when we first heard the shots, the teacher and most of the kids went to the cubby area. Like, where you couldn't shoot into, but me and the kids that were on this side we went it was probably six, seven kids we went to the front of the boardroom like where the whiteboard is and there was a file cabinet there and like immediately I moved the file cabinet so there was no angle where you could shoot us. Like I put it in front of the angle where if he was looking in it would hit the file cabinet. That was while the shots were going off, me and three others, like I grabbed them and we went down behind the thing and then a bunch of other kids came behind the file cabinet.... Two kids got shot next to me. They were, like, three feet away. I know that Nicholas Dworet, he's a blond, he was on the floor and I know that Helena, I don't know her last name but she's in my grade, and Nicholas was a senior and Helena, I know that she died, she was definitely dead because she was still with blood everywhere.

The police officer asked her about the blood she had on her white Vans sneakers. She responded, "It was probably Nick's. I mean, I would say it was Nick's because he was closer to me than Helena. But Helena was—there was a ton of blood from Helena, so it could have been her."
Nicholas Dworet, 17

Helena Ramsay, 17

When Andrew Medina reached Deputy Peterson's building, Peterson had already come outside because of what he had heard Medina call over the radio. As Medina picked Peterson up, someone radioed, "It sounds like fireworks." Campus security monitor Aaron Feis replied, "That's not fucking fireworks."

Winfred Porter, the assistant principal responsible for security, did not hear any of this. He later claimed to have had his radio on his person. Perhaps, as teachers allege is common practice, the volume was turned down. The first thing that Porter heard, more than one full minute after 18–1958 fired his first shots, was the fire alarm going off. According to reports, the fire alarm was activated by smoke from 18–1958's rifle. Experts we've consulted have expressed incredulity at the idea that a semiautomatic rifle could produce sufficient smoke to activate a fire alarm. However, MSD's fire alarm was notoriously hypersensitive and, as we've explained, several years overdue for replacement.

The fire alarm panel in the office told Porter that there was a gas leak in Building 12. The appropriate response to this alarm would have been to call a Code Brown over the intercom. This would have told students and teachers within Building 12 to evacuate and students and teachers in other buildings to shelter in place. However, Porter called an order to evacuate *all* buildings. 18–1958's original plan was to go to the third floor of Building 12 and shoot down at students as they left the school. Porter's mistaken evacuation call, based on a false signal from a faulty alarm, assured that students would pour out into the open.

On the third floor of Building 12, Kim Krawczyk had recognized the sound of gunshots before the fire alarm went off. She told all of her students to hide where they couldn't be spotted and to stay quiet. After the fire alarm ceased, a student told her, "They're telling us to evacuate, Ms. K." Kim responded, "Stay there. Shut up. Do not fucking move."

Outside the building, MSD's athletic director, Chris Hixon, understood that there was a shooting and ran toward Building 12. He entered through the west entrance, saw the shooter, and charged down the first-floor hallway hoping to tackle 18–1958. He barely made it ten yards before getting shot. Injured, Hixon retreated and took cover near the elevator door.

Then the shooter approached Room 1213. A student there told the police:

And we were in the classroom and when we heard the first shots go off, and everybody jumped to the floor. Once that happened, um, we were all crowded against the wall and then once we didn't hear shots for a couple of seconds we ran over to the designated area, which is behind the teacher's desk. Once we were there we were all crowded together, um, just hugging, listening to the shots go off. Then after a couple of seconds he shot through the glass and into the classroom and the students in my classroom didn't realize at first but he had shot four kids in my class. They were screaming and moaning for help but nobody had realized that anything had happened. Finally, once all the shots stopped going off, I stood up and I looked over the desk to see that four of the students were on the floor covered in blood.

Carmen Schentrup, 16

Deputy Scot Peterson arrived in Medina's golf cart on the east side of Building 12 eight seconds after Carmen was fatally shot in Room 1213. Hearing the shots, Peterson told Medina that there was an active shooter and that he should "get out of here!"

Peterson drew his gun. And stood there.

Ever since Columbine, police have been trained to immediately confront a school shooter.

If officers are uncertain of the shooter's location, they are trained to fire warning shots into the air. Often, the sound of these shots is enough to stop a shooting. The shooter may react to the prospect of confrontation by taking cover, fleeing, or committing suicide.

But Peterson just stood there.

As he stood there, 18–1958 walked down the first-floor hallway. He came across a wounded Hixon and fired more rounds into him.

Chris Hixon, 49

And Peterson just stood there.

Moments before Hixon was shot a second time, Aaron Feis arrived at the west side of Building 12. Chris McKenna had found him and told him there was a gunman, so Feis had no doubt about what was happening inside.

Feis ran in, entering the west stairwell at the exact moment as 18–1958. According to his brother Ray, the burns left on his hands showed that he managed to get a grip on 18–1958's rifle an instant before the fatal shots were fired. He fell in the doorway, his body visible from outside the building.

Aaron Feis, 37

As 18–1958 walked up the stairs, Peterson retreated to take cover behind a neighboring building. Peterson radioed, "I think we got shots fired. Possible shots fired in the 1200 Building."

18–1958 started walking across the second floor. Every teacher on the second floor recognized the sound of gunshots before the fire alarm went off and hid their students. Several teachers on the third floor, including Stacey Lippel, Ernie Rospierski, and Scott Beigel, did not. If a Code Red had been called, they would have directed their students to shelter. Instead, they began leading their students out of the classrooms for a fire drill. As 18–1958 walked across the empty second floor, there were over a hundred students directly above him, crowded into the hallway and totally confused as to what was happening.

18–1958 was confused too. He shot into two classrooms. By a stroke of luck, both were empty. The other second-floor teachers had hid their students out of sight of the doorway, so other classrooms appeared empty.

"Where did all the kids go?" he said out loud.

"Uh," Peterson said on his radio, "make sure we got—get some units over here. I need to shut down Stoneman Douglas, the intersection." As 18–1958 shot into his second empty classroom on the second floor, Peterson radioed, "We're talking about the 1200 Building."

By this point many, but not all, students in the third-floor hallway understood that something bad was happening. The students who had already reached the east stairwell ran down it and outside. Everything in the hallway was confusion. Some students started walking or running east, but others were being urged to continue to evacuate for the fire drill.

"We don't have any description," Peterson radioed, still hiding behind a neighboring building. "But there appear to be shots fired."

The shooter began to ascend the east stairwell to the third floor. The hallway on the third floor was bedlam. On the west side of the hallway, Rospierski told students to go back into their classrooms, with no apparent knowledge that there was a shooter. On the east side of the hallway, Lippel urged her students toward the stairwell. One of Lippel's students recalls:

We were in the hallway and then my teacher was saying, "Guys, go to Zone 10, Zone 10, go, go to the left." And then you see, like, kids. Like they're barely moving but they're like making their way downstairs. Then all of a sudden you hear "Bah! Bah! Bah!" in the stairwell and then everyone right away starts running to the right, and then my teacher, she opens the door, like, like super-fast.

So, then we all go inside the classroom. I was the first one to go inside the classroom and then we, it was not everyone from my classroom. There was in there some kids from other classrooms and then some kids from my classroom was in other ones, but then two kids from my classroom, they didn't make it. Meadow Pollack and Joaquin Oliver. They both passed away in the hallway, but I don't know where Meadow was. I know Joaquin died in the third, like, in front of the third-floor bathroom. Then, um, he shot into our classroom. My classroom was the only classroom on the third floor who got shot into.

Mr. Beigel's classroom was the closest to the stairwell. After hearing the gunshots, he started yelling down the hallway for students to run and directed his students to go back into his classroom. Then he stood in the hallway to lock his door. Classroom doors in Building 12 lock only from the outside. One student recalled:

He was standing at the door. But he didn't scream or anything. He just fell. And he was trying to close the door and then he got shot. He was, like, in the middle of the door. That's why we couldn't close the door. So, the door was open.

Scott Beigel, 35

If the shooter had peeked inside the open door, he could have taken fourteen more lives right then and there. But he didn't. He shot into Ms. Lippel's classroom next door, doubled back a few steps, and reloaded directly in front of Beigel's classroom. But he never looked inside.

There were about twenty students still in the hallway. He fired, hitting:

Jaime Guttenberg, 14
Cara Loughran, 14
Joaquin Oliver, 17
Meadow Pollack, 18
Peter Wang, 15

A student in Ms. Lippel's classroom called her father.

I mean, it took, like, a few rings and then I heard him. Because whenever I call him, like, during the day he doesn't really answer it because, like, I'm at school. I'm supposed to be learning. But, so, then he answered and I was surprised he answered because, like, he never, answers. So, then I, like, when I heard his voice...I was all calm throughout the whole thing.

Then, once I heard my dad's voice, I started bawling because I'm just like, "Oh, my God, this might be the last time I ever hear my dad's voice." And he's just like, "What happened?" I'm just like, "Oh, Papi, there's a school shooter in the class." He was like, "What, what, say that again?" Like, I was whispering really quiet. I'm like, "There's a school shooter in the classroom." He's just like, "What? Oh, my God? Are you serious?" Like, "Be careful." Like, "Be quiet." Like, "Be calm."

And my teacher, she kind of yelled at me because, like, I'm not supposed to be talking during that. Because you're supposed to be quiet and our glass is broken so, like, he could have heard every-thing in case he was, like, by our door. Then she, like, told me, like, "Put your phone away right now." I'm like, "Okay, okay." And then I tell my dad I gotta go. He's like, "No. Stay on the phone, stay on the phone." My teacher is, like, "No, put it away now." I'm like, "I gotta go."

So, then I hung up and then, like, in the hallway you hear, like, gunshots still, just in, like, so we're, like, really quiet and there's kids in my class crying hysterically. Oh, yeah, the first thing that we heard was a kid, like, a boy, like, saying, like, "Please. Please help me. Please let me in the classroom." Like, he was crying because, like, when that happens you're not allowed to let anybody in, and, like, we were scared ourselves because our door was broken.

So, like, we don't know if he was there, if Nikolas was making him do it, or anybody was making him do that. So then, we were so...that's all you heard and the kids were crying because you felt so bad you couldn't help him. Like, obviously, you knew, like, he might die. And then, sadly, he did. He died right in front of our classroom. When the police came that's, that's who was in front of our door.

But then you also heard, like, moaning from the shots. I don't know if it was, like, the shooter who was making that noise or if it was someone who got shot. And, but, then, that's also, you also heard... heard, like, laughing. And we all look at each other in the classroom we're just like, "Oh, my God, is someone seriously laughing?"

If 18–1958 had shot into any other third-floor classrooms, there is no telling how many more students he could have killed. As many as seventy ran into Robyn Mickow's classroom before the door finally closed. If 18–1958 had shot through the window of her door, he could have murdered dozens more.

After getting as many students as he could into the stairwell on the west side, Rospierski used his body to barricade the stairwell doorway to prevent 18–1958 from pursuing them. After testing the door, 18–1958 walked away from the stairwell and into the teachers' lounge.

Rospierski risked his life to give his students more time to flee. Feis and Hixon gave their lives in unarmed attempts to take down the shooter. There could be no greater contrast between those three heroes and Deputy Peterson, who drew his gun and hid outside the building next door for nearly a full hour, or the Broward sheriff's deputies who had just arrived on the scene.[5]

The Police Response

18–1958 had reached his intended destination. He wanted to shoot down from the teachers' lounge at all the students who, thanks to Porter's evacuation order, were outside. But the bullets fired from his AR-15 were too weak to shatter the hurricane-proof glass. Broward deputies Perry, Goolsby, Miller, Seward, and Stambaugh arrived on the road one hundred yards north of Building 12. Hearing the gunshots, Deputy Stambaugh realized he was not wearing his bulletproof vest. He went to back to his car and took one full minute to put his vest on as the shots were ringing out from Building 12. Then he just stood there.

Deputy Eason, who had previously told a concerned mother that 18–1958's threat to shoot up the school was protected by the First Amendment, took a position on the road three hundred yards west of Building 12.

Sergeant Miller was the supervising officer on the scene. After hearing the shots, he put on his bulletproof vest and hid behind his car. It was his responsibility to direct the response of the officers on the scene. But he did not get on his radio for five full minutes. Deputies Kratz and Seward just stood by Miller.

Deputies Goolsby and Perry began to approach, but then took cover behind trees as 18–1958 fired off his final shots in a failed effort to break through the hurricane-proof glass.

It is astonishing that 18–1958 only took seventeen lives that day. The death toll could easily have been 170. He had ten minutes alone with eight hundred children. The only one who stopped him was himself. He dropped his rifle and left the building, blending in with fleeing students.

From a position where he could have seen 18–1958 walk out of Building 12, Peterson radioed, "Do not approach the twelve or thirteen hundred buildings. Stay at least five hundred feet away."

"Stay away from the twelve and thirteen hundred buildings," the police radio dispatcher repeated.

"I had a parent tell me there was a child down. Have fire rescue stage in the area until we make contact," Deputy Perry radioed from behind his tree.

As she pulled up in her cruiser, Jan Jordan, the captain in charge of the Broward Sheriff's Office (BSO) Parkland District, could have seen 18–1958 walking away from Building 12. Her police radio wasn't working. The BSO radio system was notoriously faulty, and failed to work properly on Parkland even on a normal day. This problem was well known, especially given the fact that the radio system had failed during the disorganized and widely criticized BSO response to the 2017 Fort Lauderdale airport shooting. But Sheriff Scott Israel, who once spent $12,500 to put his face on police cruisers around election time, prioritized so-called "community outreach" efforts over replacing the radio system.[6]

According to *The New Yorker*, Israel "failed to engage sufficiently in the essential if unglamorous work of overseeing law enforcement in a large and complex U.S. county and...was overly focused on the politics of prolonging his tenure."[7] Critics allege that Israel swept out experienced commanders and installed his own, often less experienced, political loyalists.

But Israel swore that he did not bring Jordan on as his Parkland commander because of politics. Rather, he insisted, she was a "diversity" hire. According to Israel, the Parkland city manager asked him to put forward three candidates for the city manager's consideration with an eye toward "diversity." He therefore nominated Jordan (presumably because she fit two diversity categories: woman and homosexual) and the Parkland city manager hired her.[8] The MSD Commission concluded that this "diversity" hire was "ineffective in her duties as the initial incident commander. While Captain Jordan experienced radio problems that hindered her ability to transmit, nobody reported receiving command-and-control directions from Jordan in person."

Eight Broward sheriff's deputies heard 18–1958's final shots. None went in to face the shooter. Remarkably, by declining to confront an individual who could have been murdering many more children as they stood outside, these deputies were actually operating in accordance with a policy change made by Sheriff Israel. Israel changed BSO's active shooter policy from saying that deputies "shall" enter a building to address a shooter to saying that they "may."

The MSD Commission concluded that "Sheriff Israel inserted the word 'may' in the BSO policy, and it is insufficient and fails to unequivocally convey the expectation that deputies are expected to immediately enter an active assailant scene where gunfire is active and to neutralize the threat. The use of the word 'may' in BSO policy is inconsistent with current and standard law enforcement practices."

What's more, whereas the Coral Springs Police Department (CSPD) did annual active shooter training, BSO deputies could not recall the date or nature of their last active shooter training.

Jordan entered Building 1 and paced back and forth. Finally, she got a message through on her radio: "I know there's lots going on. Do we have the perimeter set up right now and everyone cleared out of the school?"

The dispatcher responded, "That's a negative."

As Jordan called for a perimeter, five CSPD officers—Mazzei, Myers, Wilkins, Mazon, and Harrison—arrived on the scene. Fortunately, their radios were on a different frequency, so they did not hear Jordan's order. They rushed straight toward the building. As officer Wilkins approached the school, a Broward deputy told him, "We all can't stand behind this tree, we're going to get shot."[9, 10]

But the CSPD officers would not hide outside while children were being murdered. They formed a group and, joined by BSO deputies Hanks and Volpe, ran into Building 12 from the west side eleven minutes after the first shots were fired. They spotted Hixon, who was not yet dead, and tried to get him medical attention. Then they began searching and clearing the building.

As they were clearing the first floor, Jordan radioed, "I want to make sure that the perimeter is set up, and the school is being...all the kids are getting out. So, we need to shut down around the school." She was then informed that, without her orders, teams had already entered Building 12.

Another group of BSO deputies, led by deputy Greetham, arrived at Building 1. Greetham spent over one full minute unslinging his rifle, taking his body camera off, putting his bulletproof vest on, putting his body camera on, and then re-slinging his rifle. When another deputy approached him, Greetham told him to wait "while I get dressed." After getting dressed, Greetham and other deputies stood there debating whether to head toward Building 12.

Before the group of CSPD officers entered Building 12 from the west side, CSPD officer Tim Burton approached Peterson in his hiding position on the east side and asked for a situation report. Peterson told Burton that the shooter might be in the parking lot behind him and to "cover his six," i.e., watch his back.

Four minutes later, after the group of CSPD officers entered from the west side, CSPD officer Best approached Peterson and asked for a situation report. Peterson told him that the shooter was on the second or third floor of Building 12.

Two minutes later, Coral Springs officers Kozlowski and Mock ran into the building from the east side and were quickly joined by officers Fernandez, Whittington, Carvalho, and Dittman and then by BSO deputies Seward, Carbocci, Valdes, and Johnson. Peterson watched them. He remained in his hiding spot for a total of about fifty minutes before finally moving further away from Building 12.

Many school districts allow law enforcement to have real-time remote access to school security video footage. But not the Broward County Public Schools. This policy set the stage for a deadly tragicomedy of errors.

Three minutes after 18–1958 left Building 12, at 2:31 p.m., Kelvin Greenleaf and Jeff Morford entered the security video room. They rewound the videotape, hoping to identify the shooter, who was now nowhere to be seen. They then related what they saw by radio to Winfred Porter and Scot Peterson, apparently without making it clear that they were describing delayed footage.

At 2:46 p.m., BSO deputy Rossman heard Porter mention that there were MSD staff in the camera room. He directed Porter to radio them for intel. Porter told Rossman what Morford and Greenleaf had told him, and Rossman radioed the intel to BSO deputies inside Building 12.

At 2:50 p.m., Porter told Rossman, "He went to the second floor." Rossman radioed, "The subject was last seen on the second floor." At about the same time, CSPD officer Best relayed the same message, which he received from Peterson, on the CSPD radio. This news halted the progress of the group on the second floor, who now believed that the shooter might be within yards of their location, perhaps in any classroom or closet. Three minutes later, Morford announced that 18–1958 was leaving the third floor and going back to the second floor. This was a twenty-six-minute delay.

"Is this live intel?" BSO deputy Rossman asked.

Porter, who was on his cellphone, replied, "This is live."

Rossman told Porter to get off his cellphone and then asked Porter, "Where was he last seen? This is live? Right now?"

"This is live," Porter confirmed.

"They are monitoring the subject right now," Rossman said at 2:54 p.m. "He went from the third floor to the second floor.... The subject is now back down on the second floor." Porter then tried to explain to Rossman that the footage was actually not live, but Rossman didn't instantly comprehend it.

A minute later, Rossman repeated, "They are monitoring the subject right now. He went from the third floor to the second floor."

"You're asking me if this is live intel?" Porter said. "Is that where he is right now? That's where they last saw him on the camera." Rossman did not acknowledge Porter's statement. BSO deputy Greetham, now inside Building 1, asked Porter if he could pull up the live feed on his phone and Porter said that he couldn't. At 2:57 p.m., Porter told Rossman, "They're looking at recorded feeds, not live feeds." Rossman did not broadcast this fact over his radio for another four minutes. At 3:00 p.m., Morford announced that 18–1958 had run out of the building. At 3:01 p.m., a group of police officers reached the third floor, thirty-six minutes after Meadow and other students there were shot.[11]

As the CSPD officers and BSO deputies were clearing Building 12, they began to triage the wounded and dying. Coral Springs deputy Michael McNally repeatedly asked Jordan for permission to send medics in. Jordan, potentially still under the impression that there was an active shooter, repeatedly denied permission. She continued to deny permission even after the delayed footage showed that the shooter had left.[12] Several parents suspect that if not for those crucial minutes of further delay, their children may have received medical attention quickly enough to have survived.

As 18–1958 attempted to flee the scene, a former classmate spotted him:

> I said, like, "I thought you got expelled last year." And he's like, "No, the school took me back in." I don't know, for some reason I believed him and he was pretty scared, like, he was all, like, terrified. I thought about trying to make a joke about it, like, "Oh, aren't you supposed to be the one [who would shoot up the school]?" But I didn't, 'cause I knew what kind of person he was and I didn't want to trigger him or anything.

The police pieced together a description from witness accounts. A little over an hour after 18–1958 left Building 12, Coconut Creek police officer Leonard apprehended him.

PART III

The Politically Correct
School District

Here's a little "what if" list of counterfactuals where, if someone had made the responsible decision, Meadow, her classmates, and her teachers might still be alive:

What if...

1. Cross Creek had never let Nikolas Cruz come to MSD?
2. Cross Creek had listened to its school psychiatrist and didn't let a psychopath who dreamed of being drenched in blood feed his obsession with guns by letting him practice marksmanship in JROTC?
3. The sheriff's deputy who got the call that Cruz had threatened on Instagram to shoot up the school had investigated it rather than idiotically telling the caller that it was protected by the First Amendment?
4. They had sent him back to Cross Creek after he threatened to shoot up MSD?
5. They had sent him back to Cross Creek after he threatened to kill his peers?

6. They had arrested him after he threatened to kill his peers like Dana?

7. They had sent Cruz back to Cross Creek instead of covering up his misbehavior all those times campus security brought him to the office his first semester, and when he wrote "I hate niggers" on his backpack and carved swastikas on the lunch-room tables?

8. They had arrested him for his hate-crime assault of Enea Sabidini, or for having bullets in his backpack after five students told Winfred Porter that he had threatened to kill people and they were worried that someday he would?

9. They had called Henderson Behavioral Health and got him evaluated under the Baker Act for any of that?

10. They had sent him back to Cross Creek for any of that?

11. Henderson had invoked the Baker Act when they were called to Cruz's house three days after the fight with Enea?

12. Henderson had invoked the Baker Act when they were called to the school and told that he had attempted suicide and was about to buy a gun?

13. Peterson had invoked the Baker Act after he thought Henderson made a mistake by not doing so?

14. Henderson had invoked the Baker Act when they got the third call about Cruz in the same week and were told that he'd written "Kill" in a notebook after his mom resisted letting him buy a gun?

15. His mom had put her foot down and refused to allow him to buy guns?

16. The Florida Department of Children and Families had done a more thorough investigation?

17. They had decided to send Cruz back to Cross Creek rather than preparing his paperwork for him to sign away with ESE protections?

18. They had gone through the modest administrative trouble to get him into a school for regular, badly behaved kids where he could still have received some support, rather than waiting

until they collected the money for him from the state and then "withdrawing" him to a school without real adult supervision?

19. The ESE specialists at Cross Creek, OCLC, or the district's ESE office had known their own policies and let him back into Cross Creek when he and his mom asked?

20. MSD administrators had agreed to let 18–1958 on campus to have the meeting he needed to transfer back to Cross Creek?

21. They'd had him arrested or tried to sit him down and talk to him when he trespassed on campus after he'd been kicked out?

22. They had helped him get back into Cross Creek after his mom died and he'd called them telling them he wanted to find a way to graduate?

23. The sheriff's office had arrested 18–1958 any of the dozens upon dozens of times they had gone out to his house?

24. A criminal record would have enabled the FBI to identify "nikolas cruz" after the tip about his YouTube comment that he wanted to be a professional school shooter?

25. Having a criminal record would have enabled the deputy whom Mary Hamel contacted to follow up on her tip that he'd commit the "next Columbine"?

26. Having a criminal record would have enabled the FBI to follow up on rather than drop Hamel's tip that he would commit the "next Columbine"?

27. The gate to the school hadn't been wide open?

28. They had fired the incompetent security monitor Andrew Medina for sexually harassing Meadow? (See chapter 13.)

29. Medina had given chase when he first spotted him on campus?

30. Medina had called a Code Red before 18–1958 ducked into Building 12?

31. Medina had called a Code Red after he heard gunshots?

32. Anyone else had called a Code Red before the fire alarm went off?

33. Winfred Porter had heard the warnings on the radio before the fire alarm went off and called for a Code Red rather than an evacuation?

34. The fire alarm had been replaced on schedule and had not gone off?

35. Peterson had gone into the building to confront the shooter?

36. Peterson had even fired his pistol into the air as a warning to the shooter?

37. Peterson had let Officer Burton enter the building rather than claim he didn't know where the shooter was?

38. Ms. Lippel had received Code Red training and knew what gunshots sounded like?

39. The bathrooms on the third floor hadn't been locked because Winfred Porter didn't want the hassle of enforcing the law?

40. Any of the sheriff's deputies had gone into the building rather than stand outside and wait to follow the Coral Springs officers?

41. Jeff Morford and Kelvin Greenleaf hadn't rewound the video-tape or had told the police that they had rewound it?

42. Jan Jordan hadn't refused to allow medics in even after she knew the shooter had left?

I could go on. But you get the point.

I can't tell you how many times people told me that I was ignorant and didn't know what I was talking about because I didn't blame the NRA for everything. Because I didn't blame the type of gun that 18–1958 used. I couldn't do that, because blaming the gun let everyone and everything off the hook. There was more incompetence here than seemed humanly possible.

But at the same time as I was investigating 18–1958, I was also investigating the Broward County school district. And I realized that maybe the most unbelievable thing about 18–1958's story is that every last awful decision makes sense given the politically correct policies and the culture of unaccountability that the policies created.

Consider what might be the most unbelievable part of what happened that day. A campus security monitor saw 18–1958, believed that he was armed, knew that he could shoot up the school, let him run into the school with a rifle bag, and even after hearing gun shots from inside, he still would not call a Code Red because it might get him in trouble by making the school seem unsafe if a mass murder wasn't actually in progress.

That's the culture of Broward schools in a nutshell.

That's the kind of thinking and behavior that these politically correct policies encourage. It's not enough to understand what happened with 18–1958. You have the understand why it happened, the policies and the culture that made the most avoidable mass murder in American history somehow inevitable. Here in Part III, I take you on a bit of a tour through the school district that became the model for the nation. The policies pioneered here, which allowed 18–1958 to slip through every crack, were forced into schools across America by Secretary of Education Arne Duncan.

I would say that these policies are "coming to a school near you," but chances are they are already there. You have to understand them in order to fight them in your kids' schools.

—*Andy*

CHAPTER 9

From Broward to Your School

It took us months to figure out everything that happened with 18-1958. But Superintendent Runcie and his colleagues had access to his full educational records from day one. Runcie could have reviewed them and said, "It's clear that mistakes were made, and it's important to learn lessons from what happened." Instead, months later when CBS News asked Runcie whether the school district had handled 18-1958 appropriately as an ESE student, Runcie told them that the district had provided him with "enormous services."[1] And when families of the victims started raising questions about the role his discipline policies played in letting 18-1958 slip through the cracks, he called the question "fake news" and called us "reprehensible" for asking it.

At first, a lot of the media attention focused on the PROMISE program, which explicitly decriminalized misdemeanors. As you've seen, PROMISE itself barely factored into 18-1958's story. But as you'll now learn, it was in a broader sense at the heart of what went wrong. PROMISE was cornerstone of a culture of leniency that encouraged school administrators and police to systematically look the other way when students misbehaved. All those red flags at MSD weren't missed by accident. They were missed by design. By administrators who were, more or less, following orders.

In this chapter, we'll show you all of Broward's leniency policies that made Runcie a national education superstar and then explain how these policies have been forced into school districts across America.

"It Is Adult Behavior that Needs to Change"

Broward's PROMISE agreement became nationally famous the day it was signed, November 5, 2013. That day, *Education Week* ran an article headlined, "Revolutionizing School Discipline, With a Flowchart."[2] The article explained, "Harsh discipline policies are falling out of favor across the country, but Broward County, Fla., is hoping to do away with them entirely." Superintendent Runcie expressed alarm that 5 percent of Broward's black students were suspended, which was twice the rate of Broward's white students. He also expressed alarm that Broward had more than a thousand school-based arrests in a school year. Those statistics fell well under the national average, but Runcie declared, "If we don't find ways to turn this around and give them an opportunity, we're wasting a lot of lives."[3]

The same day, NPR's *All Things Considered* also highlighted the PROMISE program. It explained that "one of the nation's largest school districts has overhauled its discipline policies with a single purpose in mind—to reduce the number of children going into the juvenile justice system."[4] This was a move away from "zero tolerance" and an effort to end the so-called "school-to-prison pipeline." Activists contended that the fact that students of color were disciplined more frequently than white students was evidence that teachers and principals were engaging in racial discrimination, and that by unfairly disciplining students, teachers were putting them on a path toward incarceration. NPR noted, "Civil rights and education activists say the policy can be a model for the nation."

One month later, the *New York Times* gave PROMISE a glowing review, explaining, "Rather than push children out of school, districts like Broward are now doing the opposite: choosing to keep lawbreaking students in school, away from trouble on the streets, and offering them counseling and other assistance aimed at changing behavior."[5]

In the summer of 2014, after PROMISE's first year, *Scholastic* ran a profile of Runcie. He declared that his philosophy was simple: "We are not going to continue to arrest our kids."[6] *Scholastic* noted that Runcie's leniency policies decreased expulsions and suspensions by about 60 percent in the previous year and decreased arrests by 50 percent.

Runcie told *Scholastic* that "some of my staff joke that the Obama administration might have taken our policies and framework and developed them into national guidelines." But it was not a joke. The Broad Center, a left-leaning, billionaire-funded education reform group, put it plainly in 2018, one month before the Parkland massacre: "PROMISE informed the White House's guidance on student disciplinary practices nationwide."[7]

Later in this chapter we'll explain how the federal government pressured school districts to adopt Runcie's policies. For now, it's essential to understand the ideological motivation. In his speech announcing the major federal policy shift, Runcie's old boss, Secretary of Education Arne Duncan, declared that, "Racial discrimination in school discipline is a real problem today," and pointed to data collected by the Department of Education that showed black students are suspended at three times the rate of white students. This disparity in school discipline, he added, "is not caused by differences in children; it's caused by differences in training, professional development, and discipline policies." Therefore, he declared, "It is adult behavior that needs to change."[8]

Rather than accept that differences in disciplinary rates reflect broader inequities in American society, Runcie and Duncan blamed teachers. The problem wasn't poverty, or broken families, or neighborhood crime. The problem was teachers' racial discrimination. Therefore, according to Runcie, Duncan, and their social justice activist allies, teachers must be forced to behave differently. Their judgment should not be trusted because it is tainted by racial bias. Every effort should be made to constrain teachers from enforcing rules, on the theory that students will be further "traumatized" if they face consequences for their misbehavior.

Instead of a "biased" and "punitive" approach, social justice activists argue that schools should take a "data-driven" and "restorative" approach. Instead of removing a student from the classroom, teachers should do "healing circles" and "reparative" dialogues. According to the logic of social justice activists, the more schools decrease instances of "exclusionary" discipline and phased in "positive" practices, the better off students will be. And because this was all done in the name of fighting racial discrimination, it couldn't be questioned without running the risk of being labeled a racist.

The Leniency Policies

Superintendent Runcie did much more than launch a single program to decriminalize misdemeanors. He totally overhauled Broward's approach to school safety in order to try to reduce consequences for misbehavior, no matter how mild or severe. In this section, we'll walk you through the changes that he made.

Multi-Tiered System of Supports

For low-level misbehavior, such as disrupting the classroom or cursing at teachers, Broward implemented a program called Multi-Tiered System of Supports, or MTSS. In a PowerPoint presentation to the Broward school board, Runcie's deputy Mickey Pope defined MTSS as "an *evidence-based model* of schooling that uses *data-based problem-solving* to integrate academic and *behavioral instruction and intervention.* The integrated instruction and intervention is *delivered to students in varying intensities* (multiple tiers) based on student need." (Emphases in original.)[9]

It might sound strange for parents to hear that school bureaucrats view their children as subjects who create "data" and require "interventions" in "varying intensities." But MTSS is designed this way for a reason. It is predicated on the assumption that teachers are too biased to be trusted. Therefore, decisions about students must be made according to a "scientific" process.

Because any "exclusionary" consequence is presumed to be harmful, teachers must first create "data" by documenting a range of "interventions." They must prove that they've called home, written a "behavior contract," and/or done a "healing circle," and then prove that these "interventions" have not worked and therefore the student requires a higher "tier" of "intensity" (i.e., a conversation with an assistant principal).

This "data-driven" process is labeled "evidence-based" because when schools implement MTSS, suspensions decrease. But suspensions decrease for two reasons: (1) a substantial paperwork burden deters teachers from reporting misbehavior; and (2) principals face pressure from district bureaucrats to decrease suspensions.

One teacher from Westglades Middle School, whom we're calling Mrs. Pangrace, explained that "in the old days, our principals would just trust our intuitions." But now she feels second-guessed for bringing any matter to their attention. Mrs. Pangrace told us that if she sends a student to the office, her principal often asks her, "'What are you doing wrong? What are *you* doing wrong?' This is my career, my life calling, just trust me! It's offensive. So, a lot of times, [I think], 'Oh, I'll just let it go this time.'"

We asked Kim Krawczyk for her perspective, and she told us:

> Do you want to know why we stop bothering to fill out the paperwork to take kids to the office? We began to spend more time calling parents and doing paperwork for troublemakers than planning lessons for the kids who wanted to learn. Believe me, no matter what people think about "kids these days," some kids really do come to school to learn. With all this paperwork and principals who won't want to process it anyway, the best we can do for the good kids is to just let the troublemakers disrupt the class and try to teach around them.

Teachers feel this pressure from school administrators because school administrators feel it from district bureaucrats. In a video address to principals, Desmond Blackburn, then Broward's chief school performance and accountability officer, stated that suspensions, expulsions, and arrests should be an "absolute last resort."[10]

Additional pressure was exerted privately. One Broward assistant principal, who spoke on condition of anonymity for fear of retaliation and whom we'll call Mr. Parks, explained to us, "We go to the district meeting and we're told, 'Your numbers are being looked at. We want you to do everything you can to keep kids from getting suspended and expelled.'" He told us that he sympathizes with the frustration that his teachers feel but wishes that they sympathized more with him. "At the end of the day, when your boss gives you a directive, you follow it," he said. "[Our hands are] tied by the policies."[11]

The Discipline Matrix

Once a student is sent to the office for misbehaving, the "discipline matrix" prescribes consequences that school administrators are permitted to issue. The idea of a "matrix" is also predicated on the assumption that, just as teachers need a scientific process to guard against biased decisions, so too do school administrators. Mr. Parks told us that Runcie's "matrix" has "softened things so much that things that five years ago used to be a ten-day [out of school] suspension are now a one-day internal suspension." This leniency has flipped on its head the old saying, "Do you want to take this outside?" Mr. Parks noted that students realize, "If I fight off-campus, that's a possible arrest. So, I'll fight at school where nothing will happen to me."

When asked about the substantial decrease in suspensions and expulsions, Mr. Parks insisted that they do not reflect a dramatic improvement in student behavior. Rather: "Things that used to be expellable are now only suspendable. Things that were out-of-school suspensions are now internal [suspensions]. Of course, the data looks much better. That's what happens when you change the permitted consequences."

The school discipline matrix provides a list of possible consequences from which administrators can choose. For any of the eighty-three possible violations, there are between two and ten possible consequences, and the consequences escalate after multiple instances of the same infractions. A student may be suspended for two days for the first "medium fight," three days for the second, six days for the third. Along the way, administrators could consider a "behavior contract," a "loss of privilege," or referring the student to a guidance counselor.[12]

But the most striking aspect of the matrix is this: aside from contacting the parent, all consequences are strictly *optional*. When Kenny asked Mickey Pope to justify why everything was optional, Pope explained, "We don't want school leaders to say, 'If you do this, this is what will happen.'"[13]

Serious Offenses and Crimes: Policy 5006

When it comes to more serious offenses, strong action is further discouraged by Broward's Policy 5006. According to this policy, the following crimes are automatic grounds for suspension and possible grounds for expulsion but are not possible grounds for law enforcement referral: assault, battery, grand theft auto, burglary, sexual assault, and class B weapons possession.[14]

When it comes to bringing a gun to school, a Class A offense, Broward's Policy 5006 reads:

> *Students found to have committed one of the following offenses will be expelled, with or without continuing educational services, from the student's regular school for a period of not less than one (1) full year, and will be referred to the criminal justice or juvenile justice system:*
>
> *1. Bringing a firearm or weapon, as defined in chapter 790, to school, to any school function, or onto any school-sponsored transportation or possessing, displaying, using, selling or transmitting a firearm at school.*
>
> *Note: A student may not be subject to mandatory expulsion proceedings if it is determined that the student immediately* reported or delivered the firearm or weapon to a staff member.*
>
> ** The term "immediately" means without delay as determined by the principal after considering the totality of the circumstances and prior to being reported by another individual.*

You could, perhaps, call this the "five-second rule" for bringing a gun to school. (Except that the principal is allowed to define the meaning of "immediately," so there's no telling how long a student could carry a gun in school without facing the possibility of expulsion.)

Referral to law enforcement is almost never mandatory. The policy states:

> *The following crimes committed at school shall receive the most severe consequences provided in this policy, which shall be mandatory suspension and administrative assignment to the Behavior*

Intervention Program or expulsion, referral for appropriate coun-
seling services, and may be referred for criminal prosecution to the
local law enforcement agency.

- *Sexual battery (rape) or attempted sexual battery (rape),*
- *Possessing, displaying, using, selling or transmitting a Class*
  A weapon,
- *Homicide,*
- *Kidnapping or abduction,*
- *Bringing, possessing, using or selling any explosive propel-*
  lant or destructive device,
- *Armed robbery or attempted armed robbery,*
- *Battery on a School Board employee,*
- *Battery on a law enforcement officer,*

(Emphasis added and list abridged.)

Arrests for even the most serious felonies are optional, and administrators understand that the school district wants the number of arrests to go down. As Jeff Bell, president of the Broward Sheriff's Office Deputies Association, put it when asked about the culture facing the police and school resource officers: "They don't want the police officers making arrests *on campus* and they don't want the drugs to be found *on campus* and they don't want the warrants to be served *on campus* because it looks like there's bad stats at the school."[15] (Emphasis added.)

The PROMISE "Collaborative Agreement"

The PROMISE "Collaborative Agreement" is a document signed by Superintendent Robert Runcie, Sheriff Scott Israel, State Attorney Mike Satz, and Public Defender Howard Finkelstein. Runcie has claimed that PROMISE covers "13 specific, nonviolent misdemeanor infractions," but that is a false characterization.[16] PROMISE covers ten nonviolent misdemeanors (including theft, alcohol, drugs, threats, and vandalism), one violent misdemeanor (fighting), and two noncriminal conduct offenses (disrupting a school function and disorderly conduct).[17]

Students must commit four PROMISE-eligible misdemeanors per year before consultation with law enforcement even becomes *an option.* At the fourth misdemeanor, the PROMISE agreement instructs school resource officers to issue a warning, call the student's parents, or refer the student to the PROMISE program. If "further support is needed but not available at the school level, the officer…may call the district [office] for guidance. After exhausting all of the above options, the officer may consider placing the student under arrest."[18]

Reflecting on the message this agreement sent school resource officers, Jeff Bell said, "When that program started, we took all discretion away from the law enforcement officers to effect an arrest if we choose to."[19]

For the first three misdemeanors—and plausibly for an indefinite number of additional misdemeanors, depending on administrator discretion—students are diverted from arrest and spend several days in a PROMISE center.

The next chapter offers a more in-depth look at what occurs within the PROMISE program. But the message it sends students is very clear. As Runcie tells incoming PROMISE students in a video message, "You know, this is the land of the free, home of the brave. And people aren't going to be free when they're connected and constrained by the juvenile justice system."[20]

No-Go Zones

In its effort to decrease school-based arrests, Broward went so far as to prohibit the police from coming on campus to arrest a student for any crime committed off-campus. According to minutes from the January 2018 meeting of the Broward County Juvenile Justice Advisory Committee, Runcie's deputy Valerie Wanza:

> [A]nnounced that on Monday their School Board Attorney conducted a training exercise with Principals in the District. She continued that police are not allowed to arrest children on school campus for non-school related offenses, and if a child is not being arrested for a school-related offense it should not be verified [whether] the child is in school or not.[21]

From this, it would appear that if the police were to show up and say, "We want to arrest a juvenile suspected of rape," Broward principals were trained to say, "No. Stay away. And I won't even tell you whether the suspect is here."

We're not lawyers, but it's not clear to us whether this is legal. Indeed, at the next meeting, Broward Juvenile Judge Elijah Williams "inquired how the Schools will get around the statutory rules related to school arrests." Runcie's deputy David Watkins acknowledged that principals don't want to be held in contempt of court and clarified that in some instances, such as an individual who poses an immediate threat, police could be allowed on campus.[22] (This meeting took place on the afternoon of February 14, 2018, minutes after the massacre.)

The "Prison-to-School Pipeline"

Everyone in the Broward school district knew that Runcie was trying to fix the so-called "school-to-prison pipeline" by making it harder to arrest students. But investigative journalist Paul Sperry discovered that he was also doing something that school board members like Nora Rupert said they never recalled approving: building a "prison-to-school pipeline" to funnel more and more convicted felons back into traditional schools.[23]

Attempting to reintegrate convicted felons into normal classrooms is a fraught process that should be undertaken with great care. But Runcie threw caution to the wind. According to a district handbook, students who were "convicted of a serious crime such as rape, murder, attempted murder, sexual battery or firearm-related offenses" were able to reintegrate after at most a year in the Behavior Intervention Program (BIP), housed at an alternative education center.[24]

These students are at a very high risk for recidivism but face little consequence in BIP if they continue to commit felonies. According to policy, if a student in BIP commits a "Group 3 Behavior," such as arson, making a bomb threat, weapons possession, or a major physical aggression, the consequences "will include removal from the classroom for a period of time."[25] That is to say, the punishment for repeated felonies is getting a time-out.

The number of convicts flowing into traditional schools rose dramatically: 325 incarcerated students returned to traditional schools in 2014, 570 students in 2015, and 967 students in 2016, the latest year for which there is data.[26] According to one parent, the Broward school district's chief of police told parents that there were over one thousand felons attending traditional schools.

After the April 10 school board meeting where Kenny Preston spoke, Parkland father Steven Brown privately approached Runcie about the BIP and related the conversation to us. Runcie told Brown that he had never heard of the program. Brown offered to show him documents about the program bearing his signature, and Runcie again insisted that he had never heard of it.

Brown asked Runcie whether there were any rapists attending school with his children. Runcie told him that he did not believe so. Brown then asked Runcie whether parents would be notified if convicted rapists were placed in their children's classrooms. Runcie admitted that, due to student privacy protections, parents would not be allowed to know.

Runcie's Policies Go National

At the end of the first year of PROMISE's implementation, Mickey Pope boasted to the Broward school board, "In January of 2014, while we were well into our first year of implementation of PROMISE, the Department of Education and the Department of Justice issued guidance to school districts across the nation to do exactly what we are doing here in Broward."[27]

Pope's characterization was both true and false. The "Dear Colleague Letter" (DCL) sent out by Arne Duncan at the Department of Education and Eric Holder at the Department of Justice embodied Broward's approach to school discipline, but it was much more than "guidance."[28] The DCL was the pretext for a largely secret and coercive campaign of bad-faith investigations intended to compel school districts across the country to adopt Broward's policies.

The DCL, issued two months after PROMISE was launched, fundamentally changed the standard for federal investigations into civil rights violations regarding school discipline. Before, the role of civil rights enforcement was clear: Students may not be treated differently because of their race. If a black student and a white student both curse at a teacher, it would be a civil rights violation to discipline them unequally. But the DCL changed the standard from equal treatment to equal outcomes. Statistical differences in disciplinary rates were now taken to be prima facie evidence of a civil rights violation. After the DCL, if two black students and one white student all cursed at a teacher, it could be a civil rights violation to discipline them equally (depending on the racial composition of the school district).

School districts were not explicitly told that they *must* adopt policies similar to Broward's. But they were told that they could be investigated based solely on their discipline numbers, and the aim of these "investigations" was clear. A 2014 Department of Education document, intentionally hidden from a public records request but provided to us by a whistleblower, stated that the goal of the federal investigations was to "ensure that...'the school's written discipline policy explicitly limits the use of out of school suspensions, expulsions, and alternative placements to the most severe disciplinary infractions that threaten school safety or to those circumstances where mandated by Federal or State law.'"[29] The conclusions of these investigations were essentially preordained. In order for them to end, school districts had to adopt leniency policies.

Hundreds of districts serving millions of students changed their policies because of these investigations. Hundreds, if not thousands, more changed their policies because of the mere threat of investigation.

According to a 2018 survey of school superintendents conducted by the American Association of School Administrators, these investigations were "unprecedented, intimidating, and costly."[30] Department of Education bureaucrats were told to investigate not only major disciplinary actions like suspensions, but also minor ones like loss of recess privileges and time-outs. Bureaucrats were also told to look into individual teachers, especially white teachers, for evidence of racial bias.

This presumption of racial bias is also evident in two other instructions given to investigators. Bureaucrats were told to examine cases where referrals were made but no disciplinary action was taken. Those actions merited examination because administrators act "solely on the basis of the referring teachers' opinion," a fact that "only exacerbates discrimination." Bureaucrats were also told that even though policies that allow for teacher discretion did not "per se" violate the Civil Rights Act, they ought to be very carefully reviewed for discrimination.[31]

Unsurprisingly, then, the survey of superintendents found that teachers were "so shaken up" after being interviewed by investigators that "they questioned whether they should remain in the teaching profession. There was a noticeable decline in staff morale after these investigations concluded that did not fade."[32]

These investigations were conducted almost entirely in secret. In many of the school districts under investigation, few people outside of the superintendent's inner circle were aware of them. For example, after Milwaukee Public Schools superintendent Darienne Driver signed a resolution agreement to overhaul her district's discipline policies, she explained, "We have to. It's not optional."[33] School board members told reporters that they were never aware of the four-year federal investigation.

According to the superintendents' survey, 20 percent said that they changed their discipline policies in direct response to federal investigations, 16 percent said that they changed their policies because of the DCL itself, and 25 percent weren't sure whether they changed their policies because of pressure from the federal government, state government, or activist groups. Not all these school districts went as far as Broward when it comes to lowering arrests, but they've adopted the discipline policies that encourage the same culture of underreporting.

Fortunately, in December 2018, the Trump administration's Federal Commission on School Safety—launched in the wake of the Parkland massacre—recommended rescinding the federal DCL that was forcing these policies into schools across the country.

Unfortunately, the fact that the feds aren't still pushing these policies doesn't mean that they're going away anytime soon. States such as Maryland, California, Oregon, and Illinois adopted statewide leniency policies. In New York, the attorney general forced school districts like Syracuse to follow Broward's model. (A district attorney later ordered them to reverse course after a dramatic spike in school violence.)[34] In Minnesota, the state Department of Human Rights conducted dozens of "investigations" into local districts to force them to lower suspensions.[35] Even in deep-red North Carolina, the Legislature essentially took PROMISE statewide, mandating that school districts work with local police departments to lower the rates of in-school arrests. In all, twenty-seven state legislatures have changed laws to limit suspensions, expulsions, and/or arrests in the last decade.

What's more, social justice activist groups have routinely threatened to file lawsuits against school districts for disciplinary disparities, putting additional pressure on superintendents. Indeed, at a community forum on the PROMISE program held shortly after Kenny Preston's report made national news, Mickey Pope explained that everything the school district does is closely monitored by the U.S. Department of Education, the (nonexistent) Department of Civil Rights, and liberal activist groups like the ACLU, the NAACP, the Human Rights Campaign, and the Southern Poverty Law Center.[36] Until parents learn to speak up for their children, these groups will continue to have the ear of school board members and bureaucrats, and will continue to silence the voices of teachers.

The Social Justice Industrial Complex vs. Teachers

Discipline reform is framed as an effort to combat racism, so it is politically incorrect and risky to criticize it. When it was first reported that Secretary of Education Betsy DeVos was considering rescinding the DCL, 150 activist organizations drafted a letter to DeVos telling her that doing so would send the message that she "does not care that schools are discriminating against children of color."[37] No one, certainly no teacher, wants to be accused of discriminating against minority students. And just a glance at this list of those organizations gives a sense of their collective influence over American education:

> *Achievement First, ACLU, African American Ministers In Action, Alliance for Educational Justice, Allies for Educational Equity, American Association of University Women, American Federation of Teachers, American-Arab Anti-Discrimination Committee,*

Anti-Defamation League, Autism Society, CASEL, Center for American Progress, Center for Public Representation, Children's Defense Fund, CLEAR Clearinghouse on Women's Issues, Coalition of Black Leaders in Education, Council for Exceptional Children, Council of Parent Attorneys and Advocates

Democrats for Education Reform, Dignity in Schools Campaign, Disability Law Center, Disability Rights Education & Defense Fund, EdAllies, EdNavigator, Ednovate, Education Forward, Education Justice Alliance, Education Leaders of Color, Education Reform Now, Educators for Excellence, EduColor, Equal Justice Society, Excellence Unleashed, Feminist Majority Foundation, Gay, Lesbian and Straight Education Network (GLSEN), Girls Inc., Human Rights Campaign, Juvenile Law Center, Lawyers' Committee for Civil Rights Under Law, Leading Educators, League of Women Voters of the United States, Learning Policy Institute, Legal Aid Justice Center, Legal Services for Children, NAACP, National Alliance for Partnerships in Equity (NAPE), National Association of Councils on Developmental Disabilities, National Bar Association, National Black Justice Coalition, National Center for Learning Disabilities, National Center for Special Education in Charter Schools, National Center for Transgender Equality, National Center for Youth Law, National Council of Jewish Women, National Disability Rights Network, National Education Association, National Network of State Teachers of the Year, National Partnership for Women & Families, National Protection and Advocacy for People with Disabilities Inc., National Urban League, National Women's Law Center, Native American Disability Law Center, Pahara Institute, Parent Advocate Group for an Equitable Quality Education (PAGE QE), Parent Educational Advocacy Training Center, People For the American Way (PFLAG), Public Counsel, Public Interest Law Center, Quality Education for Every Student, REACH, Restorative Schools Vision Project (RSVP), Sargent Shriver National Center on Poverty Law, Southern Poverty Law Center, SPAN Parent Advocacy Network, Stand for Children, Stop Sexual Assault in Schools, Student Advocacy, Students for Education Reform, TASH, Teach For America, Teach Plus, The

Advocacy Institute, The Alliance to Reclaim Our Schools, The Arc of the United States, The Broad Center, The Discipline Revolution Project, The Education Trust, The Expectations Project, The Fellowship: Black Male Educators for Social Justice, The Leadership Conference on Civil and Human Rights, The National Indian Education Association, The New Teacher Project, The Opportunity Institute, Third Way Solutions, Thursday Network, Transformative Justice Coalition, Turnaround for Children, UnidosUS, Union for Reform Judaism, Women's Law Project and YWCA USA.

Compared to this alphabet soup of activist groups, teachers have little voice. But in about a dozen school districts across the country, local teachers unions asked their members how they feel about these policies and found that teachers overwhelmingly oppose them.

Teachers say these policies make them less safe. In Oklahoma City, 60 percent of teachers said that offending behavior had increased since the district adopted new so-called "positive" and "restorative" discipline policies.[38] In Baton Rouge, Louisiana, 60 percent of teachers said that they had experienced an increase in violence or threats and 41 percent said they did not feel safe at work.[39] In Portland, Oregon, 34 percent of teachers said their school was unsafe.[40] In Jackson, Mississippi, 65 percent said their school "feels out of control" on a daily or weekly basis.[41] In Denver, Colorado, 32 percent of teachers said discipline issues had compromised their personal safety and 60 percent said discipline issues had harmed their mental health.[42] In Syracuse, New York, 36 percent of teachers had been physically assaulted by students, 57 percent had been threatened, and 66 percent had feared for their safety at school.[43]

Teachers say that these policies don't work. In Denver, only 23 percent of teachers said the new system improved behavior.[44] In liberal Madison, Wisconsin, only 48 percent said the new policies aligned with their values and only 13 percent said they had a positive effect on student behavior.[45] In Charleston, South Carolina, 14 percent of teachers thought that the new discipline system worked.[46] In Oklahoma City, 11 percent of teachers said that more "progressive" discipline would help them be effective in the classroom.[47]

Teachers believe that traditional discipline works. On the other hand, 65 percent of Oklahoma City teachers said that they needed greater enforcement of traditional discipline. In Philadelphia, more than 80 percent of teachers agreed that suspensions were valuable for maintaining safety, removing disruptions so other students can learn, sending a signal to parents about their child's behavior, and ensuring that other students follow the rules.[48]

In three districts, unions have allowed teachers to comment anonymously on discipline policy. The same tragic themes appeared in each district: principals refusing to manage misbehavior, turning a blind eye to violence, sweeping evidence under the rug, and even rationalizing and excusing death threats. Here are a few representative comments from each district:

Oklahoma City[49]

- "We were told that referrals would not require suspension 'unless there was blood.'"
- "I would like to see a consequence for bad behavior of some kind, such as when a male student pulled his penis out and showed it to another girl student and admitted he did so and nothing was done."

Buffalo[50]

- "I have never seen anything like it. The behavior is unreal. The students know they can get away with acting out because there are no real consequences. The kids are controlling the school—fights, furniture being thrown, students eloping, nonstop verbal abuse/swearing at staff from students. The list goes on and on. It's an unsafe environment."
- "Students are threatening teachers with violence and in many cases physically attacking teachers with little to no consequence."

Fresno, California[51]

- "Students are being allowed to throw rocks at teachers. When they are sent down to the office, they returned moments later. Students are allowed to call teachers niggas [and] break windows and classroom doors when they are mad. A student was seen touching his privates in class and sexually harassing others and was not even suspended. [Students] break into rooms and steal with nothing being done."

- "A student said he would shoot and kill me. Three students heard the threat as 'shoot and kill,' but the administration believed the perpetrator, who claimed that he said he was going to prank me with a slingshot. Administration said that since he didn't specifically use the word 'gun,' it was not as serious [of a] threat as I thought."

Unfortunately, very few teachers are willing to go on the record. In New York City, a student was stabbed and killed by his classmate in September 2017. Max Eden wanted to write a profile of why it happened and he discovered that the school had fallen into chaos once new administrators stopped enforcing consequences. A mother called to say that her son had threatened her with a knife and might start bringing it to school. Administrators ignored the call. Her son brought it and used it to kill a classmate.[52]

Max interviewed ten teachers at the school, but only one who no longer taught in the school district, Christopher Vasquez, was willing to have his name printed. Another teacher, who tried and failed to resuscitate the victim, explained, "Teachers are not going to speak out. Period. Because it's going to cost them their job." That sense of professional vulnerability is not uncommon, but it may not always be teachers' primary concern. In many schools, the bigger issue is a fear of social stigma. Vasquez explained:

So many educators are so social justice-minded that they're afraid to speak out against something that's politically correct. I mean, even if you're a minority teacher who teaches all minority students, and you see them get morally wrecked because administrators refuse to enforce any rules, and you see a bullied, bisexual Hispanic student kill a black student, you'll still be called a racist by administrators and activists and Twitter people for saying that this shit just doesn't work.

The fundamental transformation that Robert Runcie and Arne Duncan have wrought upon American education was captured in an anecdote in a *New York Times* article about the effects of discipline reform in Minneapolis:[53]

Simon Whitehead, a former physical education teacher at Southwest High School in Minneapolis, said he had watched the district's discipline policy changes play out in his classes. Name-calling escalated to shoving, and then physical assaults. Profanity was redefined as "cultural dialect," he said.

"[The reform] threw the school into complete chaos," he said. "The kids knew they weren't going to go home."

Mr. Whitehead said he learned not to call his students out in front of their peers. He did not use the word "detention," but rather "quality time." Eventually, he would just "sweep a lot under the rug."

The discipline model that he said had worked for him for 25 years—a warning, then a consequence—was no longer recognized by his bosses. He retired last year, labeled a racist.

Give a warning. Issue a consequence. Be labeled a racist.

To the social justice industrial complex, this represents "progress." We hope that to those outside that small ideologically self-obsessed bubble, this sounds like madness.

But for superintendents, there is a method to it. As Vasquez reflected, "Education reform isn't about what's right for students anymore. It's about what makes adults feel good about themselves. What gets them status."

The Superintendent's Status

It may sound astonishing that such a profound change could occur in such a short time without teachers' consent or parents' knowledge. But the incentives all line up. Superintendents risk investigation or litigation if they maintain traditional discipline policies and will receive accolades if they decrease suspensions. Principals, who report to superintendents, have an incentive to please their bosses. Even when they see their students get murdered, teachers refuse to speak out publicly for fear of retaliation or stigmatization. And a parent whose child has been bullied or beat up is unlikely to connect their child's suffering to a nationwide realignment of education policy and culture.

It all starts at the top. To understand how and why these leniency policies appeal to superintendents across the country, it's useful to return to Broward to see how PROMISE made Robert Runcie into a hometown hero. And the best way to do that is to show the tribute paid to him, and to the PROMISE program, when the "collaborative agreement" was officially re-signed after three years, in October of 2016. All of the PROMISE "stakeholders" were in attendance to celebrate.[54]

The School Board

School board member Robin Bartleman kicked off the meeting by saying, "We have created a model for the nation, brave enough to think out of the box, and to save our children."

Member Ann Murray congratulated the board for fixing the problem of racially biased teachers, explaining that before PROMISE, teachers looked at students with the attitude of, "Well, here's real jail bait going through our school." But, she said, PROMISE has "revitalized pride in the child."

Member Abby Freedman declared, "It takes a village. The wonderful thing is we have come together as a village to make that difference for all children. And I look forward to knowing that someday [PROMISE] will go into the history books."

Member Rosalind Osgood declared that PROMISE changed "the paradigm for the next generation. And this remarkable policy that took place, I say, is the most significant thing that's happened in Broward in the last ten years because it stopped locking up our children and it started educating them. What we said as a community is, we're going to choose education over incarceration."

The NAACP

Several NAACP representatives attended the ceremony to congratulate Runcie on PROMISE. Adora Nweze, president of the NAACP's Florida chapter, said, "Thank you so much again, Mr. Superintendent, for your leadership.... You are number one! You're the only school district that I know about that has gotten the United States Department of Education and United States Department of Justice to put in their report that your program is the one that works in this country for all children."

NAACP general counsel Bradford Berry declared that PROMISE was "really elegant in its simplicity," with the clear message: "We are going to do all that we can to keep our kids out of the criminal justice system." And he explained that as he stood in front of the Broward school board there, he was reminded of another lawyer, who once "stood in front of the U.S. Supreme Court and argued in support of another elegant but simple proposition: that every kid deserves an opportunity to succeed.... [T]he lawyer was Thurgood Marshall. The case was *Brown v. Board of Education.*"

After comparing PROMISE to that landmark civil rights decision (and by implication Robert Runcie to Thurgood Marshall), Berry vowed to "take the model that has been set by Broward County and introduce it and propose it to our two thousand [NAACP affiliates] across the country...in the hope that they too will have the courage to do what you have done."

The Law

Nearly every major Broward County public official was at the re-signing ceremony and praised Robert Runcie. Public Defender Howard Finkelstein, State Attorney Mike Satz, and Juvenile Judge Elijah Williams each praised Runcie and PROMISE.

Finkelstein said, "All of us know that for the last thirty years what we've been doing has been wrong. Everybody knows that we have institutionalized racism.... This is the beginning of a new future where our children are allowed to be children. This piece of paper is really the shedding of an old skin that needs to go away, shrivel up, and die as we move forward. Because our star will ascend as we save these kids, one child at a time."

Satz agreed, "We're saving a lot of kids. And that's very important."

But the man with the most rhetorical zest that day was Judge Williams, who was introduced as "the man, the myth, and the legend." His speech is worth presenting in full:

I have served as legal counsel for some of the most influential individuals in both the civilian and military world. Superintendent Runcie, I know leadership. You are second to none. We are privileged to have you here in Broward County. And as a former Air Force captain, nothing excites me more than when I'm in a room full of military folks, people who wear the uniform.

The essence of a military person is that from the very beginning, that person is willing to give up their right to live. And that's why they're so special. Because when you give up the right to live, the other rights don't really apply. That's why we respect those in the military. What happened in this [PROMISE] process is that all of the stakeholders involved began to give up their rights. They became like military folks.

You see, the school board did not say, "We control the schoolhouse. No one can tell us what to do inside of a schoolhouse." Sheriff Scott Israel, Broward Sheriff's Office, the various police departments, the Broward Chiefs of Police Association, they didn't say, "We have the right to make the arrest." They didn't say that. The State Attorney Office, Mike Satz, he did not say, "If a crime has been committed, we have the right to formally charge them." And so on and so on and so on.

All parties involved were engaged in something called collaboration. You can't collaborate unless you give up your rights. You can't collaborate coming from a position of power and strength and influence. You've got to give up your rights. So, in this sense, every single person who's a stakeholder involved in this process was just as good as any man or woman who's ever put on a uniform.

Notably absent from Williams's speech was the idea that students have rights. And we suspect that very few citizens outside of that meeting would agree that PROMISE's stakeholders have the same moral stature of veterans of the United States armed forces. But judging by their applause, everyone in the room certainly thought so.

We'd like to think that school boards and school bureaucrats across America aren't as morally bankrupt as those in Broward County. But the politically correct cancer of these leniency policies has spread to schools across America. The people you trust to run your child's schools are operating under the same perverse moral incentives as Runcie and his colleagues: pressure school administrators to refuse to enforce the rules, then pat themselves on the back when everything looks better on paper.

CHAPTER 10

The Underreporting

After the revelation that 18–1958 had been referred to the PROM-ISE program, the *Sun Sentinel* ran a front-page story headlined, "Schools' Culture of Tolerance Lets Students Like Nikolas Cruz Slide."[1] The article noted:

Broward Schools have grown so tolerant of misbehavior that students like Nikolas Cruz are able to slide by for years without strict punishment for conduct that could be criminal. The culture of leniency allows children to engage in an endless loop of violations and second chances, creating a system where kids who commit the same offense for the 10th time may be treated like it's the first.

The *Sun Sentinel* quoted Mary Fitzgerald, who taught for thirty-seven years in Broward before retiring early due to discipline concerns. She recalled, "It was so many things. I had three students bring knives to my classroom. One was out of the classroom for one day. Another had so many things on his record, he was gone for five days. None were expelled."

The *Sun Sentinel* explained that, "Many teachers and parents say Broward has created a culture in which teachers are expressly told or subtly pressured not to send students to the administration for punishment so a school's image is not tarnished."[2]

In 2015, two thirteen-year-old boys brought a Magnum revolver, knives, fifty-nine bullets, and fireworks to Sunrise Middle School. They were taken into police custody, but the school district declined to say what discipline they'd face.[3] (Recall that a student may bring a gun to school without necessarily facing even the threat of expulsion.) In 2016, a former student brought a gun to Coral Springs High School to give to a current student who planned to shoot up the school. The former student was arrested, but the current student was neither arrested nor expelled.[4]

According to the school district's official statistics, Runcie's discipline policies led to a 40 percent reduction in the number of behavioral incidents, a nearly 70 percent reduction in misdemeanors, and a nearly 40 percent reduction in felonies. The number of PROMISE-eligible infractions plummeted from over six thousand in 2013 to under two thousand in 2017.[5] But these statistics do not reflect dramatic improvement in student behavior. Rather, they represent a refusal to faithfully record and document disruptive and criminal behavior.

Case Study: February 14, 2014

Recall from chapter 4 that when Kenny Preston met with Superintendent Runcie before the April 10 school board meeting and asked why reporting felonies to the police was optional rather than mandatory, a grieving father interjected, "Obviously if someone rapes somebody in school, it's not like they're not going to take it seriously." Unfortunately, four years to the day before the massacre, that's essentially what happened at MSD.

Here is how School Resource Officer Scot Peterson described an incident involving Sheriff Scott Israel's son:

[The victim] reported that after baseball practice he was sitting on the ground near the stadium entrance when [the first assailant] came over and started to kick him. [The first assailant] then grabbed [the victim's] groin area with his hand. [The first assailant] then grabbed [the victim's] baseball bat and pushed it against his buttocks. Note: [the victim] was fully clothed and there were no attempts to remove any clothing from [the victim] during the incident. Israel's

involvement was that he held [the victim] by the ankles while [the first assailant] was committing the above actions.[6]

This is, at the very least, a description of a severe sexual assault. But Peterson consulted with Assistant Principal Denise Reed and together they determined that the incident "constituted a simple battery under the school disciplinary matrix. [The first assailant] and Israel received a three (3) day external suspension for battery. The school district disciplinary matrix requires no law enforcement action."

That same year, Scot Peterson was awarded School Resource Officer of the Year—perhaps in part because MSD appeared to have so little crime.

We spoke with the victim's mother, who said that after seeing his assailants get off virtually scot-free, the rest of her son's high school career was defined by the fact that he was the kid who got (at least partially) sodomized with a baseball bat.

When Royer Borges found this report, he and his lawyer Alex Arreaza decided to take it straight to the press. Channeling Royer's indignation, Alex exclaimed, "Is this like an alternative universe law? What happens? Because you're in school you don't have to obey regular laws?... You will never see somebody grabbing somebody's crotch and poking some kid in the butt with a bat [outside of Broward schools] and getting a simple battery for it."[7]

In June 2018, the *Sun Sentinel* ran an article headlined, "Broward School District Failing to Report Many Campus Crimes to State as Required."[8] It began:

On paper, Marjory Stoneman Douglas High looked like one of the safest high schools in Florida.

The Broward school district reported to the state that no one was bullied or harassed, no one trespassed on campus, no one was violently attacked, no one broke into campus after hours and nothing expensive was stolen during the 2016–17 school year.

It wasn't true.

The district reports only a portion of its actual crimes to the state, making it impossible to spot a school's trouble spots and inform parents about safety, the South Florida Sun Sentinel has found.

Had school administrators reported every crime that actually happened at Stoneman Douglas, it might have raised an alarm that safety was a concern, said April Schentrup, whose daughter Carmen was killed in the Feb. 14 massacre at the school.

This article was written based on discrepancies between Scot Peterson's official reports and what the school reported to the state. According to the official state numbers, the year before the shooting there was no alcohol use, battery, bullying, harassment, hazing, larceny, robbery, trespassing, vandalism, threats, sexual battery, or sexual assault at MSD. None at all. Indeed, there was no bullying, harassment, trespassing, or threats from 2014 to 2017.

The *Sun Sentinel* confirmed that those numbers did not match Peterson's official reports. But, of course, Peterson's official reports also likely understated the number and type of incidents that occurred at MSD, considering how he handled the sexual assault described earlier. In short, the official safety data for the safest school in Broward County is simply fake.

There would be another way for parents to know whether their kids are safe: student and teacher surveys. For the past two decades, the Broward school district gave an annual survey asking questions about various aspects of school climate. But the year that Runcie launched PROMISE, the district removed every question asking whether students felt safe. The year after that, the district discontinued publishing the survey entirely.

Campbell's Law, *The Wire,* and School Discipline

In the 1970s, social scientist Donald Campbell formulated what is known as Campbell's Law: "The more any quantitative social indicator is used for social decision-making, the more subject it will be to corruption pressures and the more apt it will be to distort and corrupt the social processes it is intended to monitor." As an example, Campbell cited President Richard Nixon's "crackdown on crime," which established Nixon as an effective defender of law and order but had "as its chief effect the corruption of crime-rate indicators, achieved through under-recording and downgrading the crimes to less serious offenses."[9]

Years later, this phenomenon was captured in popular culture by the hit HBO series *The Wire*, in a scene showing how the police "juke the stats":

Deputy 1: *Word from on high is that felony rates, district by district, will decline by five percent before the end of the year.*

Deputy 2: *We are dealing in certainties. You will reduce felonies by five percent or more or—I've always wanted to say this—let no man come back alive.*

Deputy 1: *In addition, we will hold this year's murders to two hundred seventy-five or less.*

Deputy 2: *I don't care how you do it. Just fucking do it.*

Officer 1: *Uh, Deputy. As familiar as we all are with the urban crime environment, I think we all understand there are certain processes by which we can reduce the number of overall felonies. We can reclassify an [aggravated] assault or a robbery. But, uh, how do you make a body disappear?*

Deputy 3: *There isn't one of you in this room who isn't here by appointment. If you want to continue wearing those [officer's stars], you will shut up and step up. Any of you who can't bring in the numbers we need will be replaced by someone who can.*[10]

Many schools and districts now operate under similar orders. NPR reported that after Miami reformed its discipline policy, thousands of fights simply "disappeared" from the official state records.[11] In Washington, D.C. principals "reduced" suspensions by refusing to record them. A recent survey showed that 63 percent of teachers in Denver and 81 percent of teachers in Buffalo, New York, believe that their administrators do not accurately report disciplinary incidents.[12] In anonymous survey comments, teachers across the country say things like: "Principal has no control [over students]—afraid she won't get tenure so keeps incident numbers down by never suspending kids. Staff bullied into not asking for suspensions"; and "No consequences for anything. And we are not allowed to write students up"; and "I was told by an administrator...that he rips up paper write-ups [of disciplinary infractions]."[13]

Unfortunately, it is—by definition—impossible to collect data on data that isn't collected. So, for the most part, we are left with stories and perspectives. Here are testimonials from two people who worked in Broward schools, which illustrate the district's culture of leniency and underreporting.

Robert Martinez, School Resource Officer

When Robert Martinez was a school resource officer (SRO) at Rickards Middle School in 2015, he got a call from the police that a student had just committed a burglary off campus. It was Martinez's duty to arrest the student, so, he recounted to us, he told the assistant principal, "I need that kid out of class because I'm taking him into custody."

"No. You can't arrest him here. We're a sovereign nation," the assistant principal replied.

"What?" Martinez asked. "Sovereign nation? What are you talking about? This is like an embassy from another country or something?"

"Oh, well...we were instructed that you can't arrest kids in school."

"I have a juvenile pickup order, signed by a judge."

"Oh, we were told that students can't be arrested here."

"You better call somebody. Because somebody is going to jail today. Him, or you."

After she consulted with the district office, the assistant principal relented. But, Martinez reflected, "This is the mentality that SROs deal with." SROs are supposed to make all their decisions on school-based crimes in consultation with school administrators who apparently believe that the law does not apply on campus.

Martinez said he "was one hundred percent supportive of PROM-ISE at first because kids do stupid stuff and make mistakes." Martinez had seen the excesses of the old "zero-tolerance" approach. He'd seen a teacher intentionally provoke a student, block his exit from the room, then call for the student to be arrested for assault when he brushed against her on his way out. But after the PROMISE program was implemented, "it's gone from one extreme to the other." He has seen teachers be repeatedly assaulted and administrators insist that he not get involved.

What's more, SROs were explicitly instructed not to arrest students for nonviolent felonies as a part of PROMISE. At the beginning of the

2014–2015 school year, shortly after the riots in Ferguson, Missouri, Martinez and his fellow officers were called in for a meeting with leadership from the school district and the sheriff's office. Martinez said, "I never wanted to remember Mickey Pope ever again after my experience that day. The way she came off was like police officers are basically bullies with badges and guns. She said that she'd instructed her college-age kids that, if they get pulled over by police officers, they should find well-lit places and make sure they follow the commands to a tee because police officers are gunning down poor black people on the streets. I was kind of offended...considering also that I'm a minority."

Martinez thought about walking out of the meeting, but he knew that could be a career-ending decision. More than her anti-police rhetoric, what stuck out to Martinez from that meeting was that "Pope made a comment that...when it comes to juveniles, kids in schools, with this PROMISE program, there are even certain *felonies* that we should not arrest for. What I found interesting is that the [Broward Sheriff's Office] command staff, Colonel [Alvin] Pollack, and the other supervisors didn't correct this lady, jump in and say, 'Wait a minute. By state law, we are required to arrest for felonies.'"

Students can assault SROs without facing any disciplinary consequences from administrators. One time, an assistant principal asked Martinez to retrieve a girl who'd run out of the school and across the street. When he caught up with her, she refused to return to school. He grabbed her by the arm, and she lunged at him and bit him. He arrested her for assaulting an officer. The police, as was customary, released her to her parents and she was back in school the next day. Martinez asked the assistant principal why the student didn't face any consequence at school and was told that the school wouldn't do anything because it happened off campus.

"Most students start off as criminals by opportunity," Martinez explained. "They see a watch on a table and swipe it." What the adults do in response is immensely important. If students see that there are consequences for criminal behavior, they'll often be deterred. If they see that nothing will happen to them, they'll often be emboldened. Martinez said to us:

[The student] becomes desensitized. He knows that there's no conse-
quence. Sometimes the parents don't even do anything. The school
doesn't do anything. The police don't do anything. What message
does that send the kid? You're setting him up for failure.

[Runcie and Israel] don't understand how they're ruining these
kids' lives with these failed policies. This system emboldens them to
continue to commit crimes until they reach that magical [adult] age
where now they're being sent to prison, and then they'll be hard-core
criminals. Because they know that they'll never get a student loan,
never be able to join the government work, law enforcement, mili-
tary—all these doors close because now they're convicted felons....

I wonder why these leaders can't see that. I mean, I'm just a cop.
I don't have the highest education in the world, but I can figure that
out.... I don't know what's in their hearts. But I can tell you right now
that they are creating that school-to-prison pipeline.

Before PROMISE, Martinez and other SROs took a hands-on
approach to students facing their first arrest. They'd try to keep them
on the right track. Sometimes they would even go to court on behalf of
the student. Martinez related, "You don't know how many times the
public defender's office thought we were there to hammer the kid.... No,
we wanted to speak on his behalf and say, 'Look, these are all the great
things he's done and is doing. He should be on probation.' And the judge
would agree." But now that students must commit four misdemeanors
a year before an SRO can even get involved, Martinez believes that the
chance for an SRO to reach out those students with a firm but caring
hand has been taken away.

According to Martinez, if the school district had actually wanted
to make a program that worked, it would have consulted with the SROs
and assistant principals—the adults working directly with students
and handling serious disciplinary issues. They would have done a
detailed analysis of the existing discipline policy, recommended incre-
mental changes, and consistently checked in with SROs and assistant
principals about whether their changes were working. But none of that
happened. And when students came back from PROMISE, Martinez

would ask them what happened in the program and they'd say, "Nothing. I sat in a classroom and did absolutely nothing."

Martinez said, "You beat your head against the wall and ask why this program was created. You have to come up with a reason for it all. At the end of the day, they're politicians and it has to do with votes or ideology.... When you see programs whose sole purpose is to make the schools look good, and something like [the shooting] happens, that's an outrage."

Martinez respected the March For Our Lives gun control students, but he had mixed feelings about the course of public debate after the shooting. Reflecting on how Sheriff Israel and Superintendent Runcie blamed the NRA, Martinez lamented, "What the students don't know is that the people who are telling them to go out and protest are the ones that are endangering them.... They're the ones who failed. These failed policies failed students miserably. Then they deflect the whole event and try to build their political careers on top of it. The students are being misled."

Anna Fusco, Broward Teachers Union President

When Kenny Preston first called BTU President Anna Fusco to ask her for insight for his report, she was eager to help. She told him that underreporting was a huge problem in the district and that there was way too much documentation required to get kids the help they need. She explained that sometimes administrators pressure teachers to not even write referrals, and sometimes principals will delete referrals when they don't want the information to exist because they want to hide the problems at their school.

Kenny took copious notes on their conversation. Fusco told him that, on the day he called, she had stood up for a teacher who'd been sexually assaulted by a student. The student had manhandled a twenty-two-year-old teacher, ripping her shirt and trying to get at her breasts. She thought she was going to be raped. But when the principal asked the student about the incident, he denied it and received a clean slate. Fusco wouldn't give Kenny precise details about the student, but implied that he was left off the hook because he was labeled "special education," even though he obviously knew right from wrong.[14]

Fusco later explained to *Weekly Standard* reporter Alice Lloyd that administrators discourage and delete disciplinary documentation to "cover their ass so that it doesn't look like they have a bad school."[15] Hundreds of teachers have complained to her about the administrators' attitude: don't write referrals, don't document.

The pressure to underreport is most acute and problematic when it comes to students with behavioral disabilities. Fusco explained to Lloyd that with these students, "documentation helps because if the problems are documented, students can get more help or extra guidance and teachers can have a better picture. It's not just about punishment. It's used to help." But even as the pressure to underreport has grown, so too has the amount of paperwork necessary to move students with extreme behavioral disabilities (like 18–1958) to specialized schools that can give them the help they need. "If the paperwork used to be a foot," Fusco explained, "now it's yards."

Fusco suggested that it's not right to point at the PROMISE program itself as having played a role leading up to the shooting. Rather, she speculated to Lloyd that the problem might have been the underreporting. "If admin are not willing to let teachers document, then you're not getting into the PROMISE program because you can't get there without documentation," she said.

Fusco told Kenny that it's a huge problem that SROs have no control over what happens to a student because the SRO cannot interfere in what the principal wants to do or what the district wants. As a result, school administrators can obstruct justice with impunity. Fusco told Kenny that just the day before they chatted, a teacher had complained to Fusco that her school's SRO refused to even let her give a statement because the school administrator didn't give her permission to talk to the SRO. Fusco fumed to Kenny that she didn't want to see one more teacher get their head smashed against the wall or their knee kicked or a desk thrown at them. Or for one more student to say "I'm going to shoot you in the face with a BB gun," and have the principal say that it's the teacher's fault for not knowing how to handle the student.

Out of everything Fusco told him, the only thing Kenny mentioned in his report is that paperwork burdens can pressure school administrators into passivity. Fusco publicly alleged that Kenny misrepresented her statements, but in reality, he substantially underreported her comments in an effort to be sensitive to her political relationship with Runcie. When Max reached Fusco for an interview, she immediately asked him whether he was in league with Kenny, who had "lied" to her. When Max asked Fusco how Kenny had lied, she explained that he didn't tell her that she'd be quoted in a report that would make Runcie look bad.

When Max explained that he was writing a book with Andy Pollack on what went wrong leading up to the shooting at MSD, and that the book would emphasize the culture of underreporting, Fusco was initially eager to help. She said that she had just polled teachers who had left the district to find out why they left and that a huge number cited discipline as the reason. She said that she intended to make the data public and would share it with us for this book. But shortly after Andy backed a school board candidate who wanted to oust Runcie, Fusco stopped responding to Max's emails and has yet to make the data public.

Fusco told Max that Runcie was a good man with a good heart who just didn't understand the impact that his policies were having on teachers. She blamed his inner circle for keeping information from him. For our part, we are prepared to believe that there's some truth to this.

But if Runcie is truly that ignorant, then much responsibility for that rests on Anna Fusco.

Fusco has a reputation in Broward as a ballbuster—almost literally. Twelve principals have accused her of harassment and filed a lawsuit against the school district for not keeping her under control. She allegedly routinely bypasses security and trespasses on school grounds to investigate teacher complaints. According to the lawsuit, Fusco allegedly pushed an administrator and threatened to castrate another who did not want her roaming his school's hallways unattended. Addressing the allegations, Fusco said, "While some may ironically call our actions bullying, we call it a public service."[16]

And yet, when a high school student shared the mildest of her thoughts on the effects of her superintendent's discipline policies, she disavowed him publicly. The irony is that these policies create a very real need for the aggressive protection that Fusco purports to offer.

But for the president of the Broward Teachers Union, it seems political convenience trumps public service.

Broward Teachers Speak Out (Anonymously)

Because the president of the Broward Teachers Union will not speak out on behalf of her teachers, it was left to the families of the victims make teachers' voices heard. Max Schachter, who lost his son Alex, solicited comments from Broward teachers—promising anonymity so that they could speak without fear of retaliation. Here are comments from a dozen:

> *Teacher 1: They do not want to report what "really" goes on in schools. The matrix they have created is a joke. For years, there has been a lack of discipline; it has progressively gotten worse with Mr. Runcie as superintendent.... A student can curse at a teacher and basically be right back in the class the next day.... I have even had an SRO tell me they could not do anything to a student who threatened me until he actually did something to me, even though the student was known to have anger management issues and was in a court-appointed program. [If the] student is ESE, then the district has made it virtually impossible to do anything, with all the documentation, RTI, meetings, limited suspension days in a school year, etc. I personally think if fingers are to be pointed, it needs to point straight to the top with Mr. Runcie.*

> *Teacher 2: We have a broken system where parents have the final word and it takes years to remove students with behavior issues.... The students and parents have all the power and we have no autonomy.*

> *Teacher 3: Please do not disclose my name or school location because I am an annual contract teacher, and I do fear retaliation.... When my son attended [school name redacted], a student that was going through the process to be labeled with a disability told my son he was going to "f***ing kill him" and took a pair of the teachers scissors and held them to his neck, and nothing was done. Nothing was put in the system. He wasn't ESE yet, so I don't know why nothing*

was done. Teachers do put in referrals, but we are scared to. I've been told by many, but I have not verified this personally because I have only written two referrals, that then some admin delete the referrals after the paper is generated for parent signatures. If it's deleted, then it doesn't stay in the system or follow the student. Teachers have told me to make copies of referrals and hold on to them to cover myself should a situation ever occur so I can prove I documented it.

Teacher 4: *It is my personal belief that the district, in order to make itself look better, has used a confusing discipline matrix and the PROMISE program to make it appear that behavior issues have decreased within the district, when the reality is simply that they go unreported. I also believe that failure by the district to follow through on issues that do arise have created a system in which teachers and administrators don't bother to report things because they know the district will not do anything meaningful about the issues.... The district has created an atmosphere in which people know that little will be done to those who break the rules, and so infractions go unreported because employees see that there is simply no point. This makes it appear that there are fewer rules being broken, when in reality the opposite is true.*

Teacher 5: *There is a culture of not reporting. I had two incidents when I was at Heron Heights. One involving a student who brought a knife to school and it was not reported.... I was told that since it didn't happen in the classroom that it wasn't my responsibility to put it in BASIS [the discipline tracking system]. In a state where teachers can be fired without just cause, there is no safety net for teachers. Generally speaking, we were not officially told not to report incidents in BASIS, but we would have to be called in to the AP's office...and discuss if we were going to report. It was a well-known fact that we didn't want high numbers in Parkland.*

Teacher 6: *[They] find a way to sweep discipline issues under the rug so that the district looks good.*

Teacher 7: *My opinion of the matrix is that it is weak and left teachers and administrators powerless in certain circumstances.*

Teacher 8: When I worked at MSD, the discipline matrix was implemented at AP discretion.... As a teacher, they would take the word of students first.

Teacher 9: Students that have IEP's are almost untouchable as far as discipline goes.

Teacher 10: The most recent principal I had NEVER would even do the discipline matrix because she did not want to create any kind record that would cause interest in her with the district. She never suspended or punished even though there were weapons and physical threats made in school. We had a fifth-grader who threatened another student on the bus with physical harm. He actually drowned their dog, because he lived next door to her. The principal did not take any interest because it did not happen on school property. He did act out in class and the AP wanted to start paperwork on him but the Principal nixed it.

Teacher 11: I also have been in a discipline matrix meeting with other school staff and county staff. It involved one of my students who had stolen school property, broke into a portable, and then written a death threat to a teacher. The staff and comity [sic] was forced to follow the discipline matrix, and since the student was ESE it was deemed that he really received no punishment.

Teacher 12: The discipline matrix is very lenient toward students and their behaviors. There is little to no consequence and it gives students who have an IEP even more of a break.... It takes a long time to get a student suspended to AES [Alternative to External Suspension] off-campus even. Even having drugs and selling/using them on campus does not qualify for expulsion; only the Promise program. Most of the time the kids gain notariaty [sic], learn to hide the drugs better, and socialize [with] other troubled kids, which causes more problems. We had a student recently who made a threat online about bringing a gun to school and shooting a student, and he is at the Promise program for 10 days. Apparently the school had made a threat assessment and told the staff and students that it was a "non-reliable" threat and we were safe on campus still. However, the student will be back to school soon, and no one can predict what will happen in the future or how that student will respond to things down the line.

CHAPTER 11

The Broken PROMISE

Compared to the culture of leniency and underreporting that it engendered, the PROMISE program itself played a relatively small role in 18–1958's story. But it's well worth showing the truth of a program that became a model for the nation.

The Broward political establishment insisted that PROMISE was a resounding success because the numbers proved it. State Attorney Mike Satz declared, "It works, it works. The numbers are terrific." Chief Judge Peter Weinstein said, "My instincts told me that this PROMISE program was going to be a huge success. I was correct. The data speaks for itself." Dwayne Flournoy, former head of the Broward County Chiefs of Police Association announced, "We're saving kids. We're making an impact. If you look at the numbers, the numbers are the numbers. The facts are the facts."[1]

But no effort was made to connect data from PROMISE to broader police records to see whether it was having a positive or negative effect on students outside of school. No effort was made to track students who participated in PROMISE after graduation. The school district repeatedly touted two numbers: a nearly 70 percent decrease in school-based arrests, and a 90 percent "non-recidivism" rate.

You have already seen the lengths to which the district went to artificially deflate school-based arrests. To get the truth behind the 90 percent non-recidivism figure, we talked to Tim Sternberg, who served as an assistant principal at Pine Ridge Education Center, the home of the PROMISE program, who explained, "Ninety percent of students don't go to PROMISE twice in the *same year* for the *same infraction*. There are thirteen infractions. The way they calculate it, a student could be sent to PROMISE fifty-two times in high school and be perfect on paper."

At first we didn't know whether to believe Tim, who appeared to be a textbook example of a disgruntled former employee. Tim routinely attended school board meetings to complain that no one was answering his emails and tweeted nonstop criticism regarding the school district. But then the *Sun Sentinel* verified Tim's claim.[2]

Despite having never met the shooter, Tim has a profound sense of guilt about what happened. Because he feels, up until a year before the shooting, he was part of the problem. He provided us invaluable insight and we wanted to tell his story, for what it reveals about the PROMISE program and the Broward school district.

"They Want Me to Hire Someone Black"

Tim began teaching in 2008 at Whispering Pines, a specialized school in Broward County for students with behavioral disabilities, similar to Cross Creek. It was the kind of school that many teachers wouldn't touch with a ten-foot pole, but to Tim, it felt like home. In his view, being a therapist is an essential part of being a teacher. The students at Whispering Pines needed therapy—and so much more. Before they could learn, many students needed to have a sense of security that was missing at home. Sometimes Tim felt that he was the only reliable adult in some of his students' lives.

Tim identified with his students because he had grown up in an unstable home with an absentee father whose gambling problems created a state of constant domestic anxiety. Tim's sister suffered from serious mental disorders growing up and could not live independently as an adult. Young Tim didn't see full-time college as an option, and for twenty years after high school he took job after job without having anything amounting to a career. But after being in the workforce for more than a decade, Tim enrolled in a part-time program at Florida International University and earned his bachelor's degree in history at age thirty-six.

After three years as a classroom teacher, Tim was promoted to be a literacy coach, and after a few years in that role, he was chosen for the highly selective PROPEL (Principal Rapid Orientation and Preparation in Educational Leadership) program, a part-time master's degree program created by a partnership between the Broward schools and Florida Atlantic University intended to fast-track talented teachers into administrative roles. One of the Whispering Pines assistant principals was departing, and the principal assured Tim that once he finished PROPEL, he'd get the job.

But then, Tim recalled to us, his principal took him aside in the spring of 2014 and said that Tim wasn't going to get the assistant principal job because the central office had told him he had to hire someone who was black.

Tim was as liberal as they come and was, generally, in favor of affirmative action. But Tim also believed that social justice requires treating people as individuals. Being passed over in favor of no one in particular, just "someone black," was demeaning, dehumanizing, and downright racist.

Tim was devastated. He resolved that he would not return to Whispering Pines the following year, even if it meant being unemployed. But his principal helped Tim land a job as an assistant principal at Pine Ridge. Pine Ridge had long been the site of the Behavior Intervention Program, a long-term program for badly behaved students without diagnosed disorders, and would now also be the home of the shorter-term PROMISE program for students who committed crimes at their traditional school.

Tim swung instantly from depression to exhilaration. He now had the opportunity to be part of the biggest dream he could have hoped for: leading a team that was on the cutting edge of combating the "school-to-prison pipeline." He couldn't wait for the fall of 2014, when he'd be leading PROMISE through its first full year.

PROMISE in Reality

On the first day of his dream job, Tim faced a shock. PROMISE had no curriculum. Teachers were making up lessons on the spot. Tim received calls from principals across the district complaining that students returning from PROMISE said that they just played games all day. Tim asked his principal, Belinda Hope, and district administrators why there wasn't a curriculum. According to Tim, Hope told him that the district didn't have the resources. The district once sent a curriculum consultant to Pine Ridge, but she merely gave Tim handouts photocopied from old textbooks.

After a few months, Hope settled on a structure: each week, teachers would focus lessons on a different disciplinary infraction.

Tim asked Hope, "How does it make sense for a student to come to PROMISE for vandalism and end up making PowerPoint presentations about bullying?" Her response, he told us, was that if the district could reduce bullying, then problems like vandalism would also decrease.

That didn't make much sense to Tim, but he soon stopped asking questions. Not because he was becoming disillusioned. Quite the contrary. He was so committed to PROMISE's mission that the only thing he could think to do was to put his nose to the grindstone and just try to work as hard as he could.

The school district frequently framed PROMISE as one part of an effectively engineered system for behavior management and modification. But at Pine Ridge, Tim fielded calls from assistant principals at traditional schools asking things like, "What gets a kid sent to PROMISE? Okay, that's what this kid did." And, "What gets a kid sent there, but just for a couple of days? Okay, that's what he did." And, "What gets a kid sent there for the longest possible time? Okay, that's what he did."

If students were caught doing drugs at school, they would go to PROMISE for six days. If they agreed to see a counselor at PROMISE, that would be reduced to three days. If they brought drugs to PROMISE, they would be kicked out of the program and sent to Juvenile Judge Elijah Williams. But, according to Tim, Williams would frequently send the student back to PROMISE. Students could return to their traditional school bragging about how they had gone to PROMISE for drugs, then brought drugs to PROMISE, then got off for it by being sent back to PROMISE.[3]

The message that Pine Ridge sent, Tim explained to us, especially for the short-term PROMISE students, was, "The world is out to get you. To profile you. To oppress you. To arrest you. But we won't let that happen because you're in the PROMISE program. What we're doing here is transforming the world, and it's our job to protect you while you're here until the world changes."

Hope told the Sarasota *Herald-Tribune*, "I have really come to believe that we are naïve in thinking students know right from wrong."[4] The goal of PROMISE wasn't so much to teach right from wrong, but to give students "strategies to withstand what they're going through."

Hope explained that punishment at Pine Ridge was minimal to nonexistent. If a student misbehaved, a teacher could threaten to not let them go on a field trip. But, per Hope's philosophy, teachers rarely followed through because Hope thought it an unconscionably draconian punishment. "If you deprive them of [a field trip], some of them won't get to live. They won't get to experience life," Hope said. "We're giving the kids here an opportunity they wouldn't have at a traditional school, because there they had a label that they were bad, they couldn't do anything, [they're] the child that's not going on the field trip."[5]

The consequence for misbehaving at a traditional school was being sent to Pine Ridge, where there were no consequences.

Tim recalled a time when a fifth-grade BIP student threw a tantrum at the end of the day. When Tim told the student to board the bus, the student replied, "I don't want to board the fucking bus," then picked up a big rock and hurled it at the bus, shattering a window. It could have struck and seriously injured one of the first graders on board. Fortunately, neither the rock nor the broken glass hit any of the students. Tim marched the rock thrower into the office and called the police. When the deputy arrived, Tim said, "I want him arrested."

"Arrested?" the deputy asked.

"Yes!" Tim insisted.

"You know we can't arrest him, right?"

"Why not?"

"You have the PROMISE program here," the deputy said. "This school is the PROMISE program."

"So what?" Tim answered, becoming flustered. "I'm telling you I want this kid arrested."

"We can't arrest him," the deputy told Tim. "The point of PROMISE is to not arrest kids in school. We can't arrest a kid at the PROMISE school. Do you realize what kind of PR that would make?" Instead, the officer called the student's mother and waited until she picked him up.

Hope and Despair

Despite the fact that PROMISE did little more than temporarily warehouse troubled students, as it gained renown, its principal, Belinda Hope, also received national recognition. A *New York Times* profile of PROMISE included her picture, and she was featured in a Russell Simmons-produced and Emmy-nominated documentary, *Prison Kids: A Crime Against America's Children*.[6] For a few years, Tim did everything he could to make Hope appear successful. But it took a heavy emotional toll.

Teacher after teacher filed grievances claiming that Hope was targeting and bullying them. Eventually, these allegations led to an official investigation and a hundred-page report that paints an extremely dark picture of Hope's leadership.[7]

According to the report, Hope would openly target teachers like Ms. Davis, whom Hope vowed to colleagues she would "do anything to get rid of." Hope harassed Davis on a daily basis. A colleague described that Davis became "a changed person; like her soul was taken out, very sad and in fear." One day, as Hope berated Davis in a particularly vicious manner, Davis suffered a stroke from which she never fully recovered. When another teacher complained about the way Davis had been treated and suggested that Hope was responsible for her stroke, Hope demoted him.

According to the report, Hope treated an assistant principal, Mr. Feldman, "like a dog" and called him a "weak ass" in front of teachers. Feldman confirmed that he "suffered abuse and intimidation, mentally and verbally, to the point where he went into deep depression and had to take anti-anxiety medications." (Feldman believed that Hope's treatment of him was motivated by anti-white racism.)

The PROMISE program itself had no dedicated administrator because Hope told her assistant principal, Ms. Reliford, "You are not the AP. I'm in charge," and tasked a newly certified teacher with all of PROMISE's administrative duties.

According to the report, Hope routinely made teachers cry. Ms. Pizam left the school, saying she couldn't take it anymore. One teacher said that his colleague, Mr. Johns, was in "anguish" after Hope reassigned him to grade levels he wasn't suited to teach, and he eventually retired early. Mr. Freehill said that he could not sleep at night for fear of what would happen at school the next day. He also ended up retiring—only one year shy of his thirty-year mark (and the accompanying large increase in his pension).

To make her school's discipline numbers look good, the report suggested that Hope pressured teachers into not issuing disciplinary referrals. Ms. Miller recounted that the better of two bad options was to accept the chaos in her classroom rather than send a student to Hope's office and get bullied for doing so. Miller also eventually left the school. When asked why, she began to cry and said she just couldn't understand how anyone could be that mean.

During all this, Tim stood by Hope's side. When he attended the PROPEL program, a top district official had taught him that in Broward, loyalty trumps everything else. If you were an assistant principal and you went against your principal, you were going against your school and against the district.

After years of receiving grievances against Belinda Hope, a top district official asked Tim to take notes on her behavior and e-mail them from his personal email account to the district official's personal email account (in order, Tim suspected, to hide their correspondence from public records requests).

Tim dutifully chronicled Hope's behavior and sent his report to the district official, trusting she'd do the right thing. She didn't. Instead, Tim recalled, he received a text: "Hey Tim, just a heads up: I showed Belinda the report you wrote."

"You did what!!??" Tim texted back.

Tim was assured that it would take some time, but that he'd be Pine Ridge's new principal. The next few weeks, working under Hope were harrowing. But it all felt worth it when the school district sent a letter to parents that Tim was the new principal. Then Tim got another text from a top district official: "Mr. Darby is coming in tomorrow. I need you to show him around the school, and he's going to be in charge."

Tim had, once again, been blindsided and passed over for a job he was explicitly promised in favor of an African-American. But it wasn't the race part that bothered him this time. At least this time it was for an individual human being and not simply "someone black." What bothered Tim was the whole damn thing. For years he felt compelled to be loyal to an abusive boss. Then he was asked to spy on her. Then he was outed for spying on her. Then he was promised a promotion. Then he was denied it via text message.

Tim was done with the Broward County school district.

Waking Up

After Tim resigned from Pine Ridge in February 2017, he spent hours each day sitting on his back porch and thinking through what had happened. He realized that he had given his heart and soul to a program that was hurting the students it was trying to help. Worse than that, he had believed in PROMISE so wholeheartedly that he would have dismissed all criticism as mal-intended and attacked anyone who questioned it.

He started to write lengthy emails to Runcie and school board members about the weaknesses of the PROMISE program and the ways it could be improved. He received nothing more than perfunctory acknowledgments of receipt. At first, he was angry about being ignored. But then he realized that two years ago, he would have ignored those emails too.

When the news about the Parkland shooting broke, the first thing Tim said to his wife was, "I bet that kid was in PROMISE." Tim felt personally responsible. He'd never met 18–1958, but Tim knew that the broken system, which until a year ago he would have vociferously defended, must have failed him. After the news came out that the shooter had been sent to PROMISE once but didn't actually attend, and that no one had followed up to figure out why, Tim was hardly surprised. What was supposedly the greatest "Restorative Justice" program in America didn't even have a dedicated administrator!

When Runcie claimed that it took three months for the district to find the information about the shooter's attendance in the student data systems, Tim felt certain that Runcie was not telling the truth. Tim knew how those systems worked.

After the shooting, Tim kept sending emails and going to school board meetings to demand that they admit PROMISE's flaws and commit to fix them. But he got nowhere, and as the district's spin machine went into full motion, Tim came to a reluctant conclusion: PROMISE just couldn't work.

At least not in Broward. Maybe not anywhere if other school districts were also led by people eager to build their reputations on statistics they knew were baloney while ignoring what was actually happening to students. Two years ago, Tim would have sworn that he was fixing the "school-to-prison pipeline" and saving students' lives. But Tim told us that the scales have fallen from his eyes. Now he believes that PROMISE is the symbol of everything that's rotten in American education.

CHAPTER 12

The "So-Called Tragedy"

Six months after the shooting, CBS News asked Andy if he had a message for Superintendent Runcie. Andy said, "Why didn't you accept any responsibility for what happened? And why didn't you look at any of the policies that were in place in Broward that led up to it? Why aren't you telling the families that you'll look into these policies?"[1]

Unfortunately, Runcie and the school board proved unwilling to accept any responsibility or reevaluate their ideas. The apparent smear campaign orchestrated against Kenny Preston when he tried to bring up questions about school discipline and school safety spending that you read about in chapter 4 was not an outlier. The school district and board routinely treated questions with condescension, and implied that parents whose children were murdered were wrongheaded—even racist—to call for change and accountability.

In this chapter, we will share three more examples of how the school district reacted in a public forum on PROMISE, in an attack on the only school board member who occasionally asked probing questions about PROMISE, and during a school board "workshop" on the PROMISE program. The culture of any organization is set from the top, and the self-righteous and contemptuous attitude displayed by Broward's leaders after the MSD tragedy helps to explain why it happened.

The PROMISE Forum

On May 6, 2018, one day before a scheduled public forum on PROM-ISE, local NPR reporter Jessica Bakeman broke the news that 18–1958 had been referred to the program.[2] Kenny, Andy's son Hunter, and Max attended, as did Ryan Petty and Lori Alhadeff (both of whom had lost children in the massacre and were gearing up to run for the school board). At Kenny's invitation, David Hogg, the most prominent and controversial of the March For Our Lives student activists, also attended.[3]

The meeting began rather awkwardly, with Runcie insisting that he had not misled the public. He explained, "I don't think anyone gave me misleading information. I had the best information I had at the time. Maybe I should have qualified [my statement] further. That's a mistake I made. But it was done trying to be as transparent as possible."

Runcie then ceded the stage to representatives from the school district, the sheriff's office, and the state attorney's office. The first speaker was Judge Elijah Williams. His speech was a rhetorical marvel, both disclaiming responsibility for PROMISE while also touting its greatness. He began:

> *We created the PROMISE program because we had to create the PROMISE program. I don't know if you've ever seen that movie The Perfect Storm. It tells about these six Massachusetts fishermen on a boat. They were like swordfishermen. And these three storms start to come in. A cold front from Canada, a hurricane, [and] something was coming off the Great Lakes. And they decided to try to deal with it. Well, it's called a perfect storm. And a perfect storm is just a situation whereby you got a combination of negative factors coming in at you at the same time. And you've got to deal with them. Back when we created the PROMISE program, we were dealing with what's called a perfect storm. We had seven things coming in. All at one time.*

Williams outlined the seven "storms" that allegedly forced the school district to create PROMISE. The first was a 2009 law prohibiting school districts from referring students to law enforcement for petty misconduct. The second was a report by the Florida Department of Juvenile Justice suggesting that the majority of students arrested in school had not committed criminal acts. The third was the statistic that more students were arrested in Broward County than in any other Florida school district. The fourth and fifth storms were national in scope and worth presenting at fuller length for their national implications:

> *And then we had a fourth storm that was coming in. The NAACP, the United States Justice Department, and other community activists were all selling me along about something called the schoolhouse-to-jailhouse pipeline. And what is the schoolhouse-to-jailhouse pipeline? Basically, everything in life is a pipeline.*

Williams explained that pipelines existed between the U.S. Air Force and commercial aviation and between college football and the NFL.

> *So there's nothing wrong with a pipeline. It's just that, we began to create a pipeline unintentionally where we began to...I guess it was in our school discipline policies, our grading systems, our school-based arrests, and so forth that began to push kids out of schools and into our criminal justice systems.*
>
> *And then we had a fifth storm that was coming in from the northeast. Lawsuits began to be filed all across the nation litigating against the schoolhouse-to-jailhouse pipeline. In fact, by the time we signed our PROMISE agreement, six counties in the state of Florida had already been served with their lawsuit.*

Williams explained that the sixth "storm" was that students who were out of school on suspension sometimes got in trouble in the community, and the seventh was that the Internet made it easier for juvenile arrest records to become public. Then Williams concluded:

> *That was our perfect storm. You know, when you deal with Mother Nature, you deal with a storm, all you really can do is bunker down or try to flee.... [But] our storm was a man-made storm. And in a man-made storm, there's no way you can really bunker down or flee. You've got to deal with it head-on. So, in October 2011, we went and hired Superintendent Robert Runcie.*

Kenny was still new to these policy issues, but he knew that his parents would flip out if they heard someone explain that his school district decriminalized misdemeanors because of pressure from the Department of Justice, activist groups, and litigation.

But Hunter caught a more fundamental problem. He turned to Kenny and asked, "Is this guy really comparing this to *The Perfect Storm?*"

"Yes, I think he's trying to say that the school district was forced into—"

"Dude," Hunter said. "At the end of that movie, everyone dies."

After Williams paid tribute to Runcie, he introduced that evening's keynote speaker: Judge Steven Teske. Williams said that he had attended a juvenile justice conference in 2012 in Las Vegas, where "there must have been a thousand judges." And all of them "were dealing with the same seven storms. So everyone began to focus on this same individual, named Judge Steve Teske," who had created one of the first major school decriminalization initiatives, in Clayton County, Georgia.

Teske took the podium and said that he would "leave it to his homies" on stage to talk about PROMISE; he wanted to provide a national perspective. He explained that after Clayton County schools had added more school resource officers, arrests skyrocketed and African-American students got arrested twelve times more often than white students. But when he implemented his program, arrests decreased. Teske said that he had flown to Broward from the college graduation of a student who wasn't arrested in high school because of his program.

Then Teske tried explaining the way he saw human nature. He said that the audience ought to appreciate that "teenagers are [the] smartest among all of us in this room," but that their prefrontal cortexes aren't developed well enough to make good decisions. When teenagers act out, it's a sign that "they are in pain!" Teske disputed the idea that his policy "looks soft. [That] it creates a 'culture of leniency.' Really?... They want me to bring the hammer out. But when I do that, it means we see all the students as nails, instead of grieving human beings trying to struggle with things at home."

Teske said that he understood that some in the audience might not agree with his philosophy. "It's like," he explained, "to the layperson, the law of relativity is counterintuitive, but to a physicist, it's intuitive. You see, this is my reality to me. This is intuitive to me."

Teske also told the audience that there was a "tragic irony" to the questions the community was raising about PROMISE. Part of the reason for his decriminalization initiative in Clayton County was so SROs could spend less time at the police station and more time guarding their schools from potential attack. "Do you know," he said, "I can only think of one worse media tragedy than what I see happening here. And that is, if you never did [PROMISE], the likelihood would have been increased that the SRO may not have even been on campus" during the shooting.

Someone from the audience shouted out, "Scot Peterson hid! What the hell are you talking about!?"

"Well," Teske continued, "that's a good point. That's why I called it a tragic irony. But you know, what happened is not an indictment of all SROs in the country.... As I talk to my partners across the country, I hear stories where SROs have done things and have prevented things because they were on campus. It's sad. It is sad."

Someone yelled that Teske should sit down. Instead, Teske just shook his head at the audience in disappointment and compared them to traumatized children.

Well, I'm not going to engage one on one. I'll leave it at this. When there's tragedy like this, it's trauma. And like the kids I talked about, trauma causes certain behaviors. And I understand it. And I want you to know...just like the kids who suffer from trauma behave a certain way, I listen to them. And I understand. Hurting people say hurting things. And that's why there's a purpose to this forum. So, whatever you have to say in this forum that may be taken as hurtful, especially to these leaders, we have to take it.

So, with that said, I just want to conclude by putting these things in perspective. Be careful not to throw the baby out with the bathwater.... And by the way, I can say this because I don't need you to like me, but just like Clayton County has twelve times more African-American youth being arrested for the same offense than white youth...

His voice trailed off, letting the insinuation of racism he leveled against the audience linger as he shook his head and then returned to his seat. A few people clapped. Most were silent. Ryan Petty texted Max:

Teske in short: 1. Lay people can't understand what we who are experts in juvenile justice know. You can't appreciate the brilliance of PROMISE because you can't understand it the way I do. 2. If it weren't for PROMISE, Peterson wouldn't have been on campus that day. A real irony. 3. If you don't keep PROMISE, you're a racist.

Most of the remaining speakers began by apologizing that they hadn't prepared remarks. All dwelt on how African-American students were the victims of institutional racism (as evidenced by the higher rates of discipline) and that PROMISE was the solution. But none provided a window into what happened inside the PROMISE program. Lori Alhadeff, who came to the meeting to educate herself on PROMISE, later reflected to us, "I felt like I knew even less about PROMISE after hearing them talk about it for two hours."

The schedule said that public questions would be entertained one hour into the program. But the program started a half-hour late, and the speeches lasted nearly two hours. Kenny started to worry that David Hogg was getting impatient and might leave, so he texted him, "Hey, thanks for coming. Sorry I know it's a little boring. I want you to hear the public speakers, though." David replied, "This is intentional. They always do this stuff. They did it with the last couple of town halls with the school board and students. It's to try to get people to leave." Kenny was relieved that David understood. Because of David's status as a national liberal celebrity, if he publicly supported their mission, then the school district couldn't label the budding campaign to flip the school board as a "right-wing" conspiracy.

After interminably long speeches and an unintelligible PowerPoint presentation by Mickey Pope, it was finally time for audience questions. The school district stationed a microphone for adults in one aisle and a microphone for students in another and posted a handler next to the student microphone. When it was Hunter's turn, he said:

Hello Mr. Runcie. My name is Hunter Pollack. My sister Meadow Pollack was killed under your leadership. I know this is off-topic. But you've never reached out to me. So I want to take this opportunity to ask you a question.

My father raised questions about your discipline policies and you called his questions reprehensible. You called them "fake news." You said there was no connection between the killer and PROMISE. You also called a report by Kenneth Preston "fake news." He said that the school board only spent five million dollars out of one hundred million dollars on safety. I haven't seen you dispute the facts, though.

One thing [Kenneth] said was that one million dollars was slated for a new fire alarm system, which Broward's former director of school safety recommended include a delay to prevent alarms from sounding unnecessarily. Now, I don't care that much about the details of the PROMISE program. I care about why my sister died. She died because she left her classroom when an alarm went off that would not have gone off if the new alarm had been installed with the recommended upgrade.

So, I'm asking you to tell me the truth: Why was the project delayed?

After a moment's hush, the moderator stammered, "I don't know if Mr. Runcie wants to answer that now, or if he—"

Hunter interrupted, "I'm expecting an answer."

The audience yelled, "Answer it! Answer it! Answer it!"

The moderator continued, "The topic for this evening is the PROMISE program. So I think—"

A man yelled, "We're all here because of the deaths! We're not here because of the PROMISE program!"

The rest of the audience broke into applause. Runcie, who had stood up as Hunter spoke, crossed his arms and hunched his shoulders.

The moderator tried to regain control. "The stated purpose of this evening is a community forum on the PROMISE program. I understand the pain that we all feel about what happened at Stoneman Douglas. And there is a forum—"

Hunter demanded, "So, when will my question be answered?"

The handler stationed at the student microphone told Hunter that audience questions were not intended to be back-and-forth debates.

"Everyone got to see the superintendent couldn't answer the question," Hunter announced and walked away.

Neither Superintendent Runcie nor anyone from his staff ever followed up with Hunter.

The Sliming of Nora Rupert

Two weeks after the forum, Runcie's political allies launched a public attack on school board chairwoman Nora Rupert, his most outspoken critic. A corporation called the Broward Black Elected Officials Inc. (BBEO) issued an open letter to Rupert that read in part:

> *The attacks on the PROMISE program and the targets on current school board members who have championed this and other solutions to the problems our children face serve to threaten the safety of our children. Thus, we assert the following positions:*
>
> - *The PROMISE program has practically eliminated the school house to jail house pipeline that has caused predominantly Black students to be shackled with lifelong criminal records and long-term consequences because of minor behavioral infractions.*
> - *We are especially concerned that there may be those in leadership, which allegedly includes you, who are using the pain of the parents who lost children to gun violence as a tool to promote your personal agendas and vendettas. That must stop immediately, and you must immediately cease any role you are playing in this unethical pursuit.[4]*

The letter became the subject of a news article in the *Sun Sentinel*. The article explained that the "uproar [about PROMISE], mostly from the right-wing media, prompted Broward Black Elected Officials Inc. to fight back."[5] BBEO had essentially accused Rupert of participating in an exploitative right-wing conspiracy to advance her own ambitions on the backs of black schoolchildren.

In Broward education politics, whether or not you face allegations of racism has nothing to do with whether you are racist and everything to do with whether you question the superintendent's policies. Whereas Nora Rupert earned the ire of the BBEO for occasionally asking critical questions of a policy she supports, board member Ann Murray retained their full support despite once allegedly referring to cheap seats in a stadium as "nigger heaven."[6]

The PROMISE Workshop

Three weeks later, on June 19, Rupert kicked off a school board "workshop" about the PROMISE program, where district bureaucrats provided presentations to the school board and the public was allowed to comment.[7] With the BBEO letter still hanging over her head, Rupert pledged her steady support of PROMISE:

> *It's no surprise that I would support the PROMISE program when children's lives are at stake. Since this important program began, I have not only supported it but have sought to understand how to evaluate its benefits, expand its successes, and improve fidelity of implementation. I take the U.S. Department of Education guiding principles seriously. And [the Dear Colleague Letter] says, "Districts and schools must understand their civil rights obligation and ensure fairness and equity for all students and continuously evaluate the impact of their discipline policies and practices using data analysis." I have done that.... It is commonly bandied about that I am not supporting this program. [But] I am.*

This was not enough for Brian C. Johnson of BBEO, the first political figure to speak during the public comment period at the meeting.

> *Superintendent Runcie, thank you. You saw the need. You had the vision. You enacted the plan to eliminate the schoolhouse-to-jailhouse pipeline that predominantly affected black children.... In the words of the great philosopher JT Money from the Poison Clan, "The truth I speak should not offend you when you hear it. But if the mother f-in' shoe fits, then wear it."*
>
> *The claims that the PROMISE program was responsible for the evil acts of one student who may or may not have spent one hour in this program five years ago are half past ludicrous and a quarter till*

dangerous. Unfortunately, there is a small group of bad-intended individuals who are peddling false narratives about the program and district leaders and as a result have unjustly incited the anger of grieving residents who are seeking to eliminate this valuable program and uproot our district under false pretenses.

Marsha Ellison, chairwoman of Broward's branch of the NAACP, took a tack both softer and harsher, thanking the board for "recognizing that all children, [including] the black, brown, [and] LGBTQ, are important. To talk about something different is to return to before PROMISE, when children were not important."

Tim Sternberg had not yet given up on trying to get the school board to take his concerns about PROMISE seriously:

I've been emailing the board, Mr. Superintendent, since May of 2017, way before anything happened in February [2018].... I have to say, there is absolutely no curriculum whatsoever in PROMISE.... There is absolutely no district support in regards to curriculum at Pine Ridge Education Center. That is important! If you want to curb the school-to-prison pipeline, you can't just house kids in a program without helping them!

Yes, we are giving them social [and] emotional support through intern counselors that come to us free of charge, who are identifying many incidences of bullying which don't even get identified at the school level, which is problematic. What is going on at the school level? The self-reporting of data? Extremely problematic!

All administrators know that every year the district looks at discipline data and the [schools with the highest numbers] are talked to. So what's the incentive for the administration to report everything accurately? There isn't any!... It's very frustrating and I hope, truly, that you look at the emails and all the correspondence I sent you.

Brian C. Johnson later tore into Tim on social media, saying, "You are a key conspirator in manufacturing many of the false narratives designed to stoke consensus outrage against Superintendent Robert Runcie and members of the Board. You are also backing a flagrant racist

[Ryan Petty] to be a school board member in a county with majority-minority children and families."

Tim replied, "There is no conspiracy. Ryan Petty is no racist. You are only protecting a board and superintendent whose leadership and that of his chiefs failed 17 lives on 2/14/2018. That is all that matters. You can't hide negligence with race baiting, sir. People truly know better."[8]

Both Nora Rupert and Tim Sternberg had invariably expressed support for the PROMISE program while also trying to ask questions intended to spark a serious conversation about how to improve it. Their reward was to be accused of participation in a racist conspiracy.

Later in the meeting, an elementary school teacher, Liliana Ruido, asked some hard questions about the district's discipline matrix:

> I would like to know how the new discipline matrix will be addressing misbehavior in the case that a student is removed from a classroom or sent to the office for misbehavior but comes into the classroom the next day with no consequences. And also, I was looking through the discipline matrix and I noticed that administrators are the primary source of the application of discipline consequences for misbehavior. However, who will follow up to make sure administrators are doing their part?

But standing right behind her was Terry Preuss, vice president of the Broward Teachers Union, who moved quickly to pigeonhole Ruido's practical concern and focus the audience's attention on the "true" problem:

> My colleague spoke about what happens when a child is pulled out of class and not disciplined and how the teacher might feel. And yeah, that's something we have to look at. And principal discretion, principal discretion, principal discretion. Yeah, some principals I can trust with their discretion and some need some oversight. But I have to tell you, if we're not ready to come way up here [she raised her hand high over her head] and see what's going on, we're not ready.
>
> You know what's going on. A lot of people, way up here, far above us, are making a lot of money from the school-to-prison pipeline. We've got privatized prisons and we've got money going into people's pockets just like it goes into their pockets for testing.

They're making laws so that they can get rich and we're here fighting amongst ourselves when the reality is: That's the problem. It's up there. That's who we're fighting. Please, let's stay focused. They're doing this because they have the power to do it. Together we can stop them.

In short, rather than try to address policies that negatively affect their classrooms, teachers should unite behind those policies in order to fight the nefarious and distant *they*, who from a position somewhere very high up above *us* are trying to profit from the "school-to-prison pipeline" somehow!

But, as ever, the speaker who stole the show that day was Judge Elijah Williams:

Two hundred and thirty-one years ago, when the Founding Fathers created the U.S. Constitution, back in 1787, they only made it for, like, white men. It wasn't made for women. It wasn't made for blacks. And essentially, even if you were a white man, you had to own land. You had to be what's called a landowner. So, if you rented property, you had no rights under the Constitution.

The Founding Fathers had to go back over the years and they began to tweak it, they began to amend it. And twenty-seven times since they created that document, they've had to go back in and add amendments to it.

The PROMISE document is our U.S. Constitution as far as I'm concerned. We knew the minute that we created this thing, back in 2013, we're going to be coming back to amend it, coming back to tweak it, coming back to change it, to make it fit what we're trying to do....

One aspect that I am concerned with is what's called a precursor. A precursor is a thing that comes before another thing. There's no doubt in my mind that the February 14 incident had nothing to do with PROMISE. But when we take a look at the misdemeanor offenses, you have to concede Nikolas Cruz, if he had not committed trespassing initially, never could have committed the so-called tragedy.

None of the school board members batted an eyelash when Williams called the massacre a "so-called tragedy." In fact, several board members said they were inspired by his words. Laurie Rich Levinson declared, "I want to thank Judge Elijah Williams for his comments, because those really spoke to me. About the Constitution and about living documents that are created." Patti Good agreed, "As Judge Williams said, [PROMISE is] our Constitution. And it's a constitution that we will continue to ensure develops with time."

Williams concluded his speech with a flourish, declaring,

Whenever I travel across the country, every judge asks me, "Man, how'd you guys get such a great document?" It's nationally famous! The thing is the greatest thing, I think, that—as one Supreme Court judge told me—we've seen in juvenile delinquency in a lifetime. So it's not going to go anywhere.

At least in those final two points, Williams was onto something. PROMISE may very well be the "greatest thing we've seen in juvenile delinquency in a lifetime," just not in the sense that he intended. And it would not go anywhere so long as Broward was led by people so committed to their ideology and given to self-congratulation that they would applaud a speaker who referred to the murder of seventeen human beings under their leadership as a "so-called tragedy."[9]

PART IV

The Fight to #Fixit

Before my daughter was murdered, I didn't pay a whole lot of attention to what was going on in my kids' schools. Maybe you are like I was. That's why I wrote this book—so you could learn from what happened, and figure out what's going on in your schools, and take action to keep your kids safe.

I hope that your school board members and district leaders aren't as morally challenged as the ones in Broward County. But I hope what you've seen is that bad policies create a corrupt culture. If people get rewarded for sweeping things under the rug and tell themselves that they're doing it because of social justice, then schools will get more dangerous. Even when kids get murdered, education bureaucrats will treat parents with contempt for asking why. This politically correct cancer started here in Broward and spread to school districts across America.

It's little wonder that Superintendent Robert Runcie and Sheriff Scott Israel instantly pointed a finger at the National Rifle Association. Because all the attention for months after the massacre was devoted to the gun control debate, they might have succeeded in avoiding accountability. But me, I wasn't going to let anyone off the hook.

People have called me pro-gun. I'm not pro-gun. I'm not anti-gun. I'm just pro-accountability. I think that if people do their jobs, then

211

things like this won't happen. I think that the way our country is supposed to work is that we hold our local officials accountable. And if they fail, we get new and better people into office who can #Fixit. This shouldn't be a conservative position. It's an American position. And I think that if Americans saw what really happened here in Broward, we wouldn't have become divided against each other by another culture war debate. We would have united in disgust over Broward's leaders and moved forward with a bipartisan consensus on school safety.

But that's not what happened. So, I made it my mission to expose everything and hold everyone accountable. By mid-summer, my investigation was mostly complete and I turned all my attention, my energy, my life toward trying to bring some accountability to Broward schools by electing Richard Mendelson to the school board. I didn't have time to grieve because I was in a battle every day for justice and for change. That's what the last part of this book, "The Fight to #Fixit," is about. I don't think America has ever seen a school board race anything like what we did. And I hope that our story can inspire parents across the country to step up and take action to keep their children safe.

—Andy

CHAPTER 13

Graduation Week

By Andy Pollack

I thought that burying Meadow was the hardest thing I'd ever have to do. But watching her friends go to prom without her was just as brutal. I couldn't even bear to go to her graduation on June 3. My sons, Huck and Hunter, and Meadow's boyfriend, Brandon, went in my place. I bought them all matching pink ties to honor her memory. I helped them tie those ties, but would you believe I never knew how to tie one myself until all this happened? I'd never had to wear a tie before in my life. Then all of a sudden, I had to talk to the media and lobby politicians to try to make some good come out of all this.

I saw them off to graduation and then I drove up to Polk County, Florida, where some of that good was taking place. Sheriff Grady Judd was training a new generation of armed guards to protect schools under the Coach Aaron Feis Guardian Program. It meant the world to me to watch those guards get trained. Because I know that if Aaron Feis had had a gun, Meadow would be alive. Part of her spirit lives on in that program.

Another place her spirit lives on is at the playground that I built to honor her and the other sixteen victims. I raised the money for it through motorcycle rides and other charity events and then pulled all the strings to get the permits. Unless the school or the city ever gets their act together, which I doubt, it may end up being the only monument to the victims. (The school district did commission a small statue; it misspelled one of the victims' names.)

The playground, the Guardian Program, Rich Mendelson's race for school board, and my investigation were the main things I focused on after Valentine's Day.

The investigation was the most surreal part because the list of "what ifs" kept growing and growing. It would have been one thing if the school district had taken some time to review everything and then gone public with what went wrong. Instead, they stonewalled. I had to fight for every last detail, but things kept trickling out. With each new revelation, the victims' families and the broader MSD community were re-traumatized. Runcie could have spared them all those months of pain by being an honest guy. But of course, he just couldn't. The hits just kept coming.

So much of this book is through the eyes of others. But in this chapter, I want to tell you about everything that happened in just one week of my life—the first week of June. Graduation week.

The Scot Peterson "Pity Party"

The weekend of graduation, Deputy Scot Peterson went on a media offensive. The guy couldn't take one step toward Building 12 during the shooting, but he ran to NBC's *Today* show to insist that he hadn't done anything wrong.[1] He told the country, "Those are my kids in there. I never would have sat there and let my kids get slaughtered. Never." Except that's exactly what he did. Incredibly, he even told *Today* that he "never thought for even a moment of being scared or a coward because I was just doing things the whole time."

But Peterson couldn't even keep his story straight. Campus monitor Andrew Medina had told him there was a shooter in Building 12. But Peterson told *Today* that no one had ever told him that, and that he heard just two or three shots. Dozens of shots rang out while he was hiding outside. Then Peterson told *Today* that he thought the shots were coming from *outside.*

Then, when *Today*'s main coanchor, Savannah Guthrie, reminded Peterson that he had said over his police radio that the shots were coming from inside, he said that he knew they were coming from inside but "didn't think they were shooting at the kids; I thought they were shooting out [from] the building." Guthrie asked him why he didn't go in, and he replied that he didn't know that the shooter was inside. Then he said that he was trained not to go in but to contain the area. (That's not true either.) Guthrie asked him why he didn't go in anyway, and he claimed that "it just never even dawned on me those initial first few minutes because I never believed there was even an active shooter inside." Guthrie asked him how that could possibly not occur to him after hearing shots fired from within the school, and then Peterson said that he didn't realize that there were shots coming from within the building.

Did you follow all that?

You'd think that any journalist worth her salt would have concluded that Peterson's story didn't add up. But I guess that wasn't the conclusion that *Today* wanted to reach. After the segment, Guthrie's colleague Hoda Kotb said, "Certain things you think are so black and white, you know? Before that interview you only had one side of the story and now you got to hear his."

Guthrie replied, "Well, I hope that people see the complexity. I don't know that people will."

To the media, literally everyone is a victim these days. Even if they let seventeen people get killed and then lie about what they did on national TV.

A bunch of media wanted to talk to me about Peterson's interview, but I didn't want to say anything more about that scumbag. Besides, the other parents were all over it. Fred Guttenberg (who lost his daughter Jaime) went on the *Today* show with Max Schachter (who lost his son Alex) and Manuel Oliver (who lost his son Joaquin). Fred said, "I listened to [Peterson's interview], and I got enraged.... Don't call them 'my kids.' Those were not his kids. Okay? They were Max's kids, they were my kids. He didn't go to a funeral.... He feels sorry for himself, and he wants us to feel sorry for him. I'm not joining him in this pity party." Manuel said, "I don't want Mr. Peterson to become another victim. You are not a victim, sir."[2]

The Secret Service Agent

Later that week, the *Sun Sentinel* broke a story I already knew about but that others had dismissed as fake news.[3] Two months before the shooting, a retired Secret Service agent, Steven Wexler, gave MSD administrators a free security consultation and warned them that their lax security made MSD particularly vulnerable to a school shooting.

Wexler's kids had gone to MSD, and he had been trying to offer this consultation for years. Finally, in December 2017, MSD took him up on it.

Wexler gave a dramatic demonstration. He told Assistant Principal Winfred Porter to watch as he walked around campus and handed out blank Post-it notes to every adult he passed. No one stopped to ask this stranger what he was doing. The adults just took the Post-it notes. After the twentieth Post-it note, Wexler went back to Porter and said, "I ran out of numbers. You want me to keep going?" Each one of those Post-it notes represented someone he could have shot. And he had only handed them to adults—he'd skipped the countless children that crossed his path.

Then he gave Porter a presentation about the school's flaws and said, "This stuff is so blatantly obvious. You've got to fix it." Here are a few of the things he said:

- The gates should be locked during the day. They're supposed to be, per district policy, but MSD didn't follow the policy.
- Any adult should be allowed to call a Code Red so students know to shelter in place. This is also district policy, but MSD didn't follow the policy. Principal Ty Thompson decided that only he was allowed to call a Code Red.
- Administrators shouldn't immediately call for an evacuation after a fire alarm has been pulled. They first need to make sure it's not actually a school shooter. Wexler told them, "We learned that from Columbine."
- There should be a plan in place for who is in charge when the principal is off campus.

The administrators didn't act on this advice. And on Valentine's Day, the shooter walked straight through an open gate. No one called a Code Red, even after they heard shots fired. Porter called for an evacuation as soon as the false alarm sounded. Thompson was off campus that day. Wexler told the *Sun Sentinel*, "It didn't have to happen. Those kids didn't have to die." If they had listened to his recommendations, Meadow could still be alive.

Kenny's Diploma

Another fact that bothered me during graduation week was that Kenny Preston couldn't graduate. In April, he told me that he was worried that the district would retaliate against him. Because he was homeschooled and nineteen years old, the district was under no obligation to keep him enrolled; it could find a technicality to kick him out and then he'd be out of luck. I thought he was paranoid. But then it happened.

On May 23, three weeks before he would have graduated, Kenny got a letter from the district. It told him that because he didn't reply to an earlier letter (which he didn't receive), he was no longer a student in Broward and couldn't finish his online coursework through Florida Virtual School. He called to ask what the problem was, and they said it was because there were semesters when he didn't have as many credits as he should have. He told them, "Of course not, I had Lyme disease. And by the way, I have a lingering cognitive issue from that, so you are legally bound to evaluate me as an ESE student, so I'd be entitled to an education until I'm twenty-two." At this point, Kenny really knew his stuff. But they just said, "Nah."

Kenny called a bureaucrat in the Palm Beach County School District, hoping they'd sponsor him so he could finish his courses. At first they said sure, they just needed to call Broward first. Then they called back and said, "Nah." No explanation given. Until then, Kenny had wanted to believe that it was an honest mistake. But what other explanation was left? Broward denied him a high school diploma out of spite for making them look bad. He'd have to wait another whole year to go to college. Think about it: At the end of the school year, Kenny was the only person in the entire Broward County school district to face any consequence from what happened on February 14.

Resigning from the MSD Commission

The Marjory Stoneman Douglas High School Public Safety Act established a state MSD commission to investigate everything that went wrong. I was named to the commission along with two other dads, Max Schachter and Ryan Petty. But during graduation week, the chairman of the committee, Pinellas County Sheriff Bob Gualtieri, gave me an ultimatum: either drop my wrongful-death lawsuits against Peterson and the Henderson Behavioral Health or resign.

He said that the lawsuits created a conflict of interest. I didn't see how it could be a conflict of interest if everyone's goal was to expose the truth and hold people accountable. There was no way I'd drop my lawsuits. But I also didn't want to resign. I'd never resigned from anything in my life.

I called my friends and asked their advice. Kenny told me he thought it was purely political. He pointed out that if I was on the commission, the press would cover me hammering at every witness. But without me, it would be Gualtieri's show.

Max pointed out something funny: they wanted me off, but they kept Desmond Blackburn on. Blackburn was Runcie's protégé in Broward. He oversaw PROMISE and all these policies at the time we were investigating. Then he became superintendent of Brevard Public Schools, and brought leniency policies there. Shortly after the news broke that 18–1958 had been referred to PROMISE, he resigned from Brevard.

Blackburn was practically looking into himself on the commission. Talk about a conflict of interest! Max told me that with Runcie's right hand serving as the commission's education expert, I shouldn't have high hopes for them.

I wrote a resignation letter, saying, "It is my intention to get individuals elected to our school board who will take preventative measures to keep our schools safe. I will also be spending my time and resources on an independent investigation that will get to the bottom of who is responsible for the atrocities that occurred in our school on Valentine's Day 2018, the last Valentine's Day I will ever spend with my daughter."

I got a bad feeling from Sheriff Gaultieri. At the next meeting, he declared that PROMISE was a "red herring" because one vandalism incident in middle school wouldn't have prevented Cruz from buying a gun.

But literally no one was arguing that. We were talking about the culture of leniency that it created, and the alleged felonies Cruz committed that he wasn't even disciplined for.

Gaultieri and his team did a great job with the law enforcement response. But they phoned it in on the school system. They didn't reach out to students who came forward to the media. They didn't even reach out to Tara Bone, whose name was all over Cruz's paperwork at MSD. In their final report, they basically cited the "independent" analysis by the Collaborative Educational Network (CEN) and left it at that. It was disappointing. But I had expected it. And that's why I resigned to do my own investigation. Because as my father always told me, if you want something done right you have to do it yourself.

Stonewalls and Cover-Ups

A few weeks before graduation week, the *Sun Sentinel* ran an article headlined, "School District Shuts Down Information after Stoneman Douglas Shooting."[4] It began, "Statements that Nikolas Cruz had not been in a controversial disciplinary program fit a pattern of an institution on the defensive and under siege." The article noted that the district consistently released untrue and misleading statements, fought in court to keep surveillance video out of the public eye, and might have violated state law in how it stonewalled basically every other request for information with the response: "At this time, *any* records pertaining to Stoneman Douglas High will not be released." (Emphasis in original.) The *Sun Sentinel* article also noted that the district hadn't given the MSD Public Safety Commission 18–1958's discipline records, two months after the commission requested them. When the paper asked the commission if it had received all the records another two months later, the commission declined to comment.

Covering Up 18–1958's Education History

When Runcie commissioned the CEN report, he said, "While we can't undo what happened, we must understand what led to the violence and avoid it in the future."[5]

The report was supposed to come out in early June, around graduation week. But 18–1958's lawyers sued to block its release. One of his lawyers said, "There is a danger in releasing this report at all. It's a whitewash. It is a disservice to the public to be able to put it out there, and it's intended only to absolve the school board from its responsibilities."[6]

I figured it would be a whitewash. And eventually, the *Sun Sentinel* proved that it was.[7] They found the contract, which charged CEN to keep all the details secret and "further assist the client in ongoing litigation matters." CEN only analyzed whether the school district had directly violated the law. They weren't tasked with evaluating whether decisions made about 18–1958 were responsible or negligent, nor asked to look into whether the school district had failed to act on any of the myriad allegations of his troubling and criminal behavior at school that weren't officially recorded. Runcie said that other agencies would be interviewed for this report, but none were.[8]

The *Sun Sentinel* obtained all of this from a simple public records request. The school district couldn't even cover up its cover-up. As you'll read in the next chapter, even though the report was every bit the whitewash that 18–1958's lawyers alleged, it still proved a disaster for the district.

Covering Up MSD's Graduation

The school district's stonewalling reached comic proportions when they denied the media any access to MSD's graduation, claiming that this had always been their policy. *Sun Sentinel* reporter Scott Travis dug up and tweeted an old photo from 2012, when Runcie had welcomed Vice President Joe Biden as a graduation speaker, which received plenty of media coverage. By this point, the school district was trying to tweet "corrections" to Travis's work. When Travis informed the public that Runcie would not attend MSD's graduation, the school district tweeted a "correction" that Runcie had a good reason: his daughter's graduation from Princeton University. (MSD's graduation was on Sunday and Princeton's was on Tuesday.) Travis was not permitted to attend the ceremony. But NBC News was. The network broadcast the surprise graduation speaker: Jimmy Kimmel, whose speech made national news and warmed viewers' hearts.[9]

The Police Foundation

When I first heard that the Broward County commissioners had hired the Police Foundation to do an independent investigation of the tragedy, it didn't make any sense. They're a respectable organization, known for doing a thorough job on other major tragedies. So, I wondered: How could Broward have hired them?

My friend Mike Johnson was tasked with doing part of their report. He was initially excited, and a bit daunted, by the ninety-day deadline set by commissioners. But then around graduation week, he told me that the county had changed the contract. Instead of doing its own investigation that summer, the Police Foundation was re-tasked to wait for the state commission report and then fill in its holes. Johnson told me the Police Foundation had never seen anything like it, and he thought about resigning. He ended up staying on, though, because the more I talked to him about what teachers were telling me, the more he was convinced that he had a duty to stay on so that, someday, people could read his report and learn from it.

18–1958's Lawyers

18–1958 has an $800,000 trust fund from his mother, which he'll get when he turns twenty-two. His attorneys at the public defender's office were trying to give away all his money, presumably in a play for leniency and so he could remain qualified to be represented by the public defender.[10] This made Kenny suspicious. His thought: If 18–1958 had that kind of money, the first thing he would do would be to buy a high-caliber defense attorney who would defend him by attacking Broward, showing how badly the school district, the police, and the mental health clinic had failed him.

Fortunately, this is one case where Kenny was too suspicious. Eventually, I approached 18–1958's attorney and said, "Give me all of his files and I will take the stand as a witness for the defense to talk about how badly the school district failed him." They took me up on the offer, and that's how we got some of what's in this book.

Still, I don't want them defending 18–1958. They're well-intentioned and working hard, but the public defender's office is understaffed and overworked. I hope that 18–1958 gets the best defense attorney that money can buy. Any would-be Johnnie Cochran could make his career on this case, tearing Broward County apart limb from limb. That would be the trial of the century: a monster vs. the system that created him. The question of where the scales of justice would fall would be a drama that

America needs to see. He murdered my daughter and he deserves the death penalty. But I would testify as a witness for the defense, because whether or not he gets the needle matters less to me than whether our country sees what went wrong, learns its lesson, and does what it needs to do to make sure that this never happens again.

The Campus Monitor

The day before graduation, prosecutors released the sworn statement of Andrew Medina. You know the key details from chapter 8: Medina saw "Crazy Boy," who he thought could be a school shooter, walking on campus with a rifle bag; he thought 18–1958 was armed but didn't call a Code Red; he heard gunshots but didn't call a Code Red. He had one job. If he had said two simple words, Meadow would be alive.

That was hard enough. But what I learned next was even worse. After his statement was released, my ex-wife told our son Hunter that Medina was the guy who Meadow had complained was sexually harassing her. Meadow and her mom went to Assistant Principal Jeff Morford to file a complaint, as did another girl. (Since the news broke, so many parents have called me saying that their daughters were also sexually harassed by this creep.) Neither Meadow nor her mom had ever told me about it. If they had, I'd have made sure that he'd be gone and there would have been someone competent at the gate that day and Meadow would still be alive.

Instead, here's what happened: The district launched an official investigation in May 2017. It collected statements and found evidence that Medina had told my daughter she was "fine as fuck" and said things like "damn, mami" to another girl as she passed him in the halls. He'd ask them to come to his apartment to have a drink. He was such a fucking creep that Meadow found different ways to walk to her classes so that he wouldn't see her.

The school district's Professional Standards Committee reviewed the case and unanimously recommended that Medina be fired. But the superintendent's office overruled that recommendation and gave him a three-day suspension instead. There was a note written with a Sharpie pen on the Professional Standard Committee's official report that said, "SPEAK TO CRAIG FIRST."[11] Craig Nichols is Runcie's HR director and the person who made the final decision on Medina's punishment. Despite the fact that Nichols was acting officially as Runcie's administrative designee, Runcie told the press he had absolutely no idea about it.[12] A few months later, Nichols resigned. When a *Sun Sentinel* reporter asked him why, Nichols said, "I just won't be here. Everyone twists everything around."[13]

The district issued a press release in which it explained that Medina got that dramatic commutation of his sentence in part because "there was no inappropriate physical contact" between him and my daughter.[14] I guess here in Broward, you have to actually physically molest schoolgirls to face any consequences. If the Broward school district took sexual harassment seriously, Medina would have been gone, a competent person would have been at the gate, and Meadow would be alive.

A Trip to the Principal's Office

After reading Medina's statement in the paper, I realized that the last time I visited MSD, in May 2018, he was still the guy manning the gate. Even after his failure to call a Code Red had cost students their lives, he was still working there. Those kids simply weren't safe with a guy like him at the gate. I called another dad, Joe Valko, whose son survived the shooting, and Fred Guttenberg, whose daughter Jaime didn't, and we decided to pay Principal Thompson a visit about Medina.

We went to the school two days after graduation. Max Eden was in town that week. He spent about one out of every three weeks with me from April to September, staying at my house. He could only spend a few days or a week here on any trip because whenever he was in Parkland, he just couldn't sleep. "I can't handle more than a few days of this at a time," he once told me. I know exactly what he meant. But it was my life, so I had no choice.

Before I picked up Joe and Fred, Max and I walked over to the Little Coffee Shoppe with my dog Sonny, like we did almost every morning when he was in town. There was so much on my mind.

One thing was that I couldn't find anyone who was willing to help me do a fundraiser for the victims of the school shooting in Santa Fe, Texas. That was such a painful thing for me. Because two weeks after the Parkland shooting, as I was pushing to pass the MSD Public Safety Act, I stood next to Governor Rick Scott and I said, "The reason I'm here right now is, I want this country to come together. As one party. We're not the Democrat Party, the Republican Party, we're one country. We all have to come together. Because, you see me here? I don't want to do this. But you guys, look at me. I want to be the last father of a murdered kid."

But we didn't come together as a country. For the next three months, the only thing the media wanted to do was turn Americans against each other on the issue of gun control. At that point, the only public legacy of my daughter's murder was a bunch of talking heads and Twitter mobs going after one another about whether or not to ban AR-15 rifles.

Then on May 18, there was another school shooting. Ten people died. The media gave it barely a day's worth of attention. To the extent that they covered it, they folded it back into their clickbait arguments about AR-15s.

On our walk, I said to Max, "Can you believe that Harley-Davidson won't even help me on putting together a motorcycle ride for those families?"

"Yeah," he said. "The sad thing is I can."

I said, "If the Santa Fe kids had been killed with an AR-15 rather than a shotgun, it would have had all the attention in the world."

It was just sick to me. What's more, the Santa Fe shooter used a shotgun *from his dad's closet*. It didn't fit any partisan gun control political agenda. As a result, it was almost totally ignored. I guess I expected that from the media. And I didn't expect any big tech companies to do anything for those Texans, because it was the kind of charity that didn't fit any politically correct agenda. But I figured I could at least get Harley-Davidson executives to introduce me to their Texas dealership presidents so I could work with them to organize a motorcycle ride for the victims. I knew that Texans would flock to it, and it had the potential to be even bigger than the Ride for Meadow. But the executives refused to even send an email introduction. I wasn't asking them for money, just a few hours of their time. If a company like Harley-Davidson wasn't willing to do that for the families of kids who were murdered in school, I didn't know what America was coming to.

We talked about that, we talked about what we were hearing from students and teachers, and we talked some more about these policies. Max had explained this stuff to me before, but I still had a hard time believing the whole thing.

I asked Max, "Are schools still getting federal funds to do this PROMISE program stuff?"

"Not really," he said. "But it's worse than that. The grants from the stimulus package have run out. But the Department of Education is still threatening to investigate school districts and take away their federal funds if they don't adopt these policies."

I asked, "Why is DeVos still doing that?"

And Max told me that every time DeVos was asked a question about school discipline, the media set it up as a trap to make her sound racist.

"I'll call them and tell them that I can take the lead on it," I told Max. "They can't call me racist. I'm doing this because of my daughter."

"It doesn't matter," Max said. "Look how the PC mob went after Ryan Petty for suggesting that students should be kind to each other.[15] If you actually argue *against* these policies, they'll call you a racist."

"I don't care," I said. "They already killed my daughter. They can't do anything worse to me."

Joe Valko joined us at the Little Coffee Shoppe, and I started talking about Medina and Peterson again. After a while, we went to pick up Fred Guttenberg and the four of us, plus Sonny, drove to MSD.

Thankfully, Medina wasn't manning the gate anymore. But the new guard told us to wait. He looked like he was having a panic attack, and eventually school security and police started coming out of the building toward my truck. But they weren't going to stop me, so I just went through and parked.

When we entered the building, we heard over the loudspeaker, "All security personnel to the principal's office. All security personnel to the principal's office."

Max asked me nervously, "Are they going to try to kick us out?" I told him of course not. Every time I looked up, the security officers had no idea what they were doing.

"Joe," I said, "look at these security guys right now. How are you going to send your kid back to this school in the fall?" Joe just shrugged.

I asked Fred the same question. But Fred was looking down at his phone, distracted. He said gravely, "My son is getting texts that some lunatics are holding David Hogg hostage in his own home."

"Jeeeez," said Joe. "So that's what all of this security is about?"

Just then, Principal Thompson came out of his office and said that they were dealing with an emergency and asked if we could we wait another ten minutes. His staff had been discussing whether to call a Code Yellow to lock down the school to outsiders. Finally, they called a Code Yellow. Right after, my car alarm went off. Somehow Sonny had set it off. I got up to go out to my car and Max said, "We're on a Code Yellow. They might not let you back in."

"Look at these guys," I said. "They can't stop anyone from walking into this school."[16, 17]

I went out to my car, turned off the alarm, settled Sonny down, and came back inside. Then I turned to Joe and said, "You can't send your kids here, Joe. You gotta homeschool."

It turned out that someone had made a prank call to the police that Hogg was being held hostage. The police sent a SWAT team to Hogg's house to try to rescue him. Faking a hostage situation to get a SWAT team called to someone's house is a sick thing to do. People have died that way. Fortunately, the situation was defused and no one was harmed. With that sorted out, Thompson finally invited us back.

We told him we were there because we couldn't sit back and let Medina work at the school after how he failed everyone during the shooting. I wasn't even going to bring up the fact that Medina harassed my daughter.

Thompson said that Medina's failure was news to him. "I don't know if any of you guys know this, but I don't get information before anyone else."

I say, "We didn't get the information either until the other day. I knew that there was some guy that saw the shooter. But I didn't know to what extent and how incompetent he was. I can't have this guy working at your school."

Thompson told us that he was on the same page, that right after he read about it in the Sunday paper, he decided that Medina shouldn't keep working at the school.

"It's unbelievable," I said. "A ten-year-old would have called Code Red."

Thompson said that he also had a hard time understanding it, and pointed out that just the other month they had been trained that anyone could call a Code Red.

"I'm glad to hear you say that," Fred said. "And especially this morning, after listening to that Peterson interview with the *Today* show, I'm in a rage. It is unacceptable the way these guys failed our kids. And unfortunately, we do not get to hold Peterson accountable."

"Don't say that," I said. "I got Peterson on the hook. I got him."

I turned back to Thompson and said, "I'm telling you, I think it's disrespectful having Medina at the school after what he did. I really don't want the guy here. Joe's kids, any kid at this school, any parent does not want that. To me, it's disrespectful having him at the school after you read the article. That's it."

Thompson said he agreed with us, and the meeting ended on good terms.

After we left Thompson's office, I turned to Joe and Max and commented, "He said he just found out about Medina."

"What would be worse?" Max asked. "If he was lying to you? Or if he really just found out key facts about what happened the day of the shooting at the school he leads three months later?"[18, 19]

"They kept Medina at the gate for three months," I said. "Thompson said Medina was trained to call a Code Red."

"The Secret Service guy, Steve Wexler, said the policy was that only Thompson could call a Code Red," Max said. "Sounds like one of them is not telling the truth. Wexler has no reason to lie."

I didn't want to think about it anymore that day. I turned to Joe. "There are three thousand kids at this school. I don't even have a kid at the school anymore. How's it only you, me, and Fred who have a problem with Medina being there?"

Joe didn't have an answer. Out of everything that happened that week, out of almost everything that happened since after February, this was maybe the thing that stuck with me the most. I asked Kim Krawczyk if any other parent had gone to the school or called the school to tell them that Medina shouldn't be working there. She said she hadn't heard of anything else.

Here is a guy who everyone knew was harassing girls and whose incredible incompetence at his one job function had cost seventeen lives. Then the school keeps him at his post like nothing happened for three months. Then, when the news breaks, parents don't say anything about it.

Superintendent Runcie wanted to let Medina keep working as a security monitor for another school. Then, after I hammered them in the media, the school board finally decided during the summer not to let him keep his job. They also fired David Taylor, the campus security monitor who hid in a closet and never called Code Red.

I guess some accountability was better than none. But it sickened me that the only people who faced any consequences were two guys getting paid $19,000 while nothing was happening to anyone higher up the food chain who was responsible for creating 18–1958.

I want you all to understand this: Schools are not going to do the right thing unless you give them a reason to. If you don't get involved at your school, then your daughters will be guarded by Medinas too.

I was already planning on leaving Broward before all this happened and I realized what an utter hellhole it truly was. But for the sake of other kids, I wanted to do something to #Fixit before I left. I wanted to get someone elected to the school board who could be a wrecking ball for accountability: Richard Mendelson.

CHAPTER 14

Flip the Board!

After the April 10 school board meeting, three parents, Lisa Olson, Nathalie Adams, and Steven Brown, approached Kenny Preston in the parking lot. They were appalled by the scorched-earth campaign the superintendent and school board had waged against a teenage student journalist, and as they talked, they all reached the same conclusion: they needed to run a slate of candidates in the upcoming school board elections to flip the board and oust Runcie.

The first time Kenny brought this idea to Andy, Andy wasn't sold. But two weeks later, at a barbecue at Joe Valko's house, Kenny pitched it again. Andy said, "Okay, kid. Less talking, more doing."

There were about a dozen other Parkland parents at the barbecue, and within minutes everyone started to strategize. Maybe Joe's wife could run. Maybe Kim Krawczyk could run. Kenny wanted April Schentrup to run. But April told Kenny she was nervous about retaliation from the district. (Kenny had a hard time believing that the district would retaliate against an elementary school principal and a grieving mother, but this was before he learned that the district had docked her pay.)

They approached other parents of victims, and Ryan Petty and Lori Alhadeff expressed interest in running. Within a week, Andy, Kenny,

Ryan, and Lori met to form plans for a slate of candidates with a clear message: safety, accountability, and new leadership.

They'd need at least a 5-4 majority on the board to get anything done. The election was in four months, on August 28, so they had no time to waste. There were only two board members willing to criticize the superintendent: Nora Rupert and Robin Bartleman. They needed at least three more. Jim Silvernale, who worked for the teachers union, had a well-funded campaign to oust incumbent Ann Murray and appeared critical of Runcie. Lori could run in the district representing Parkland against incumbent Abby Freedman (who ended up dropping out shortly after Lori announced). Ryan could run for the countywide at-large seat against incumbent Donna Korn. But who could run in District 6 against incumbent Laurie Rich Levinson?

Kim was open to running. But she had recently moved to neighboring Palm Beach County, so she would need to establish a residence in Broward to run. Andy thought about Richard Mendelson, who had sent him a Facebook message saying that he taught Andy's son Huck and wanted to do anything he could to help. Mendelson had taught at MSD for thirteen years and was now a professor of institutional and organizational psychology at Keiser University. As an overweight, bearded, bald guy, he didn't look like the most electable school board candidate. But when Andy met with Rich, it became clear that no one would work harder. It would be a battle, but there was no doubt: Rich would stop at nothing to win and make a difference.

Why Rich Ran

Aaron Feis was one of Rich's best friends. After Aaron died on Valentine's Day trying to take down the shooter with his bare hands, Rich knew he had to do *something*. Because at the darkest moment in Rich's life, Aaron had been a beacon of hope. Rich's son Jake was born six weeks premature in 2008, three months after his wife, Becky, had lost her job as a teacher in a charter school. Rich's health insurer declined to add Becky and Jake to his plan, and after three weeks in the hospital Becky went home with a frail infant and nearly $300,000 in medical debt. Jake's specialized formula alone cost $1,600, about half of Rich's monthly income. Rich had already taken out substantial student loans to pursue his PhD, and the housing market collapse had put his home underwater. The family had no choice but to move in with Becky's parents.

On moving day, Aaron helped Rich with the heavy lifting. After everything Rich owned was packed into a U-Haul van, he went back inside to do a final sweep. He walked upstairs, looked at the room he had thought Jake would grow up in, looked down at the hardwood floors he had installed with his own hands, and collapsed in tears.

He was moving in with his wife's parents. He would never own a home. He would never be able to do better for his son than his parents did for him. He couldn't see a light at the end of the tunnel. Within two minutes, Rich heard Aaron coming up the stairs. Rich looked up at Aaron's giant silhouette in the doorway and tried to pull himself together. Aaron stood there silently for a few moments, his eyes inscrutable behind the sunglasses he never took off. Then he extended his hand to Rich.

Rich cried out, "My life is a total failure. There's no coming back from this." Aaron grabbed Rich, pulled him up, gave him a tight bear hug, and whispered, "You've had to fight for everything your whole life. Sometimes when you fight, you get knocked down. You got knocked down hard this time. But when you're knocked down, you have a choice: stay down or get up. You're going to choose to get up. Because that's what you do. So, get up." Rich got up. He went to the bathroom to splash some water on his face, walked down the stairs and out the door, and with his head held high kept moving forward.

A few days after Aaron's funeral, Rich sent Andy a message on Facebook to say that he wanted to do anything he could to help. When Andy met him, each sensed in the other a kindred spirit with an iron will. When Andy asked Rich to run against Laurie Rich Levinson, Rich said he was all in. All summer, he knocked on doors, wearing Aaron's MSD hat.

Rich vs. Rich

There could hardly have been a greater contrast between two candidates in terms of background and privilege than between Rich Mendelson and Laurie Rich Levinson.

Rich Mendelson

Rich's mom, Carol, met his dad, Steven Mendelson, in 1975 when they were both teachers at Franklin Delano Roosevelt High School in Brooklyn, New York. Rich was born in 1978 and his family moved to Broward County in 1986. Carol and Steven could make ends meet, but when Rich entered middle school his parents got divorced. His mom took a second job, and Rich had to work part time to help her make the mortgage payments. As a teenager, Rich juggled school, a part-time job and effectively raising his little sister with his athletic passion, wrestling.

Rich went to college at San Francisco State, near where his extended family lived. He walked onto the wrestling team his freshman year and received a scholarship for his last three years. He still worked a part-time job on top of that to have spending money. After he graduated in 2002, he moved back to Broward County to follow in his parents' footsteps and become a teacher at his alma mater, MSD.

Rich met his wife, Becky, in August 2006 and got married a little more than a year later. The next year, Rich enrolled in an online, part-time PhD program through Capella University in hopes of providing more financial stability and security for his family by someday finding a job that paid better than his high school teaching position. But after the crippling medical debt the family incurred with Jake's birth in 2008, those hopes appeared to be dashed.

It took three jobs to keep his family afloat. Rich's second job was as a graduate assistant for online courses at Capella University. After earning his PhD in 2011, he added a third job as an adjunct professor at Keiser University. He was also pursuing a part-time master's degree through Broward's PROPEL program, which he hoped would fast-track him into a position as an assistant principal.

Rich suffered another financial setback in 2012 when Superintendent Runcie's teacher pay reforms took a huge bite out of his paycheck. Before Runcie's reforms, high school teachers taught five classes. Additional classes or especially large class sizes meant larger pay. Runcie retained that workload but took the financial bonuses away. Rich took nearly a 30 percent hit to his paycheck even as he taught another forty students. Teaching was no longer economically viable for him. Rich sent out 863 job applications in 2013 and was offered a position as a full-time professor at Keiser in 2014. The salary afforded him a path to long-term solvency, and the flexible hours let him spend quality time with his wife and son. Eight years after Aaron told him to get up, Rich finally felt that he had his feet back under him.

His whole life, Rich Mendelson had to fight for everything he had.

Laurie Rich Levinson

Laurie's mom, Nan, met her dad, David Rich, the heir to a large and successful carpet company, in college in 1960. Nan dropped out and Laurie was born in 1962. Nan became an active volunteer in Jewish philanthropy, eventually serving as president of the National Council of Jewish Women from 1996 to 1999. Then she entered politics, serving two terms in the Florida statehouse from 2000 to 2004 and as a Florida state senator from 2004 to 2012. She was among the most liberal Democratic members of the state Legislature and became minority leader in 2010. After a failed run for governor in 2014, Nan was elected to the Broward County Commission in 2016.[1]

Nan's daughter Laurie describes herself as an experienced businesswoman. However, aside from a brief stint out of college at the now-defunct Abraham & Strauss department store, her business experience, as described on the Broward school district website, is largely confined to her family's companies, which were shuttered in the late 1990s and early 2000s. Laurie Rich married Neil Levinson, a Broward school district lobbyist, and was elected to the school board in 2010 after raising $100,000, much of which came from her mother's deep-pocketed political supporters (sugar producers, for example, don't usually take an interest in school board races). In her 2018 campaign against Rich, she raised $73,000—more than half of which came from big-dollar donors to her mother's county commissioner campaign. On the school board, she helped expand Broward's debate program, became one of Superintendent Runcie's biggest supporters, and earned a reputation in the community for being prickly and aloof.

After Mendelson and Levinson met with the *Sun Sentinel* editors to vie for the paper's endorsement, the paper's editorial board wrote:

Levinson was grumpy from the time she entered the room. Mendelson's criticisms clearly irked her. She is unhappy with the Sun Sentinel, too.

"Every article written is negative," she said.... Others tell us they see Levinson's prickliness, too, including with constituents. Frankly, this choice was a tough call. But Levinson comes prepared for board meetings, is strong on facilities issues, attends meetings she doesn't have to, and was active in public education before she ever ran for office. Mendelson is a good candidate, but would be stronger if he had been an advocate for public schools before seeking to join the board.[2]

Never mind that Rich had been a public school teacher at MSD. Still, Rich wasn't surprised when he read the newspaper's reluctant endorsement of Laurie. As the daughter of one of the most powerful Democrats in a two-to-one Democratic county, Rich figured that Laurie was perhaps literally entitled to it.

The Slate Falls Apart

Rich knew that the race would be an uphill battle. Nearly all of his friends were working-class, and he didn't know more than a dozen people who could afford to donate a hundred dollars. Still, Rich figured he had one big thing going for him: he would be part of a united slate with a powerful message.

But at his first meeting with the other candidates on the slate, Rich felt uneasy. The meeting was run by two political consultants with whom Rich was unfamiliar, Eric Johnson and Sean Phillippi. Rich and Kenny recounted to us the following conversation.

"I don't want to be disrespectful," Rich said. "But I've introduced myself. Who are you and why are you here?"

They told him that they were political consultants who had done extensive local, state, and federal work.

Rich asked, "But how did you end up here?"

They repeated that they'd done extensive campaign work, especially in Broward.

"Who have you worked with in Broward?"

"Nan Rich."

"Just so you know," Rich looked around the table, "that's the mother of my opponent."

Sean said, "Look, if you were running against Nan Rich, I wouldn't be here. I love her. She's a great leader. But Laurie is not Nan. I don't owe her loyalty."

"Okay," Rich said, "so you're really going to work with me to defeat your boss's daughter?"

They said that they would, but Rich didn't believe them.

After the meeting, Rich told Kenny, "These guys are here to sabotage our slate."

Kenny thought Rich was being dramatic and said, "Everyone is here to flip the board."

"No," Rich insisted, "they're here to make sure we don't. Lori is sure to win. They'll put her victory on their résumés, take money from the PAC we set up, and work against Ryan and me. Then, when we lose, they'll report back to Nan Rich, 'Mission accomplished.'"

"Do you honestly think that?"

"Absolutely," Rich nodded. "You know how much money flows through the school board. Our majority would pose a big political problem. I mean, last time anyone looked into the school board, people went to jail. They're here to sabotage this."

Kenny wasn't sure whether to believe Rich, whom he suspected was prone to bluster and exaggeration. But after he filed his paperwork to run, Rich recalled, "Everybody disappeared. Lori wasn't taking calls. Her campaign people wanted nothing to do with me."

Then Kenny learned that, behind the scenes, the campaign consultants were trying to convince Lori and Ryan that a slate was a bad idea. Ryan recalled to us that his consultants put it to him quite plainly: "If you run as a slate against the superintendent and/or his policies, you will be branded as a racist and lose." Lori and Ryan suspected that the consultants were correct. They were running to win, so they took the advice.

Kenny tried insisting that Ryan and Lori at least have Rich in the background when they announced their candidacy. But that didn't happen, and when Lori and Ryan announced on May 15, the campaign consultants physically prevented Kenny from speaking to Lori before she took the microphone. The *Miami Herald* ran the headline, "Parents of Slain Parkland Teens Want to Work with Runcie on School Board."[3]

After the announcement, Rich called Kenny. "I told you so," Rich said. "I don't know why you're helping Lori. She's going to win, and I need all the help I can get. I need you to help me convince Andy to throw everything he has behind me. I can't raise any money myself. And he has the power to mobilize who knows how many volunteers."

"All right," Kenny said. "I'll talk to Andy again. But I can do more for you from Lori's campaign because I can help make sure that they distribute the PAC money to you."

"Don't be an idiot, Kenny. I'll never see one cent of that PAC money. That's how the consultants are paying themselves. They'll marginalize you until they find an excuse to cut you out entirely."

Kenny figured Rich was being too cynical. Lori had asked him to be her campaign manager! But two weeks later, Kenny coauthored an op-ed for the Daily Wire with Kyle Kashuv, an MSD student, arguing that Runcie should resign.[4] The morning after it was published, Kenny awoke to texts from the consultants and Lori. When Kenny called Lori, she told him that because of that op-ed, they had decided that he shouldn't be associated with her campaign. He told her he thought he was on her campaign *because* he was critical of Runcie, but Lori insisted that they needed to part ways.

Kenny realized Rich was right. Getting a school board majority would depend on Rich, and he was going to have the hardest race. Rich and Kenny implored Andy to devote as much time and energy as he could to Rich's campaign. Andy didn't give them a firm answer at first, but after meeting with Ty Thompson about Andrew Medina, he called Rich to say, "I'm all yours. We have to hold these people accountable."

The BTU Endorsement

With Andy's support, Rich could run a real campaign. But Rich knew that in school board elections, with low turnout and teachers often the only voters paying attention, the teachers union president is often the kingmaker. Rich set up a meeting with BTU President Anna Fusco.

When Rich showed up for the meeting, he chatted amicably with BTU Vice President Terry Preuss while they waited for Fusco.

When Fusco walked in, the tone completely changed. Rich recalled to us that she immediately became hostile, accusing him of leaving public education for a for-profit university and wanting to arm teachers.

Although the conversation started hostilely, it ended cordially. Rich explained to Fusco that he only left public education because of what had happened to his salary under Runcie, that his online university was a nonprofit, and that he didn't want to just arm teachers. He told her that in his opinion, the choice should be clear: if she liked the status quo, she should stick with Laurie, but if she wanted someone who would stand up for teachers, he was her guy.

By the end of the conversation, Fusco brought up Rich's friend Aaron and said that the BTU wanted to honor him by providing funding to have his name engraved on a memorial in Kansas for educators who had lost their lives at school. Rich put Fusco in touch with Aaron's little brother Ray Feis, and Fusco made good on her word.

Kenny told Rich he was crazy if he thought he was going to get Fusco's endorsement. But Rich was confident. The way he saw it, Fusco was practically obligated to endorse him because he had been MSD's union representative. Rich explained:

> The way unions work, the core of their ideals and belief structure is: You don't cross union lines. Ever. My opponent was never a teacher. She was in business, which unions are supposed to stand up against. But actually, she wasn't ever really in business. She inherited her business. She inherited her political career. She lives at the privileged nexus between business and government. When unions talk about how the system is rigged, they're basically talking about people like Laurie Rich Levinson.

But Rich was wrong. When the union announced its endorsements in mid-July, the *Sun Sentinel* ran the headline, "Teachers Union Not Endorsing Any Candidate with Ties to Stoneman Douglas."[5] The BTU had endorsed Levinson, Ryan Petty's opponent Donna Korn, and no one for the district that represented Parkland. It ended up pouring in more than $150,000 to defend Runcie's majority.[6]

Ray Feis texted Fusco, "I know you're a good person, but it's extremely disheartening to see how far Nan Rich's reach is."

Fusco replied, "This is not about Nan. Trust me, she's gone after me too."

Door-Knocking

Losing the endorsement was a setback, but they knew it would be a tough battle from the start. In a two-to-one Democratic county, any voter walking to the polls with a Democratic or a teachers union endorsement sheet would vote Levinson by default. The school board race was technically nonpartisan, but Andy and Rich were registered Republicans—an instant disqualifier to many Broward voters. They had to play like they were starting 40 percent down.

What's more, they knew that they could never raise as much money as their opponent. In addition to Nan Rich's and Anna Fusco's financial backing, Levinson and Runcie also had the full backing of the Broward business community. Keith Koenig, the CEO of City Furniture and chairman of the Broward Workshop, a consortium of business leaders (many of whom have lucrative contracts with the school district), declared, "The business community has confidence in Bob Runcie 100 percent."[7,8] The good news for Rich was that elections ultimately come down to votes, and historically very few people vote in school board elections, especially those held during the primaries. In 2014, Laurie Rich Levinson was reelected with 8,738 votes to her opponent's 3,962. Rich figured if they could get 12,000 votes he would be guaranteed to win. While Rich couldn't afford professional consultants, many people were telling him the same thing: the most persuasive thing in politics is a face-to-face appeal.

Nearly every evening for two months, Rich, Andy, Hunter, and Kenny knocked on doors. If this were a movie, now would be the time for a montage with the *Rocky* theme song playing in the background (because, corny as it may sound, Rich and Andy listened to it whenever they drove around together).

Rain or shine, didn't matter. Rich recalled, "Sometimes it was like Forrest Gump's Lieutenant Dan at the top of the rigging in the monsoon level of rain. We'd be running out of the truck and putting out yard signs and scrambling back. There were nights my wife and I were out in the car until eleven p.m. or midnight planting yard signs in people's houses. We didn't even know who they were. They'd just requested them through Facebook or Twitter."

A core group of about a dozen volunteers showed up at most public events Rich attended and knocked on doors at least a couple of times a week. A few dozen more came out at least once a week for door-knocking. Andy's wife, Julie, helped organize all the volunteers. Nearly two hundred people did something for Rich's campaign, be it knocking on a door, holding a sign, making phone calls, or handing out flyers.

The message was simple and powerful. The leaflet that Team Mendelson handed out to voters had a picture of Rich on one side along with what he stood for: Safety, Accountability, and Fair Teacher Pay. On the other side was a picture of Andy and Meadow. Rich's volunteers would explain that the school district had not only abdicated any responsibility but had misled the families in the wake of the tragedy. What's more (as you'll read in the next chapter), the district still could not get its act together on school safety. Each volunteer closed the conversation by asking if Rich could count on their support—almost everyone said yes.

On a weekend day, twenty volunteers could knock on fifty doors each in just a few hours. On their biggest days, Team Mendelson could hit nearly a thousand doors, only counting a door "knocked" if they made direct contact with a voter. And at the end of each week, Rich uploaded a Facebook video to give an update on the running tally.

All told, Team Mendelson knocked on over thirty thousand doors and left flyers at forty thousand where no one was home. They handed out fifteen thousand flyers at public events and reached eight thousand voters by the phone. They knew they couldn't count on every "yes" they received to translate into a vote. But they figured that if even a quarter did, the election would be a landslide.

Strangers Became Family

One day in July, Andy turned to Rich and asked, "How do you know all of these people?"

"I mean, they're your friends, right?" Rich asked.

"I don't know any of these people," Andy replied.

"I don't know them either," Rich said.

"Well," Andy said, "who the fuck are they, then?"

"It was unbelievable," Andy later reflected. "Family and friends came and then left. But total strangers came and they never left. They became like another family. Like cousins and sisters and brothers."

Kenny gave his entire summer to Andy and the campaign. At one point, they did a podcast interview together for TheBlaze. After the interview was over, the hosts forgot to immediately turn off the recording. "That interview was so weird," one host said.

"Yeah, it really was. But why?" the other asked.

"Because I figured that the kid was just a volunteer. But the way they talked, I know they're not, but it sounded to me like father and son."

Part of why Kenny dedicated himself to Andy that summer was the righteousness of the cause. But most of it was just Andy.

For Kenny, the most powerful moment of the whole campaign came in early August, after an especially long day of door-knocking with about twenty volunteers working their way through several apartment complexes. As Kenny and Andy were walking back to Andy's truck to drive to a new site, Kenny was so tired that he wanted to call it a day.

Kenny turned to Andy and said, "Why not take a few days off? You're out in the sun five hours a day campaigning. We have enough volunteers that you can afford to take some time to yourself."

Andy stopped in his tracks. He started to tear up. And then, more slowly and haltingly than Kenny had ever heard him speak before, Andy said, "This is how a father honors his daughter. I am going to do this every single day. This is the only thing I can do."

CHAPTER 15

Free Campaign Ads

Rich could feel the momentum building with every door knocked. And what he lacked in funding for campaign advertising, the *Sun Sentinel*'s invaluable reporting more than made up for with their coverage of the school district's embarrassing incompetence.[1]

This chapter will give you a flavor of the failures of the school district that a local newspaper brought to voters' attention, and a few other stories that did (and didn't) make the news.

The Bond Money

In April, Superintendent Runcie called Kenny's report on the school district's bond program "fake news." But in June, Florida TaxWatch reported that five years into the seven-year schedule, the district had completed only 10 percent of its more than 1,500 projects and had only begun just another 12 percent. School board members who had been mum on the issue started pressuring Runcie for answers. One member, Heather Brinkworth, exclaimed, "We are desperately behind and we need to know why."[2]

Runcie blamed his staff. "I share the frustration," he said at a school board meeting. "I'm going to sit down with staff. We need to come better prepared. When we enter a public forum, we've got to acknowledge the problem, have answers, and explain how we're going to move forward. I haven't heard enough of that."[3]

In July, the *Sun Sentinel* reported that with some projects running between $10 million and $23 million over budget, the school board would likely run out of money before all the projects could be completed.[4] By August, school board members were demanding detailed answers. Nora Rupert asked for a report on the status of bond projects.[5] When she didn't receive one, she demanded to know why not. Runcie insisted that "no one has ever requested any of these reports from my office." But upon further questioning, Leo Nesmith,[6,7] who was Runcie's chief of staff's right-hand man, admitted that he had received the request but did not act on it.[8]

The Guardian Program

At the April 10 school board meeting where Kenny spoke, the board also unanimously rejected the idea of using additional state funding from the MSD Public Safety Act to fund armed guards under the Coach Aaron Feis Guardian Program. Their rationale was that they didn't want to arm teachers. When Laurie Rich Levinson voted no, she declared, "I have not met one teacher or one student who is in favor of arming teachers in Broward County."[9]

But the law explicitly prohibited arming teachers.[10] Instead of allocating state money for trained guards, the school board decided to increase the number of school resource officers, who were three times as expensive, without a plan to pay for it.

By late June, Andy and other parents had raised enough political heat to make the school board reverse course and agree to hire eighty additional armed guards. But the late start to the hiring process left the school district scrambling. By mid-July, they had received 140 applications, but only 35 passed the basic screening requirements to serve as armed guards, and the vast majority of those were expected to fail the intensive training requirements.[11]

The week before school started, the district announced that it had filled all eighty positions. But the day before school started, it backtracked and admitted it had only filled eight. Fort Lauderdale Mayor Dean Trantalis was frustrated that Runcie had personally assured him that all the schools would be covered, only to turn around and ask him to assign police to work overtime to make up for the school district's shortage. "It's disappointing," Trantalis said. "It's terribly disappointing." [12]

The Secret Service Review

Three weeks before the start of school, Runcie hired retired Secret Service agent Steven Wexler to review and report on MSD's preparedness for and response during the shooting. Wexler was the consultant who had given largely ignored tips on how to make the school safer months before the shooting. One week later, Runcie reversed course and canceled the review. [13]

The Metal Detectors

Throughout the summer, the school board promised that MSD would have metal detectors the next school year. But two weeks before school started, Runcie announced that would not happen. [14] When board member Robin Bartleman pressed the superintendent on his reversal, Runcie analogized the case to the tragedy of the *Challenger* space shuttle in 1986. [15] Despite the fact that one component of the shuttle, known as an "O-ring," was not approved for use at temperatures below 54 degrees Fahrenheit, the launch proceeded when it was 30 degrees, in part due to political pressure, and the *Challenger* exploded, killing everyone on board. Therefore, Runcie said, he was wise to ignore political pressure and reverse course on the metal detectors because his security consultants said there would be logistical difficulties.

The analogy was odd, given that there are no documented instances of metal detectors exploding or causing fatalities. Robin Bartleman pointed out that the reversal right before the start of school made the school board appear incompetent.

> We are the six largest district in the nation. We have told everyone, in every every club I've been to, every meeting, we have discussed these metal detectors, and now, a week before that the implementation is supposed to happened, all of a sudden we have all these issues?... You're telling me there was some sort of epiphany that they

were going to be issues with metal detectors a week before school started? All of a sudden everyone knows. People knew about this before... The day before school starts, after promises army to this community, we have no credibility as a board.[16]

Later, it was revealed that the order for metal detectors was never actually put in. The school district and the school board had been misleading the MSD community for months. It seems probable that school board members like Robin Bartleman genuinely had no clue. Either Runcie knew that they were never going to be installed and let his colleagues mislead the community, or when Runcie gave his *Challenger* speech applauding his last-minute decision not to install metal detectors, he actually had no idea that they were never even ordered.

Redactiongate

The Collaborative Educational Network's whitewashed review of 18–1958's education history was finally released at 5:00 p.m. on Friday, August 3. It was almost entirely redacted. The district released a statement that "CEN's findings show that the District provided significant and appropriate services to Nikolas Cruz," and Runcie commented that he was "pleased with the overall review."[17]

For the first two hours after the report was released, the headlines were positive. The *Miami Herald*'s piece was titled, "Schools Handled Nikolas Cruz's Education Properly, Probe Finds."[18] But then someone on Facebook tipped off a *Sun Sentinel* reporter that the district hadn't redacted the document properly. Rather than print it out, black it out by hand, and scan it back into a computer, they just highlighted portions of the PDF file in black. When the file was copied and pasted into Microsoft Word, the text became visible. When the *Sun Sentinel* reached Runcie for comment over the weekend, he said, "I didn't even know that was possible."[19]

The report contained some damning facts covered in previous chapters: the school district encouraged 18–1958 to sign away his special education rights and refused to let him restore them. These facts made national headlines. The *New York Times* story was headlined, "Parkland Shooting Suspect Lost Special-Needs Help at School

When He Needed It Most."[20] Angry that these details became public, the school district filed a motion to hold the *Sun Sentinel* reporters in contempt of court. *Politico* Florida reporter Marc Caputo tweeted that the school board was "declaring war on the First Amendment."[21]

The school board found out that they had filed a motion to throw *Sun Sentinel* reporters in jail by reading about it in Monday's *Sun Sentinel*.[22] The next day, at the school board meeting, Robin Bartleman plaintively demanded that the board address what had happened.

> *I hear everyone saying I'm not allowed to talk about [the motion against the Sun Sentinel]. But when am I supposed to talk about it? Next week, when everything is said and done?... I mean, I wanted to talk about metal detectors this week. I wasn't able to talk about [that] either. When do I get a say in any of this? How am I allowed to represent where I stand on certain issues? What am I allowed to do?*[23]

Barbara Myrick, the school district's general counsel, stepped in to explain her actions. She said, "Dealing with this over the weekend with Mr. Runcie [and our] cadre attorneys...we were appalled [by the *Sun Sentinel*'s decision to publish]. It was our decision. The verified motion was not a motion from the school board. It was a motion by me, which obviously implicates you."

Nora Rupert declared that it was "ridiculous" that no one contacted any member of the school board about it. But then Myrick interjected again to change her story.

"Let me just say that Mr. Runcie was not part of this decision. Um..."

Rupert asked, "He was out of it too?"

Myrick had previously spoken for six straight minutes without as much as a stutter. But now she stammered, "So, I'm, I'm, I'm not saying what, uh, that, that Mr. Runcie did not, was uh, I discussed, uh, there were other things that Mr. Runcie was involved in over the weekend, but he was not part of this decision, so it's not him that kept anything. If, if, if you have anybody to blame, it's me. And I will take full responsibility for what I, uh, for what, what occurred. I'm just saying I want that to be clear."

It certainly appears as though Myrick changed her story to cover for Runcie. But it's also entirely possible that she filed a motion to throw local newspaper reporters in jail without Runcie's knowledge. It's not clear which of these two possibilities would reflect more poorly on his leadership.

At any rate, even after the district's failures became undeniable, Runcie continued to deny them. When CBS News asked him later that month whether the district had dropped the ball on the shooter, he replied, "You know, I will say this: We had an independent review that was done. We, as a district, provided enormous amount of services to this individual."[24]

Begging for a Tweet

Hunter and Kenny spent many weeks trying to create a major news story that could turn the tide decisively in Rich's favor: an endorsement from the March For Our Lives student activists. Those students had a national platform and were beloved in Democratic circles. With just one tweet they could make Rich's campaign into a national story and shield the effort from being labeled a right-wing conspiracy.

Hunter had been in touch with David Hogg since shortly after the tragedy. When Hunter introduced David to Kenny, David said that he'd read his report and was also disgusted by the school district's actions. In late May, Hunter, Kenny, Andy, and Ryan Petty's son Patrick had lunch with David Hogg and Emma Gonzalez, the second-highest-profile student activist, to discuss the school board races. Emma told them that she'd support Ryan and do anything for Rich; her older brother once had Rich as a teacher and loved him. Emma said that March For Our Lives was about to announce a national bus tour, the "Road to Change," to mobilize young voters on the issue of gun control. But she said she'd fly back to Broward to campaign for Rich, host an event, or do whatever he needed.

After the lunch meeting, David tagged everyone in a tweet using Andy's favorite hashtag: "Lots of great work ahead to make our schools and communities more safe. Time to #Fixit." Emma retweeted it with the comment, "This lunch honestly Healed my Soul I've never felt more Excited to work on student and Societal safety with these guys :'-)."

After the bus tour started in early June, Emma and David simply stopped responding to Hunter's texts. For a couple of weeks Hunter was patient.

But after many weeks of silence, Hunter decided to apply some public pressure. In late July, David tweeted, "These Midterms could be the last election of our lifetime. VOTE." Hunter retweeted with the comment, ".@davidhogg111 would be great to see you encouraging your followers who live locally to get out August 28th, and vote for the school board election!"

David called Hunter, furious, telling him that Hunter shouldn't criticize him and that everyone has to stay "united." Hunter said, "Listen, man, the only reason you have your platform is that my sister got murdered. You want to go on tour like the Beatles trying to ban AR-15s? That's fine. But how about you just send out one tweet so we can hold the people who let this happen accountable?" David said that he couldn't endorse particular candidates but promised to tweet something helpful.

By this point, Hunter had become convinced that David would never help. Rich was a Republican running against a Democrat. David was making his reputation as a liberal firebrand and anti-NRA warrior. There was no way, Hunter thought, that David would go off-brand and suggest that there was any problem other than a gun, let alone tweet something that reflected badly on a Democrat politician. Kenny thought Hunter was too cynical and they arranged for another call.

Hunter insisted that David at least get on the phone with Rich Mendelson.

David practically shouted at Hunter, "I've met with your candidate three times!"

"No, David," Hunter said. "You met Ryan Petty, who lost his daughter Alaina. We're talking about Rich Mendelson, who lost his best friend Aaron. Have you been following any of this?"

Apparently not. Even after the call, Kenny kept chatting with David, offering him ideas for tweets that could highlight the school board's failures. Eventually, Hunter told Kenny that he was being pathetic and should just quit, because David would never help.

When David endorsed New York City's socialist Democratic congressional candidate, Alexandria Ocasio-Cortez, Hunter retweeted with the comment, "So you can endorse Alexandria Ocasio-Cortez as future president, but not Lori Alhadeff and Ryan Petty—both parents whose kids were killed in Parkland—as candidates for Broward school board?" He couldn't. (But after the August 28 school board election in Broward, David tweeted an endorsement of a left-wing school board candidate running in Denver.)

In mid-August, *New York* magazine ran a front-page profile of David, titled "David Hogg Takes a Gap Year at the Barricades."[25] In the piece, David marveled about himself: "We really only remember a few hundred people, if that many, out of the billions that have ever lived. Is that what I was destined to become?" Hunter could only shake his head at this self-declared world-historical figure who couldn't even spare one tweet to hold local officials accountable for the tragedy that made him famous.

Kenny was genuinely surprised and let down. Then one day in early August, out of the blue, March For Our Lives co-founder Cameron Kasky reached out to Kenny to say that he'd been following the campaign and wanted to help as soon as the road tour finished in early August. Cameron didn't have the kind of star power to create a national story with a single tweet, but he pitched an op-ed to the *Sun Sentinel* endorsing Rich, Ryan, and Lori. The *Sun Sentinel* rejected it, but Cameron told Kenny that he would still try to help out by volunteering at early voting and on Election Day. And Cameron made good on his word.

Parkland Parents Unite

Whereas Cameron Kasky was the only student from March For Our Lives to take an interest in the school board election, the families of all the victims united to appeal to the community for a change in leadership at a press conference on August 9. Tony Montalto, who lost his daughter Gina, spoke first:

> *After this tragedy, members from our group and the entire MSD community have attempted to work with the Broward County School Board and superintendent in order to make things better.*

We have focused on issues, but the school board has not provided answers. So today, we would like to make the citizens of Broward County aware that the current school board has failed to properly prepare the county's 234 schools for the upcoming school year, which begins next week. The constant reversals of policy positions continue to leave our county's students and teachers at risk, and clearly show that there is no unified plan to keep them safe.[26]

Montalto ticked off failure after failure: the bond spending, the metal detectors, the canceled internal investigation, the armed guards.

The most poignant moment of the press conference came when April Schentrup took the microphone. Her voice seemed to strain with the effort of not crying. She said:

This morning I attended the State of the District address where our school board member Donna Korn stood up in front of all district administrators and said that last year was an amazing year. In fact, she said it was the best year in Broward schools.

Being an employee of the school district and a mother who has endured such tragedy, it was difficult to hear those words. Because I know that we are not the only ones in Broward County who struggle. We know that it wasn't an amazing year. We know that it wasn't the best year in Broward schools.

So, this is the kind of leadership we have.... And if you do not understand what we're saying, pick any school board meeting. They're on the school board website. Pick one and watch it in its entirety. And just think, "Is this the kind of leadership we want in our Broward County schools?" And if it isn't, then you as a community have the power to make that change.

We've been hearing it from our own children, from our community. We've been hearing that inaction is not leadership. And we have the right to vote and make change.[27]

CHAPTER 16

The Election

During the nine days of early voting before the August 28 election, Team Mendelson had a least three volunteers stationed at each of the four early voting stations every hour that polls were open. Sometimes barely a handful of voters showed up in an hour, but Rich's volunteers were there to catch each and every one.

Every volunteer had his or her own approach. Andy told voters about Meadow. Rich showed voters a copy of the Behavior Intervention Program policy and pointed to where it mentions putting convicted rapists back into normal classrooms. Aaron Feis's younger siblings, Johanna and Ray, were there every day telling voters about their brother and what he would want if he hadn't been murdered trying to save students' lives. Neither Ray's nor Johanna's employer would agree to allow them two weeks off. So, they both quit their jobs in order to honor their brother.

Other volunteers had their own stories to share. But everyone had the same closing line: "Can I count on you to vote for Rich?" And everyone reported the same result. It seemed like they were getting 70 percent of the vote. There are a handful of stories from early voting that stand out in the collective memory of Team Mendelson.

Kim: "One little thing..."

Kim Krawczyk recounted to us that on August 23, as she stood outside the Plantation High School early voting site, a woman across the street wearing a Broward Teachers Union shirt kept shouting, "Teachers are for Levinson! Teachers are for Levinson!"

After about ten minutes, Kim shouted back, "I'm a teacher! And I'm not for Levinson!"

"She's done a great job!" the woman declared. "I've been out here supporting her for years! I'm a teacher and I've had to fight tooth and nail for a raise! I know all of the players in this game!"

"Well," Kim rebutted, "why would you want to reelect someone you've had to fight for a raise? Why can't we agree to try something new? Let Rich replace Laurie and see what he does for our pay."

"You just don't understand how the system works," the woman insisted.

"I think you're making a big mistake by backing Laurie," Kim said. "Her husband's firm is receiving money from school board contracts. There's so much corruption and nepotism in the schools, and it is time to show that these people aren't entitled to their jobs."

"You know what?" the women harped back. "Here's the problem with you people. One little thing happens and everybody just rolls out here like they're going to change the world."

"One little thing? One little thing!?"

A young man in a BTU shirt crossed the street to try to defuse the situation. "Ma'am, maybe I could give you my point of view."

"Do you know who I am?" Kim demanded, straining not to lose her temper.

"A very concerned parent, and I'm sure you want to make our schools great," he said.

"Honey, I'm a third-floor teacher at Marjory Stoneman Douglas. My name is Kimberly Krawczyk. I had to walk twenty-five kids over six dead bodies to leave Building 12. That was not 'one little thing!' There was a mass shooting at a high school in our county with Runcie as the leader and Laurie as his rubber stamp. And you're going to tell me that you think that keeping that board intact is the right thing to do? Not just for teachers but for these children?"

Kim paused, then burst out, "And where's my fucking fire alarm!?"

As the young man walked away with his tail between his legs, Kim regained her composure and started to feel a bit guilty for snapping at him. Then the woman crossed the street and approached Kim.

"I didn't mean to upset you," the woman said. "I'm a concerned parent too. My special-needs son couldn't even graduate from a Broward high school. They didn't have the accommodations to help him. I had to send him to New York City."

"So, change that! Maybe your kid couldn't get the support he needed, but other kids could if we change the system. So, let's change it!"

"Listen, we're all on the same side here."

"No. We're really not."

"We're all teachers. We're all friends. Why don't we take a picture together right now?"

"No. Why don't you walk away right now?"

"I'm really sorry. I didn't mean to upset you. I do think we're on the same side. But I don't think that putting new people in is going to fix any of this. "

"Well," Kim said, "I guess that's where we differ."

Gurmeet: "Where Have You Been?"

Gurmeet Matharu was a stalwart volunteer for Team Mendelson. He moved from New Jersey to Parkland in 2016, close enough to MSD to see Building 12 from his kitchen. Gurmeet was immediately struck by the lax security at the school. After the 2012 Sandy Hook shooting in Connecticut, his son's elementary school moved quickly to bolster its security. But when Gurmeet complained at community forums about MSD's open gates, he was brushed off and labeled an alarmist. His oldest son, Dev, was at the neighboring Westglades Middle School the day of the shooting. Because Dev would be a freshman at MSD the next fall, Gurmeet gave as much of his summer as he could to electing someone who could help keep his son safe.

Traditionally, the only people who stand outside the polls for school board races are folks who are paid by teachers unions. But in this election, Rich's supporters significantly outnumbered the BTU work-ers. BTU Vice President Terry Preuss was apparently exasperated to see so many volunteers for an opposing candidate and said to Gurmeet on the last day of early voting, "A lot of people have been asking, 'Where have you been? Where have you been?'"

Gurmeet could hardly believe he and dozens of other parent volun-teers were being dismissed as Johnny-come-latelies. "Where have *we* been?" Gurmeet asked. "Where were you guys when they put these policies in place?"

"I didn't put these policies—" Preuss protested.

"Fine," Gurmeet conceded. "But you're *supporting* policies that allow criminals and felons to sit next to our children?"

"That's not true."

"When I attended the Parkland City Commission meeting," Gurmeet said, "the chief of police for the Broward County schools told us that there were felons sitting next to our kids."

Preuss tried to interrupt, but Gurmeet continued: "You want to talk over me because you know what I'm saying is the truth. That is the truth."

"No," Preuss said. "I don't want to argue with you and your misin-formation anymore."

"It's not an argument. It's the truth."

"I believe in the PROMISE program," Preuss declared. "It helps kids to stay out of the, the, the—"

"Okay, that's fine," Gurmeet said. "But the chief of police told us, 'Felons are sitting next to your children in their classrooms.' How can you deny that when that message is coming from the Broward chief of police for the Broward County school district?"

"Because I've been in the classroom for thirty-five years."

"But he's the Broward chief of police for the Broward County school district!"

Johanna Feis, who was standing nearby, handed Gurmeet the offi-cial policy document and Gurmeet said, "We have [the policy] right here. I'll read it to you—"

"Hey, listen, I've had my experience with you—"

Gurmeet held out the policy document and said, "Students 'convicted of a serious crime such as rape, murder, attempted murder, sexual battery, or firearms-related crimes' are allowed to sit back in the classroom next to my children!"

"So what? So?" Preuss asked. "This has been out for years. Why are you only now noticing it?"

"Oh, you know why?" Gurmeet retorted. "Because you guys didn't. Did you send these out to families? And say, 'Hey, guys!'"

"It's been online for a long time. I don't want to be adversarial. I really don't."

"I'm stating facts. And you have no answer for them."

"I do have an answer. Where were you then?"

"Your answer is, 'Where were you then?'" Gurmeet demanded. "Guess what—if I were to receive this in the mail, my attorney would have been calling."

Johanna Feis cut in, "Yesterday didn't you say that this didn't exist? This statute didn't exist? That's what you told us yesterday."

Preuss shook her head. "I don't want to argue with you."

Gurmeet said, "Their answer is, 'Where were the families when we passed this?'"

Johanna turned away, saying "She didn't even know about it yesterday. It didn't exist. That's what she said."[1]

Rich: "When Is Your Mom Going to Clean All This Up?"

On a daily basis, someone called the cops on Andy, Rich, and other volunteers at other polling places. Rich assumed this was a dirty trick by the BTU, but then Andy told Rich that he'd heard an elections official walk up to Laurie Rich Levinson, point to Andy's volunteers and ask, "When is your mom going to clean this up?" Rich assumed that all the phony police calls were part of Nan Rich's cleanup operation. Whenever the police confronted Rich, he recorded it.

During the first conversation, Officer Green approached Rich and told him that she'd received a call from people that involved Rich "saying certain things to certain people passing by."

"Can you give me an example of these 'certain things' that I've been accused of saying?"

Officer Green couldn't. She then told Rich that she'd heard that his volunteers had been harassing people. Rich insisted that there was absolutely no basis to that and demanded to see a report detailing the complaints, but Green did not provide one. This became a common practice. The police would say they were responding to a report but never show the report. Officer Green asked Rich whether he would talk to his volunteers about the complaints.

"I will not," Rich replied. "We have our script. We're talking to people who choose to talk to us."

The officer put her foot down. "Just so you know, there's a trespass agreement here. If we're called back out, you or whomever will be trespassed from the library parking lot."

"That would be campaign tampering, which is against federal law," Rich explained. "If you choose to take me off of the grounds here, I will file a federal lawsuit against the police department."

Green backtracked, saying, "Okay. So, we're letting you know, you're letting us know. We're getting out of here."

Rich posted the video on Facebook and it went viral, getting nearly one hundred thousand views.[2] He hoped that this would dissuade the police from responding to whoever was calling in the bogus accusations. But the cops kept coming back. Rich kept recording the conversations, holding his ground, and reminding officers that he could put the videos online and tens of thousands of people could see.

The wrestler in Rich relished these small victories. But the budding politician in him knew he was taking a beating. The BTU broadcast the message on social media that Rich's volunteers were so out of control that the police had to be called, and the *Sun Sentinel* ran an article about it.[3] Rich knew that anyone who saw these posts or read that article would become less likely to vote for him. But there was nothing to be done but to keep shaking every voter's hand.

Johanna: "You Are Utilizing a Death"

Aaron had been almost a father figure to his sister Johanna, who was fifteen years younger. For Johanna, volunteering for Rich was her way of honoring her brother's sacrifice. She was out there for every hour of early voting, and when voters asked her about the eagle statue on the table next to her, she explained that MSD had given it to her family in Aaron's honor.

On the second day of early voting, Johanna was having a conversation with a voter and Laurie Rich Levinson's husband, Neil, approached them. As she told the voter about how the school board allows convicted rapists back into normal classrooms, Neil became very angry.

"That's not true! She doesn't know what she's talking about! She doesn't know what she's talking about!"

"Sir," Johanna said, trying to keep her voice calm and level. "Can you please stop yelling?"

Instead, Neil started shouting, "She's too emotionally unstable to give you reliable information. You can't believe her!"

"Sir," Johanna said, "I'm two feet away from you, and your hands are in my face. Can you please stop yelling?"

"You can't listen to her!" Neil screamed. "Her brother just died. She's too unstable to tell you anything about what's going on!"[4]

The nod Johanna received from the voter suggested to her that Rich had his vote. Rich recalled that Neil continued to pace angrily, appearing not to calm down at all. Now it was Team Mendelson's turn to call the police; according to Rich, Neil hopped into his car and drove off when he saw a police car approaching.

But this was far from the worst indignity Johanna endured during early voting.

Johanna and Rich were at the same polling site for nine days. When they worked the same side of the parking lot, Rich would frequently introduce himself by saying, "Hi, my name is Richard Mendelson. My best friend Aaron Feis was murdered trying to defend students at Stoneman Douglas High School."

About halfway through early voting, the BTU's professional development coordinator, Shafeza Moonab, who was stationed in a booth ten yards away, started to laugh every time Rich introduced himself. Appalled, Kenny turned on his camera to record her laughter, and Rich walked over to confront her.

As he approached, Moonab said, "Ha, ha, ha, ha! Wow, wow, wow! Ha! So, Rich Mendelson! When did he become your *best* friend?"

"When I was fifteen years old," Rich said.

Johanna walked up to Moonab and said, "I've known Mendelson since I was in my mother's stomach. I'm Johanna Feis. Aaron was my big brother."

"I know," Moonab replied.

Kenny walked up too, holding his phone to record the exchange, and said, "It's incredible that you would laugh over something like that."

"I'm sorry for your loss," Moonab said.

"Are you really, though?" Kenny asked. "Because you're laughing whenever we mention the fact that her brother was killed."

Moonab explained, "I am concerned that you are utilizing a death to justify negativity."

"The family is not 'using a death,'" Kenny said. "The family is honoring him."

Moonab looked down and saw that Kenny was recording her. "I'm so sorry for your loss. I'm so sorry for your loss. I'm so sorry for your loss, sir. I really am."

"You changed your tone when [you noticed] my camera," Kenny said.

Moonab became alarmed. "You're filming me without my permission! You're filming me without my permission, sir! Please don't film me! I'm asking you nicely not to film me!"

"I'm asking you nicely not to laugh at them," Kenny said.

"I'm not laughing at him," Moonab insisted. "I wasn't laughing at him! Please don't judge me!"

The next day, a BTU organizer brought an eagle statue to the BTU table. Not an MSD eagle, just a generic statue of an eagle. Rich recalled to us that he approached the organizer and said, "Are you serious? What is this eagle about?"

"Well," he replied with half a smirk. "We live in America. It's a symbol of America."

"That's pretty disgusting that you would bring an eagle statue and put it on your table across from Aaron's." It felt to Rich like they were trolling the Feis family by putting a knockoff eagle statue across from the one that Aaron gave his life to earn.

"Well, the symbolism of an eagle is even bigger than your friend. So you're going to have to get over it."

Rich struggled to suppress the urge to sock him, and he turned away to provide Johanna some words of comfort. But she didn't need them. She took the slight on the chin and continued to introduce herself to every voter.

Momentum Building

Rich and Andy took the shameful conduct of the BTU as a sign that the union knew they were losing. Andy told the *Sun Sentinel*, "They've never been beat before, and they're getting beat to a pulp. They're going to try everything, and nothing is going to work."[5] Everyone was feeling great at the end of each day. Sure, maybe a fifth of the voters sped past, holding up a Democrat endorsement card and saying, "No, thanks, I did my research." But it seemed like more people came saying, "Don't worry, I came here to vote for him." People said, "You knocked on my door," or "You called me. No one has ever done that for a school board race before." It felt like the countless hours that everyone had put in all summer long were finally paying off.

Kenny's favorite moment of the whole campaign came when he was volunteering at early voting alongside Cameron Kasky. Cameron wasn't wearing a Mendelson T-shirt, and Laurie Rich Levinson approached him to thank him for his inspirational work on gun control. She told him that she was working to ramp up the debate program he had participated in so that the next generation of Broward students could be just as outstanding as he was and that she hoped she could count on his vote. Cameron listened politely, then said, "First of all, I was never in the debate program. Second, I can't vote yet. And third, I would never vote for you in a million fucking years."

The last day of early voting was Sunday, August 26, giving Team Mendelson one day of downtime before the final twelve hours at the polls on Election Day. Andy spent most of the day calling voters, but Rich and Kenny needed some downtime and they spent that afternoon at Rich's house with Max, rehashing everything that had brought them all to this point.

"Max," Rich said, "give it to me straight: Do you think we're going to win this?"

"I don't know," Max replied. "I'm the least optimistic guy I know. But after all of this...I feel like you have to. You've worked too hard and reached too many voters not to win."

"I think it's going to be a landslide," Rich proclaimed.

"I don't think anything like this has ever happened before," Max said. "I mean, you're running for school board on a wrecking-ball platform, to expose everything—the data manipulation, the lies, and the corruption. It would be a hell of a thing to write about."

"The minute I get in office," Rich continued, "I'll file for whistleblower status. Everything will come out. I hope you'll be up for more stories."

"It could be huge," Max agreed. "Showing everyone what really happens behind the scenes. And you've heard the way Andy has been talking about Americans for CLASS? He'll start a 501(c)(4) and use this race as a template for a nationwide campaign to pressure school boards to repeal these leniency policies, a grassroots organization that can undo what these activists and bureaucrats have pushed from the top down. Prove to parents that they still have a say in their schools. Yeah, Rich, I think you're going to win. You have to."

Rich turned to Kenny and asked, "What do you think?"

"I think we're going to lose."

"Dude, do you actually believe that they're going to rig it?"[6, 7] Rich asked.

"No, Rich," Kenny said. "I mean I think we're going to lose. I was talking to Abby Freedman. She's a realist. She dropped out because she knew Lori would beat her. She said that Petty's campaign was dead the moment that article on his tweets was published. And she said our campaign was dead before it began. She said that it's cute that we tried so hard but that you're a registered Republican going up against the daughter of Broward's most influential Democrat in a two-to-one Democrat district, and up against the union. Also, Levinson's campaign has been saying that you want to arm teachers."

"Nonsense, Kenny," Rich insisted. "People aren't dumb enough to believe that 'arm teachers' talking point. And sure, Broward is heavily Democrat, but people are mothers and fathers first, Democrats or Republicans second. Levinson didn't even get nine thousand votes last election. We've knocked on thirty thousand doors. We've left flyers at another forty thousand. We've handed out almost fifteen thousand flyers at events. Not to mention all the people Andy has reached through social media and the weekly beating the district has taken in the *Sun Sentinel*. Turnout has been way up compared to her last race in 2014. People aren't coming out in droves to give the status quo a resounding vote of confidence after a mass shooting."

Kenny shrugged. "Abby is a realist, and that's what she said. I'm just not as optimistic as you guys."

"Listen, Kenny," Rich said. "We've put in all the work all summer. We crushed it at early voting. It's not going to be close. We just have to finish strong. So, what am I supposed to do tomorrow? Be at one site all day or be driving around or what?"

"Dude, just listen to Julie," Kenny said. "She's organizing everything. Just do what she says."

Whereas there were only four early voting stations, there were sixty-one precincts to cover for Election Day. Andy's wife, Julie, coordinated the volunteers and made sure that at least one Mendelson supporter was at each precinct at all times. The BTU had a handful of temp workers, but in most polling places Rich's volunteers stood unopposed, talking to any voter who would stop and listen.

Rich stood alone at a polling precinct for the first three hours, but shortly after 10:00 a.m. a husband and wife parked and approached him.

"Are you Rich Mendelson?" the man asked.

"I am."

"We came here to help you," the man said. "Sorry we're a few hours late. It was a long drive. We came here from Santa Fe. You'd have had more Santa Fe parents here, but they had a school board meeting last night. We represent them, because everyone there believes in what you're doing here."

Rich thanked them, then stepped away for a minute to compose himself. They'd driven halfway across the country from Santa Fe, Texas—the site of a school shooting all but ignored by the media—because they'd believed in what Andy and Rich were doing. Rich headed for the bathroom and was in tears before he got there. After a minute,

Rich splashed a little water on his face and walked back outside to stand with them.

The Victory Party

When the polls closed at 7:00 p.m., everyone from Team Mendelson headed to the victory party at Wings Plus in Coral Springs. Spirits were high as over two hundred supporters awaited the election results. Max, Kim, Robyn Mickow, and Tim Sternberg sat down and debriefed one another on what it felt like at the polls and how their lives were going.

Robyn said the least. After the minimal and horrible mental health attention she received from the school district, Robyn gave up on seeking professional treatment, and her friends were growing more worried about her by the week.

Tim was finally feeling good about life. After a year of unemployment, he had found a job teaching civics at a local charter high school, and the new school year was off to a great start.

Kim's year was off to a rocky start. There was still no new fire alarm, and some prankster kept pulling it, triggering horrible PTSD episodes in students and staff. Principal Ty Thompson later sent an email explaining that this student was ESE and all but blamed his teachers for not keeping a closer eye on him.[8]

"I do have one kind of funny update, though," Kim said. "I was walking by Ty Thompson's office and he was on a conference call with someone. He was asking whether he should still be using the #MSDStrong hashtag. I guess they decided he shouldn't, because he doesn't say it in morning announcements anymore. It served its purpose, I suppose."

As they chatted, Tim kept thumbing the refresh button on his phone's Internet browser waiting for the results to roll in. Finally, Tim's eyes widened. "Absentee and early voting results now in. District 1: Lori Alhadeff ahead at sixty-five percent. District Two—"

"Don't care! Mendelson!" Kim urged.

"District Six: Laurie Rich Levinson ahead at sixty percent."

"We lost," Max said.

"Really?" Kim asked.

"It's over."

Robyn's head sank slowly. "It honestly didn't occur to me that we could lose," she said. "We knocked on thirty thousand doors. We were out there every day." She finished her beer and left to get another drink.

Tim announced, "District Eight: Donna Korn at fifty-point-three percent. Ryan Petty at thirty-four percent. Elijah Manley, sixteen percent."

"How could that happen?" Kim shook her head wildly. "Ryan lost his daughter and Donna just said it was an amazing school year!"

"There will be no runoff if she stays above fifty percent," Max said

"Is there any chance Rich can come back from this?" Kim asked.

"None."

Neither Rich nor Andy had arrived yet. Kim and Max sat in silence. Tim kept refreshing his phone. Kenny walked by to give everyone a hug and a word of encouragement.

"How are you feeling?" Kenny asked Max.

"Empty."

"Well," Kenny said, "all you can do is the best you can do. And we did the best we could."

After Kenny left, Tim said, "That kid is an American hero."

Max replied, "Yeah. But he still doesn't have a diploma. And now he has to figure out what he's going to do for a year before he can go to college."

A few minutes later Andy walked in, and everyone at Wings Plus, the two hundred volunteers there for the party and seventy-five others just there for dinner, gave him a standing ovation. Andy was smiling, cracking jokes, and holding the cigar he had saved for when Rich won.

"Does he know yet?" Kim asked.

Andy made his way through the crowd and eventually reached Kim's table. Noticing Tim still glued to his phone, Andy asked, "How's it looking, Tim?"

"Early voting and absentee only: Laurie Rich Levinson, sixty, Richard Mendelson, forty," Tim recited.

Andy glanced at Tim's phone. "We're down by four thousand? We can't make that up. How is that even possible? We must have talked to a hundred thousand people. We crushed it at door-knocking. We crushed it at early voting. How is that even possible?"

Andy wasn't asking rhetorically. Max sullenly offered, "Maybe nobody gives a shit."

"Everyone was saying they'd vote for Rich. Like, I thought we'd get seventy percent, easy. How is that even possible?" Andy stepped away and headed toward the restroom.

"I'm worried about what this will do to him," Kim said. "His whole life since Meadow died has been about fighting for change and accountability. He gave his whole soul to this. He was totally convinced it all happened for a reason and would somehow be for the greater good. And he just lost."

Andy came back and sat down at a nearby table. From a distance he seemed fine, drinking beer and eating wings. But he kept asking, "How can that be possible?" And no one could give him a satisfactory answer.

"I didn't think we were this far gone as a society," Kim said to Max and Tim. "How can you have the mass murder of schoolchildren, have the district treat the survivors like shit as our leaders showboat on CNN, have Runcie get caught twice covering up key facts and flip-flop on everything. And then have everyone endorse the status quo?"

Max was too deflated to respond. Tim was still refreshing his phone, hoping that the results would shift as more precincts reported.

"I'll tell you how," Kim wound up. "We've been thinking this was the school system's fault. We were wrong. This is on us. This is society. This is what America has come to. My generation just decided that we all wanted McMansions, so we maxed out our credit cards and doubled down on the rat race, thinking we could have it all. But someone always pays. And it's the kids who are paying because we're not paying any attention to them. Not really. We send them off to day care, to summer camp. We buy a house near the picture-perfect school: the best school in Florida! Then we congratulate ourselves on being great parents. But do we ever actually *go* to the school? Do we take any interest in what happens there? No! We let activists and bureaucrats force policies down teachers' throats to make the school look better on paper. Then, if we even notice, we applaud ourselves for sending our kid to the safest school in Florida! I mean, there was a mass fucking murder and even after the news broke that the security monitor who sexually harassed Meadow and other girls just fucking let him walk into the building, knowing who that psychopath was and thinking he was armed. Even then, it's only Andy who went to the school to object to him still being there!"

"I mean," Kim continued, "I really think we've lost the ability to *look*. Because if you start pulling on that thread, if you start asking, 'What's actually happening in my child's school?' then you have to start asking all sorts of questions. Why did I stick a tablet into his hand to keep him quiet as a toddler rather than give him a stick and tell him to play outside? Why did I never volunteer at the school? Should I have spent those extra hours that I worked or drank with friends with my kids instead? Looking into our schools would mean looking into our souls. And I don't think anyone wants to hold up that mirror."

For a few moments no one spoke. Then Tim said, "Okay, Kim. I won't argue with a word of that. I'll just add to it. They call all this stuff that's destroying our schools 'social justice.' So you can't question it. I mean, I actually *couldn't*. I was so caught up in thinking I was ending racism. And if anyone questioned me, I would have dismissed it and just attacked them. This stuff is just destroying the next generation of minority students, but you're not allowed to question it because of 'social justice.'"

"I'm sorry, but," Kim looked up as she crossed herself, "how can you even believe in God after this? I'm not even talking about my astrologer. I'm not even talking about how we all let ourselves think that there was a bigger meaning to this. I'm not even talking about how the school district conjured up this demon killer and then tried and failed to cover it up and then no one cared. I'm not even talking about Rich and Andy and everything we've been fighting for. Well, I am talking about that. But...Ryan Petty! You couldn't find a more goodly, godly man. A better father. A more beautiful family man. His daughter was murdered. He tries to set up a foundation to promote kindness, and he gets attacked for it. He tries to run for school board to make schools safer, and he gets smeared for it. And now he won't even make a runoff?"

"All precincts now reporting," Tim said a few minutes later. "Final count: District Six: Levinson beats Mendelson fifty-six to forty-four percent. At-large: Donna Korn beats Ryan Petty with fifty-point-two percent. A few hundred votes short of making a runoff. Looks like Ryan won the Parkland precincts handily. But voter turnout there was only thirty-four percent."

The After-Party

Later that night, Hunter, Kenny, and Max sat in Andy's living room ruminating.

"The worst part of tonight wasn't even losing," Hunter said. "It was having a hundred fifty people try to make you feel better about losing."

Max and Kenny remained silent. After another minute, Hunter said, "I don't know what's worse. That we lost, or that they're all laughing at my dad right now."

"It's not all over," Max said. "Your dad said his mission is to expose everything. Rich didn't win, but we'll still expose everything. He has filed lawsuits. We'll find a publisher for our book. We'll expose how the district failed Nikolas Cruz, how many ways this could have been avoided if not for their policies and incompetence, how awfully the district treated students and families. We'll still expose it all."

Hunter replied, "I don't think anybody gives a shit about Nikolas Cruz. I don't think anybody gives a shit about Parkland. Or the victims. Or the families. I think the only thing anyone cares about is the fact that guns exist."

After about a minute of silence, Kenny tried, "Well, Lori won her race. Jim Silvernale made it to a runoff. Maybe he wins. With Nora Rupert and Robin Bartleman, that could make four. Then if they just get one to switch sides, maybe Heather Brinkworth, then that would be five and they could oust Runcie and bring in a real leader."

"Stop it, Kenny. Just stop," Max said. "Lori will be good. But right now, Rupert is Runcie's strongest critic. And she was literally willing to lie and defame you rather than publicly admit to privately criticizing Runcie. There will be no majority. And Runcie isn't even the problem."

"He's not?"

"Not at this point," Max said. "He's a symptom. You want to see the true disease? Look at what just happened. Seventeen dead. The most preventable school shooting in history. Runcie got caught covering up key facts, and every week for the past two months there has been a story on how incompetent he and the school board are. We had people who lost their loved ones run on the most powerful message imaginable: my daughter died, no one is being held accountable, and no one is taking the safety of your children seriously. And we lost. That's the disease: apathy. That's why Runcie will remain in office. And that's why he doesn't matter."

"This is a pretty shitty ending for your book," Kenny said.

"Yeah, but it's what happened," Max continued. "Like Andy kept saying, if we can win in Broward, we can win anywhere. And if we can't win in Broward, we can't win anywhere. We couldn't do it. We lost. That's it. It's over."

"Is there really nothing we can do for Parkland anymore except tweet?" Hunter asked.

"I still think," Kenny said, "if we keep meeting with some of the school board members and the stars align just right—"

"Kenny! Fucking stop it," Max said. "Figure out how to get your high school diploma. Apply to a good college. Figure out what you'll do for the next year. This is over."

"Yeah." Kenny hung his head. "Well, it's going to be a lot harder to get my diploma without Rich on the board."

"There's the playground," Hunter said.

"Huh?"

"Princess Meadow's Playground. My dad raised all the money himself. Pulled all the strings. The city didn't do anything. The school didn't do anything. They probably never will. My dad built the only memorial for the seventeen victims. That could be how your book ends."

You Have to #Fixit

By Andy Pollack

It took me about a month to recover from that election. I couldn't have been more disappointed with the people of Broward. They had an opportunity to unite around families who had lost their loved ones and to press for change to make our schools safe again. They had an opportunity to hold the people accountable for the most avoidable mass murder in American history. But instead, they voted the incumbents back into office.

I did not want this book to be political. I was never a political guy. I never even voted until 2016. After Meadow was murdered, I wanted to fight for something that I thought all Americans could come together on: school safety. I wanted to hold off on giving you my political opinions about all this until the end, so that you could know the facts first and think for yourself. But right here I'm going to tell you exactly what I think. Not because I want to be partisan, but because this has to be said for the safety of our children.

I've been over every inch of what happened. The NRA had nothing to do with it.

This happened in a Democrat county with a Democrat sheriff, a Democrat superintendent, and a Democrat school board, implementing Democrat ideas on criminal justice, Democrat ideas on special education, and Democrat ideas on school discipline. And after Democrat voters gave all these Democrats a resounding vote of confidence in the school board election, the Democrat teachers union president, Anna Fusco, wrote in a Facebook group about our campaign for accountability: "Now you can all shut up!"

Meanwhile, at the national level, Democrat organizers swooped in and weaponized my daughter's murder for their Democrat agenda and to fund-raise to elect more Democrats.

My friend Royer is right. Broward County really is the closest thing America has to Venezuela. When local officials do something awful, they can just pick a distant enemy who wasn't responsible, whip up public anger, and grow their own power. In Venezuela, it was anyone that President Chavez or Maduro didn't like. In Broward, it was the NRA.

And aside from the great reporters at the *Sun Sentinel,* the media totally went along with it because it fit their agenda too. After the murder of my daughter and sixteen others, there should have been a deep look into what went wrong like there was after Columbine. There should have been a constructive debate about how to keep schools safe. And there should have been a lot of soul-searching.

Instead, the media exploited this tragedy as an opportunity to pit Americans against one another for higher ratings. They made it all into a Twitter showdown between a few teenagers and the Republican Party over a policy issue that didn't have anything to do with what happened. Short of banning guns altogether, nothing in the gun control agenda would have prevented 18–1958 from getting a gun because he looked totally clean on paper. But rather than try to figure out why a student who everyone was saying had committed plenty of crimes had nothing on his record, the media treated the question as a threat to their agenda and marginalized it as a "right-wing" thing.

Again, though, I'm not saying this to be partisan. These are facts. And they have to be said because while I used to think school safety could be a nonpartisan issue, I am not so sure anymore. I only ever wanted to talk about school safety. I never wanted to say anything either way about guns. But because I didn't want to only focus on guns, the politically correct media labeled me as being on the "other side of the gun debate." As I hope this book has shown you, there are so many school safety problems that have nothing to do with guns. But if these people think that any school safety idea that isn't about gun control is pro-gun, then I just don't see how Democrats can ever be for school safety.

I really don't like saying that. But look at what happened after President Trump released the findings of the Federal Commission on School Safety that he launched after the Parkland shooting. Four cabinet secretaries and their teams researched and took testimony about best practices in school safety for almost a year. The report had about one hundred recommendations across a wide range of issues, the sort of things that we could all agree on, that every parent would want, and that would keep students safe if school boards and superintendents took them seriously.

And what was the response from Nancy Pelosi and the mainstream media? They attacked the report because it didn't advance the gun control agenda. They basically tried to delegitimize it in order to attack President Trump. I fear that because of the way they attacked it, school boards and superintendents won't even want to read it. And because of that our students will be less safe.

It's just sick to me. It shouldn't be this way. I don't think Democrat parents care any less than Republican parents. I have to take some hope by looking at Kim Krawczyk, a Democrat who doesn't fall for the politically correct nonsense that she knows is wrecking American education. I have to believe that there are many people out there who are like her.

I have to believe that it's the politically correct politicians and media who have made it this way. We should be able to put the interest of students and teachers above the self-satisfaction of distant bureaucrats and social justice activists and come together on things that ninety-nine percent of Americans agree about.

But it's the politically correct one percent that has the most power over our schools right now. When my friend Max Eden told me about the education reform movement and the "social justice industrial complex," I thought it sounded too strange to be true. Like, that can't really be the way things work.

But in October, the Council of the Great City Schools, a nonprofit coalition of urban public school systems, gave Robert Runcie a "Courage Under Crisis" award. They tweeted, "The courage you all exhibited after a tragedy and the stand that you all took after to make ensure [*sic*] schools become safe is absolutely amazing!"

On the one hand, Runcie provided awful mental health services to students and no mental health support to teachers, totally ignored the victims' families, misled the public, stonewalled the press, reacted to questions and criticism with open contempt, flip-flopped on every promise, and failed to make good on the easiest action items to make schools safer.

On the other hand, he held a press conference the morning after a mass murder that occurred under his leadership and, with the bodies of dead children lying on the cold floor in the building directly behind him, he made a partisan argument about gun control.

In the eyes of public education's politically correct overlords, this is apparently literally award-winning courage.

To be clear, I am not telling you that your school superintendent is like Robert Runcie. But I am telling you that he wants to be like Robert Runcie. Because it's the people like Robert Runcie who get ahead these days. Between the federal bureaucrats, the state bureaucrats, the district bureaucrats, and the billionaire philanthropists who fund a cottage industry of politically correct social engineers, this social justice industrial complex has more power over our schools than parents and citizens. Runcie became a national superstar for lowering discipline and arrests by not enforcing discipline and the law. Then his old Chicago boss, Secretary of Education Arne Duncan, pushed Runcie's policies into your kids' schools without you knowing about it.

Fortunately, President Trump and Betsy DeVos rescinded that Dear Colleague Letter on school discipline that we explained in chapter 9. School districts no longer have to fear bad-faith federal investigations that will force them to adopt Broward's discipline policies no matter the damage. School leaders at least have the freedom once again to choose their policies.

Unfortunately, they'll still face a lot of pressure to keep these leniency policies. The social justice industrial complex, all those bureaucrats, and left-wing activist groups like the Southern Poverty Law Center will keep on prodding and threatening and suing to advance their agenda. On autopilot, this politically correct cancer will only metastasize.

The only thing that can #Fixit is you, the parents. I couldn't #Fixit here in Broward. The best consolation my friends have given me is that running against an incumbent Democrat and politically correct policies in a two-to-one Democrat district and losing by only 9 percent is amazingly good. Maybe it is.

I have to think that progress is still possible, even in places that are overwhelmingly Democrat, where school board leaders aren't as corrupt and morally challenged as they are here in Broward. I do have one ray of hope to offer you from Baltimore County, Maryland. My friend up there, Nicole Landers, managed to #Fixit. She started bringing parents to school board meetings and connecting teachers to the local TV media. The teachers were too scared to go on record, but with their faces concealed by shadow and their voices changed, they talked about all the bullying and violence that school administrators refuse to address. At the end of one school board meeting where Nicole brought parents and local press, the superintendent ran away so she didn't have to answer questions about school safety.

Nicole teamed up with her school board representative, Ann Miller. Ann helped parents file ethics complaints against her superintendent and ended up getting the superintendent sent to jail for perjury (though Ann says that it was basically like Al Capone getting locked up for tax evasion). Ann and Nicole found candidates, organized a campaign, and appealed over the head of teachers unions directly to parents. They built a large coalition and actually elected a new majority to overturn these dangerous discipline policies.

So maybe there's some hope for Blue America beyond Broward. But don't think that what you read in this book doesn't apply to your kids' school just because you live somewhere Purple or Red. Superintendents everywhere are facing the same policies and incentives and operate in the same culture. You have to push back on it everywhere.

And now, because President Trump rescinded the federal policy that coerced school districts to do this no matter what parents thought, your voice can actually be heard again. The only credit he got for it was being called a racist by the media. But this has nothing to do with race. It's about holding kids accountable and empowering and trusting teachers again.

I wrote this book to expose and to educate. When I started my investigation, I thought that school safety was simply an issue of preventing shootings. I figured we could #Fixit simply by making sure our schools have a single point of entry, metal detectors, and armed guards. After all, students can't bring weapons into the classroom if there is only one way to enter the school, a metal detector there, and an armed guard watching over that entry point.

Sometimes when I say that I think schools should have metal detectors, someone else will say, "We can't make our schools feel like prisons!" But that's a dumb and dangerous talking point. Sports stadiums don't feel like prisons. We protect our athletes better than we protect our children, and that should change.

Sometimes when I say that I think schools should have armed guards, someone else will say, "We can't arm teachers!" But that's also a dumb and dangerous talking point. No one is talking about just handing a teacher a gun to slip into her desk. We're talking about things like the Coach Aaron Feis Guardian Program, where we have retired cops, veterans, or very highly trained professionals carrying a firearm. For some reason, the idea that there would be a guard with a gun in a school scares some people. Let me tell you something that's scarier: a mass murderer with a gun in a school alone with hundreds of kids for ten minutes.

But I've also realized that school safety is about so much more than physical hardening. You've learned about the danger of diversionary programs, like PROMISE, where the aim really is to reduce arrests no matter the effect on school safety. I used to look at this and think that Broward was prioritizing the rights of criminals over the rights of good students. But the more I talked to teachers and school resource officers, the more I realized that these programs do the greatest harm to the troublemakers. They get sent the message that they're untouchable, and they never get the help they actually need. As my friends Tim Sternberg and Robert Martinez will say, PROMISE and programs like it are actually building the "school-to-prison pipeline." And if we pathologically refuse to arrest anyone under the age of eighteen, then as soon as they hit eighteen they'll be able to buy a gun. Just like 18–1958.

My friend Ann Miller once said, "We hear about school shootings and external threats, but as horrific as they are, if you take the cumulative effect, I think that it pales in comparison to the daily instances of bullying, assaults, and violence that occur in every school across the country."

Personally, if I had heard that back in February 2018, I would not have agreed at all. But now I understand it. Because so much bullying and violence happens in our schools for the simple reason that school administrators refuse to enforce the rules. They refuse to enforce them because that's what's in their own professional interest under these politically correct discipline policies. Kids need adults to enforce rules. Behavior doesn't magically get better when you decide to not punish mischief. What happens is that things get worse for students and teachers but look better on paper for bureaucrats and activists. This leads to a thousand tragedies a day that you'll never hear about. And it lets troubled kids just slip through the cracks.

Max told me that he'd been studying this problem for years and it never occurred to him that it could lead to a mass shooting. But here in Broward, it did. And it certainly could elsewhere. There are hundreds if not thousands of other students like 18–1958 out there. School shootings don't happen every day because those kids are not hard to identify, to help, or to stop. It only happened here because the Broward County school district was even sicker than 18–1958.

I expect that politically correct people who won't read my book or even try to understand my argument will attack me by saying that I want to treat every troubled student as a potential school shooter.

Not at all. The students we should treat like potential school shooters are the ones that threaten to kill everyone all the time. We shouldn't take students who are so dangerous that they require a security escort to walk through the hallways and put them in a room alone with pre-teen girls. We shouldn't let students who are obsessed with guns and dream of being covered in blood and gore into traditional schools and literally let them practice marksmanship. And we shouldn't cover up their behavior until it becomes too late to help.

For other students with disabilities, I hope that how badly the Broward school district treated 18–1958 can help spark soul-searching in our policy makers and school leaders. We can't just push troubled students into classrooms where they won't get the help they need and celebrate ourselves for being "inclusive." The idea that all students with disabilities must be taught in the "least restrictive environment" ends up just becoming a way for school district bureaucrats to save money and congratulate themselves for being politically correct even as they do things to students that teachers know are wrong.

You have to step up and #Fixit. Talk to your kids' teachers. Talk off the record so that they'll tell you the truth. And if they're telling you that the social justice discipline stuff is a problem, then take the issue to your school board. Tell them to get rid of restorative justice or Multi-Tiered System of Supports or Response to Intervention or whatever else they call it. Tell them to get back to the old system that the social justice activists say is now politically incorrect: rules, warnings, and consequences. And if you can't convince them, vote them out of office. You have the power to #Fixit in your community. (Unless you live in Broward. If so, you should just move.)

If anyone in the Broward County school district made a single responsible decision regarding Nikolas Cruz, then my daughter Meadow would still be alive. This wasn't just incompetence. They all did the wrong thing every single time because that's what these policies pressured them to do. And even after these policies led to the murder of seventeen people, it's somehow politically incorrect and "reprehensible" to question them.

The only reason that our schools work this way is because we, the parents, allow it. You simply have to step up, get involved, and make a difference for your children. You can't let your schools be run like the Broward County Public Schools district.

As for me, I'm going to keep fighting to make our schools safe again. Because Meadow is still on my shoulder, saying, "Daddy, keep going."

And she wants us to #Fixit.

Endnotes

Chapter 1

1 Kimberly Krawczyk. Letter to Michael Ramirez. 2018. "Thank You!!!" Email.

2 Bryce Wilson Stucki, "Reversing Broward's School-to-Prison Pipeline," *The American Prospect*, December 4, 2013, https://prospect.org/article/reversing -broward-countys-school-prison-pipeline.

3 *Anderson Cooper 360 Degrees*, "Pres. Trump Offers Condolences, Doesn't Mention Guns; Gunman Confesses to Florida High School Shooting; 17 Dead, at Least 14 Hurt in Florida School Shooting; Shooter Charged with 17 Counts of Premeditated Murder; Shooter in Court Today, Denied Bond; Sheriff: Uber Dropped Shooter Off at the School at 2:19." Aired on 8–9p ET (transcript), CNN, February 15, 2018, http://transcripts.cnn.com/TRANSCRIPTS/1802/15/acd .01.html.

4 *Megyn Kelly Today*, "Mother of Slain Parkland Student: We Are Fighting to Make Our Schools Safe Again," NBC, March 13, 2018, https://www.today. com/video/mother-of-slain-parkland-student-we-are-fighting-to-make-our-schools-safe-again-1184583747746.

5 Author's calculations based on presentation by Florida Department of Law Enforcement on April 24, 2018, https://www.fdle.state.fl.us/MSDHS/Time-line.aspx.

6 Broward County Public Schools, "SBBC Meeting 04-10-18," https://becon. eduvision.tv/Default.aspx?q=d0F7qPKKlcfmtjfULqo9AQ%253d%253d.

7 Jessica Bakeman, "Stoneman Douglas Shooter Was Assigned To Controver-sial Broward Discipline Program, Officials Now Say," WLRN.com, May 6, 2018, http://www.wlrn.org/post/stoneman-douglas-shooter-was-assigned-contro-versial-broward-discipline-program-officials-now; Scott Travis, "Broward Approves Raise for Leader of Controversial Promise Program," *Sun Senti-nel*, May 22, 2018, https://www.sun-sentinel.com/local/broward/parkland/ florida-school-shooting/fl-florida-school-shooting-promise-board-meeting-20180522-story.html.

8 *Sun Sentinel* Editorial Board, "Big Raise, Bad Optics at Broward School Board," *Sun Sentinel*, May 25, 2018, https://www.sun-sentinel.com/opinion/editorials/ fl-op-editorial-broward-schools-runcie-20180525-story.html.

9   Scott Travis, "Broward Schools Give Big Raises to Administrators," *Sun Senti-nel*, September 27, 2018, https://www.sun-sentinel.com/news/education/fl-ne-broward-schools-raises-20180927-story.html.

10   Ibid.

11   Scott Travis, "Broward School Board Members Blast Way Administrators Got Raises," October 18, 2018, https://www.sun-sentinel.com/news/education/fl-ne-broward-school-board-runcie-evaluation-20181016-story.html.

12   Scott Travis, "Broward Schools Hold Off on Money to Boost Public Relations," *Sun Sentinel,* September 18, 2018, https://www.sun-sentinel.com/local/broward/parkland/florida-school-shooting/fl-ne-broward-school-pr-posi-tions-20180917-story.html.

13   Broward County Public Schools, "SBBC Meeting 05-22-18," https://becon.eduvision.tv/Default.aspx?q=d0F7qPKKlcfmtjfULqo9AQ%253d%253d.

Chapter 2

1   Anthony told his father that it felt like it took an hour for the police and medical attention to arrive. At the time, Royer assumed that his son's sense of time was skewed by the pain. He later learned it wasn't. Anthony lay on the ground for forty-three minutes before the police arrived on the third floor and started to triage victims for medical attention. Forty. Three. Minutes.

2   "How the Polices [*sic*] of the Progressive Left Directly Caused the Florida Massacre #NRA #2A #Liberty," Charles Carroll Society, March 1, 2018, https://charlescarrollsociety.com/2018/03/01/how-the-polices-of-the-progressive-left-directly-caused-the-florida-massacre-nra-2a-liberty/.

3   Elizabeth Chuck, "Anthony Borges, Parkland Teen Who Was Shot Shielding Classmates, Rejects 'Hero' Label," *Today*, April 4, 2018, https://www.nbcnews.com/news/us-news/anthony-borges-parkland-teen-who-shielded-class-mates-speaks-first-time-n862636.

4   Mark Osborne, "Parkland Shooting Victim Criticizes Sheriff, School after Release from Hospital," ABC News, April 7, 2018, https://abcnews.go.com/US/parkland-shooting-victim-criticizes-sheriff-school-release-hospital/story?id=54302725.

5   Kathleen Joyce, "Parkland Shooting Hero Blames Sheriff and Superintendent for Failing to Prevent Massacre," Fox News, April 7, 2018, https://www.foxnews.com/us/parkland-shooting-hero-blames-sheriff-and-superintendent-for-fail-ing-to-prevent-massacre.

Chapter 3

1   Tim Craig et al., "Teachers Say Florida Suspect's Problems Started in Middle School, and the System Tried to Help Him," *Washington Post*, February 18, 2018, https://www.washingtonpost.com/local/education/teachers-say-florida-shooters-problems-started-in-middle-school-and-the-system-tried-to-help-him/2018/02/18/cdff7aa6-1413-11e8-9065-e55346f6de81_story.html.

2   Washington Post Editorial Board, "Bowser's Pick for New D.C. Schools Chan-cellor is a Safe Choice," *Washington Post*, November 22, 2016.

3   Rachel Cohen, "How D.C. Became the Darling of Education Reform," *The American Prospect*, April 19, 2017, https://prospect.org/article/how-dc-became-darling-education-reform.

4   Diane Ravitch, *Reign of Error: The Hoax of the Privatization Movement and the Danger to America's Public Schools*, Knopf, New York, NY 2013.

5   Washington Post Editorial Board, "Test Scores Point to School Reform Success in the District," *Washington Post*, November 7, 2013.

6   Max Eden, "D.C. Public Schools Deserves an F for Bogus Reforms, Faked Successes, and Disastrous Failures," *The 74*, March 4, 2018, https://www.the74million.org/article/eden-d-c-public-schools-deserves-an-f-for-bogus-reforms-faked-successes-and-disastrous-failures/.

7   Kate McGee, "What Really Happened at the School Where Every Graduate Got Into College," NPR Ed, November 28, 2017, https://www.npr.org/sections/ed/2017/11/28/564054556/what-really-happened-at-the-school-where-every-senior-got-into-college.

8   Alvarez & Marsal, "DCPS Graduation Review SY 2016-2017 Audit and Investigation: Final Report District of Columbia Public School Audit and Investigation," January 26, 2018. https://osse.dc.gov/release/osse-announces-overall-four-year-graduation-rate-685-percent-2017-18-school-year.

9   Nat Malkus, "DC's Dishonest Graduation Rate is a Disgrace: Here's How To Fix It," *Washington Examiner*, March 12, 2018.

10 Alejandra Matos and Emma Brown, "Some D.C. High Schools Are Reporting Only a Fraction of Suspensions," Washington Post, July 17, 2017, https://www.washingtonpost.com/local/education/some-dc-high-schools-reported-only-a-small-fraction-of-suspensions/2017/07/17/045c387e-5762-11e7-ba90-f5875b7d1876_story.html.

11 Washington Teachers' Union and EmpowerEd, "Survey of DCPS Teachers on Grading, Promotion Policies," January 25, 2018.

12 *In Class Not Cuffs: Rethinking School Discipline*, Center for American Progress, Washington, D.C., January 17, 2018, https://www.americanprogress.org/events/2018/01/08/444673/class-not-cuffs-rethinking-school-discipline/.

13 Frederick M. Hess and Grant Addison, "Education as Reeducation," *National Review*, October 25, 2018, https://www.nationalreview.com/magazine/2018/11/12/higher-education-junk-science-wokeness/.

14 Xiomara Padamsee, "Interrupting White Dominance to Make Good on the Promise of Equity," Promise54, May 17, 2018, https://promise54.org/interrupting-white-dominance-to-make-good-on-the-promise-of-equity/.

15 Rachel Cohen, "How D.C. Became the Darling of Education Reform," *The American Prospect*, April 19, 2017, https://prospect.org/article/how-dc-became-darling-education-reform.

16 See Tapper's full interview with Sheriff Israel, CNN video from "State of the Union with Jake Tapper," February 25, 2018, https://www.cnn.com/videos/politics/2018/02/25/scott-israel-parkland-shooting-response-entire-sotu.cnn.

17 Curt Devine and Jose Pagliery, "Sheriff Says He got 23 Calls about Shooter's Family, but Records Show More," CNN, February 27, 2018, https://www.cnn.com/2018/02/27/us/parkland-shooter-cruz-sheriff-calls-invs/index.html.

18 Max Eden, "How Did the Parkland Shooter Slip Through the Cracks?" *City Journal*, February 26, 2018, https://www.city-journal.org/html/how-did-parkland-shooter-slip-through-cracks-15741.html.

19 Ann Coulter, "The School-to-Mass-Murder Pipeline," Townhall.com, February 28, 2018, https://townhall.com/columnists/anncoulter/2018/02/28/the-schooltomassmurder-pipeline-n2455793.

20 Scott Travis and Megan O'Matz, "Broward Schools Backtrack on Gunman Nikolas Cruz's Promise Program Connection," *Sun Sentinel*, May 7, 2018, https://www.sun-sentinel.com/local/broward/parkland/florida-school-shooting/fl-florida-school-shooting-cruz-promise-20180507-story.html.

21 Robert Runcie, "Schools Chief: Focusing on Safety and Security, and Toppling 'Fake News,'" *Sun Sentinel*, March 23, 2018, https://www.sun-sentinel.com/opinion/commentary/fl-op-viewpoint-broward-school-security-safety-measures-20180323-story.html.

22 Broward County school district, "Statement Regarding Broward County Public Schools PROMISE Program and Collaborative Agreement on School Discipline," March 5, 2018.

23 Michael Stratford and Caitlin Emma, "Politico's Morning Education: Trump School Safety Plan Targets Obama Discipline Directive," *Politico*, March 13, 2018.

24 Erica L. Green, "Trump Finds Unlikely Culprit in School Shootings: Obama Discipline Policies," *New York Times*, March 13, 2018, https://www.nytimes.com/2018/03/13/us/politics/trump-school-shootings-obama-discipline-policies.html.

25 Paul Morgan et. al, "Are Students with Disabilities Suspended More Frequently than Otherwise Similar Students without Disabilities?" *Journal of School Psychology*, Vol. 72, Issue 1, pp 1-13, https://www.sciencedirect.com/science/article/pii/S0022440518301171.

26 Scott Travis, "Schools Could Have Done More for Shooter Nikolas Cruz, Experts Say," *Sun Sentinel*, March 4, 2018, https://www.sun-sentinel.com/local/broward/parkland/florida-school-shooting/fl-florida-school-shooting-cruz-mental-health-20180302-story.html.

27 Alexander Russo, "Worst Education Journalism of the 2017–2018 School Year," Phi Delta Kappan, May 30, 2018, http://www.kappanonline.org/russo-worst-education-journalism-of-the-2017-2018-school-year/.

28 Marjory Stoneman Douglas High School Public Safety Commission, April 24, 2018, http://www.fdle.state.fl.us/MSDHS/Meetings/April-Meeting-Documents/PublicSafetyMeeting04-24-18.aspx.

Chapter 4

1 Meghan Keneally, "After Parkland Shooting, Some Call For Mental Health Reforms While Others Want Gun Control," ABC News, February 15, 2018, https://abcnews.go.com/US/parkland-shooting-call-mental-health-reforms-gun-control/story?id=53114225.

2 Monica Scott, "Bernard Taylor, Other Superintendent Finalist, Face Broward Residents Tonight at a Public Forum," Michigan Live, September 13, 2011, https://www.mlive.com/news/grand-rapids/index.ssf/2011/09/bernard_taylor_other_superinte.html.

3 Florida Supreme Court, "Final Report of the Ninetheenth Statewide Grand Jury, Case # SC-09-191-0," June 11, 2011, accessed January 9, 2019, https://browardoutrage.wordpress.com/2011/06/18/broward-school-board-grand-jury-report-scary-stuff-and-nothing-has-been-done/.

4 Scott Travis, "Broward Schools Fought Against 2013 Plan for More Security Money," Sun Sentinel, February 12, 2019, https://www.sun-sentinel.com/local/broward/parkland/florida-school-shooting/fl-ne-broward-school-board-forgoes-safety-money-20190211-story.html.

5 Ibid.

6 William Hladky, "Public Won't Help Pick Companies to Manage Broward County School Construction Spending," Miami Herald, May 30, 2015, https://www.miamiherald.com/news/local/community/miami-dade/article22724217.html.

7 Brittany Shammas, "Runcie Stands By Hiring of New Facilities Chief amid Debate over Audit's Findings," Sun Sentinel, October 22, 2015, https://www.sun-sentinel.com/news/education/fl-facilities-director-audit-20151022-story.html.

8 Ericka Mellon, "Audit Finds HISD Exceeded Contract Limits without Approval; Trustee Demands Accountability," Houston Chronicle, September 9, 2015, https://www.houstonchronicle.com/news/education/article/Audit-finds-HISD-exceeded-contract-limits-without-6494427.php.

9 A full timeline of Sun Sentinel articles on the bond project can be found: Scott Travis, "Promises and Setbacks: the $800 Million Broward School Bond Timeline," Sun Sentinel, December 14, 2018, https://www.sun-sentinel.com/news/education/fl-broward-bond-project-timeline-20160814-story.html.

10 Emanuella Grinberg and Steve Almasy, "Students at Town Hall to Washington, NRA: Guns Are the Problem, Do Something," CNN, February 22, 2018, https://www.cnn.com/2018/02/21/politics/cnn-town-hall-florida-shooting/index.html.

11 Scott Travis, "Report Criticizes Broward Schools' Management of Bond," Sun Sentinel, February 27, 2017, https://www.sun-sentinel.com/news/education/fl-sb-broward-bond-committee-report-20170227-story.html.

12 Records provided to author by Kenny Preston.

13 Kenny Preston, "An Investigation Into Broward County's School Board and Superintendent," Medium, April 26, 2018, https://medium.com/@kennethrpreston/an-investigation-into-broward-countys-school-board-superintendent-4789bbd5b2e5.

14 Judicial Watch, "Education Official Got Secret Cash Bonuses as Office Lost Billions to Fraud, Corruption," The Judicial Watch Blog, May 31, 2017, https://www.judicialwatch.org/blog/2017/05/education-official-got-secret-cash-bonuses-office-lost-billions-fraud-corruption/.

15 Ibid.

16 Molly Hensley-Clancy, "An Education Department Official Resigned after DeVos Demanded He Testify Before Congress," *BuzzFeed*, May 24, 2017, https://www.buzzfeednews.com/article/mollyhensleyclancy/an-education-depart-ment-official-resigned-after-devos#.beL4Pe8K4B.

17 Team DML, "Report: Broward County Schools Was Sitting on $100M Allocated for School Safety Since 2014," DennisMichaelLynch.com, March 27, 2018, http://dennismichaellynch.com/report-broward-county-schools-was-sitting-on-100m-allocated-for-school-safety-since-2014/.

18 Alice B. Lloyd, "The Broward Blame-Game," *Weekly Standard*, April 13, 2018, https://www.weeklystandard.com/alice-b-lloyd/the-broward-blame-game. Quotes in this section are from Lloyd's article or notes.

19 Broward County Public Schools, "SBBC Meeting 04-10-18," https://becon.eduvision.tv/Default.aspx?q=d0F7qPKKlcfmtjfULqo9AQ%253d%253d.

20 Timothy Sternberg, interview with authors, August 15, 2018.

Chapter 5

1 Carol Marbin Miller and Nicholas Nehamas, "Nikolas Cruz's Birth Mom Had a Violent, Criminal Past. Could It Help Keep Him Off Death Row?" *Miami Herald*, https://www.miamiherald.com/news/local/community/broward/article216909390.html.

2 Alan Weberman, *The Miscreant: The Nikolas Cruz Story* (CreateSpace Independent Publishing Platform: 2018).

3 Max Jaeger, "Alleged School Shooter's Mom Paid $50K to Adopt Him from 'Drug Addict,'" *New York Post*, February 27, 2018, https://nypost.com/2018/02/27/alleged-school-shooters-mom-paid-50k-to-adopt-him-from-drug-addict/.

4 Ibid.

5 This and all details about Cruz before middle school, as well as some details from his time at Cross Creek and MSD, are from a report commissioned by the Broward school district conducted by the Collaborative Educational Network Inc. The story of how the contents of this report became public is covered in chapter 12 and is accessible at Brittany Wallman and Paula McMahon, "Here's What Broward Schools Knew about Parkland Shooter—Details Revealed by Mistake," *Sun Sentinel*, August 3, 2018, https://www.sun-sentinel.com/local/broward/parkland/florida-school-shooting/fl-florida-school-shooting-con-sultant-report-full-20180803-story.html.

6 Laura Italiano, "Accused Florida School Killer Watched His Father Die," *New York Post*, February 25, 2018, https://nypost.com/2018/02/25/accused-florida-school-killer-watched-his-father-die/.

7 There is no clear evidence in his disciplinary record of Cruz being caught masturbating. There is, as will be discussed, plenty of evidence that his sexually charged statements and actions were regularly recorded as mere "profanity."

8 Ibid.

9 The education records were provided to us by the Broward public defender's office, which is representing Nikolas Cruz in his criminal trial.

10 Cruz's grades in the first quarter of eighth grade: Intensive Reading: F; Language Arts: F; Pre-Algebra: F; Exp Wheel: F; Physical Science: F; US History: C+. His second-quarter grades were similar.

11 Another anecdote, recorded by another teacher, from October 28: "I asked him to stop cursing and interrupting other students while they work. He told me, 'You are creepy. Just looking at me is creepy.' I then asked him, 'What would you rather be doing?' His response was, 'I would rather be on the street killing animals and setting fires.'"

12 Ibid.

13 Isabelle Robinson, "I Tried to Befriend Nikolas Cruz. He Still Killed My Friends," *New York Times*, March 27, 2018, https://www.nytimes.com/2018/03/27/opinion/nikolas-cruz-shooting-florida.html.

14 Scott Travis, "Nikolas Cruz's Record in PROMISE Program Is a Mystery," *Sun Sentinel*, July 9, 2018, https://www.sun-sentinel.com/local/broward/parkland/florida-school-shooting/fl-florida-school-shooting-cruz-promise-participation-20180709-story.html.

15 If Cruz had been arrested for vandalism, that would not have affected his ability to buy a firearm. But at an MSD Public Safety Commission meeting months later, Polk County Sheriff Grady Judd pointed out to Robert Runcie that, "There is a multi-billion-dollar system in place across this country today to hold people accountable, to set checks and balances and responsibility and to be able to force people into mental health counseling, into probation checks, into curfews. And that's the criminal justice system." By preventing Cruz from being referred to the criminal justice system, the school district passed up another opportunity to help him.

16 Scott Travis, "Report Finds Flaws in Broward Special Ed Services," *Sun Sentinel*, July 12, 2014, https://www.sun-sentinel.com/news/education/higher-education/fl-broward-special-ed-report-20140711-story.html.

17 Advance Education, Inc., "Executive Summary: Cross Creek School," September 29, 2016, http://www.broward.k12.fl.us/ospa/ospa-central2/_sip_plan_files/3222_10222018_3222_10032018_3222_09292016_EXECUTIVE_SUMMARY.pdf.

18 Henderson Clinic's in-home therapist, however, counseled Lynda to allow Cruz to have a BB gun so long as she made it part of a plan of rewarding him for good behavior. So, he got one.

19 Michael Vasquez, "Parents Decry Closing of Two Broward Schools for Special-Needs Kids," *Miami Herald*, February 16, 2013, https://www.miamiherald.com/latest-news/article1947381.html.

20 Michael Vasquez, "After Closing, Sunset School Campus Could Become Offices—Or Another School," *Miami Herald*, April 22, 2013, https://www.miamiherald.com/latest-news/article1950591.html.

21 Ibid.

22 Ibid.

23 E-mail correspondence with author.

24 Ibid.

25 Ibid.

26 Advance Education Inc., "Executive Summary: Cross Creek School," September 29, 2016, http://www.broward.k12.fl.us/ospa/ospa-central2/_sip_plan_files/3222_10222018_3222_10032018_3222_09292016_EXECUTIVE_SUMMARY.pdf.

Chapter 6

1   Megan O'Matz, David Fleshler, and Stephen Hobbs, "Deputies Faulted over Parkland Shooter Tips, But Neither One Is Fired," *Sun Sentinel*, September 7, 2018, https://www.sun-sentinel.com/local/broward/parkland/florida-school-shooting/fl-school-shooter-broward-deputies-disciplined-20180907-story.html.

2   Gabrielle Fonrouge and Ruth Brown, "Alleged School Shooter Was Abusive to Ex-Girlfriend: Classmate," *New York Post*, February 15, 2018, https://nypost.com/2018/02/15/alleged-school-shooter-was-abusive-to-ex-girlfriend-classmate/.

3   Remy Smidt, "The Florida School Shooting Suspect Snapped Into A Jealous Rage When Another Student Began Dating His Ex-Girlfriend," *BuzzFeed*, February 17, 2018, https://www.buzzfeednews.com/article/remysmidt/cruz.

4   Sarah Rumpf, "The Broward Sheriff's Juvenile Arrest Conspiracy Might Actually Be True," RedState.com, February 27, 2018, https://www.redstate.com/sarah-rumpf/2018/02/27/the-broward-sheriffs-juvenile-arrest-conspiracy-might-actually-be-true/.

5   Curt Devine and Jose Pagliery, "Sheriff Says He Got 23 Calls about Shooter's Family, but Records Show More," CNN, February 27, 2018, https://www.cnn.com/2018/02/27/us/parkland-shooter-cruz-sheriff-calls-invs/index.html.

6   Citing a laundry list of grievances, Broward Sheriff's Office Deputies Association President Jeff Bell held a vote in April of 2018. Eighty-five percent of deputies expressed "no confidence" in Israel's leadership, Once, when accused of corruption, Israel commented only, "Lions don't care about the opinions of sheep." When asked for comment about the opinions of his deputies, Israel said, "I will not be distracted from my duties by this inconsequential…union vote, which was designed to extort a 6.5 percent pay raise from this agency." In response, Bell commented, "The sheriff is a complete liar, capital letters on that."

7   Robby Soave, "When Broward County Sheriff Scott Israel Was Accused of Corruption, He Responded: 'Lions Don't Care About the Opinions of Sheep," *Reason,* February 23, 2018, https://reason.com/blog/2018/02/23/broward-county-sheriff-scott-israel-accu; Terry Spencer, "Union Votes No-Confidence in Sheriff After School Massacre," *Washington Post,* April 26, 2018, https://www.washingtonpost.com/national/union-no-confidence-in-sheriff-after-school-massacre/2018/04/26/1416e1fa-4993-11e8-8082-105a446d19b8_story.html?utm_term=.8309ce6f22bb.

8   Remy Smidt, "The Florida School Shooting Suspect Snapped Into A Jealous Rage When Another Student Began Dating His Ex-Girlfriend," *BuzzFeed*, February 17, 2018, https://www.buzzfeednews.com/article/remysmidt/cruz.

9   Remy Smidt, "The Florida School Shooting Suspect Snapped Into A Jealous Rage When Another Student Began Dating His Ex-Girlfriend," *BuzzFeed*, February 17, 2018, https://www.buzzfeednews.com/article/remysmidt/cruz.

10 Twitter,https://twitter.com/ArianaLopez_MSD/status/1067862435728642049.

11 Kim Greene, "Leadership Profile: Robert Runcie," *Scholastic*, Summer 2014, http://www.scholastic.com/browse/article.jsp?id=3758419.

Chapter 7

1   Carol Marbin Miller, "Authorities Considered Committing Future School Killer Nikolas Cruz. Here's Why They Didn't," *Miami Herald*, March 20, 2018, https://www.miamiherald.com/news/local/community/broward/article205972224.html.

2   Ibid.

3   Patricia Mazzei, "School Officials Wanted Florida Gunman Committed Long Before a Massacre," *New York Times*, March 18, 2018, https://www.nytimes.com/2018/03/18/us/nikolas-cruz-baker-act.html.

4   Only 1 percent of individuals who are Baker Acted end up being adjudicated as mentally defective and lose their right to buy guns. We have tried to steer clear of either side in the gun control debate. But everyone agrees that dangerous psychopaths should not be allowed to buy guns. If we make it impossible to label someone as a dangerous psychopath, we are going to continue to have a major gun problem. Anyone who calls mental health "a distraction" from gun control should have their head examined.

5   Florida Department of Children and Families, Case of Nikolas Cruz, http://www.myflfamilies.com/press-release/dcf-records-nikolas-cruz-was-receiving-mental-health-services-taking-medication-and.

6   Public Safety Commission, "Marjory Stoneman Douglas High School Public Safety Commission," *Florida Trend*, January 2 2019, https://www.floridatrend.com/public/userfiles/news/pdfs/MSD-Commission-Report-Public-Version-UPDATED.pdf.

7   David Fleshler and Brittany Wallman, "More Than 30 People Didn't Report Disturbing Behavior by Nikolas Cruz Before Parkland Massacre," November 13, 2018, https://www.sun-sentinel.com/local/broward/parkland/florida-school-shooting/fl-ne-florida-school-shooting-fdle-day-1-story.html.

8   Nicholas Nehamas, "Parkland Shooter Had a Friend. She Was 13 and Lived Across the Country," *Miami Herald*, October 19, 2018, https://www.miamiherald.com/news/local/community/broward/article220328395.html.

9   Megan O'Matz and Stephen Hobbs, "Parkland Shooter Trespassed at Stoneman Douglas Months Before the Shooting," *Sun Sentinel*, October 12, 2018, https://www.sun-sentinel.com/local/broward/parkland/florida-school-shooting/fl-sfl-school-shooting-cruz-trespass-20181012-story.html.

10 Nicholas Nehamas and Sarah Blaskey, "'I'm Going to Watch You Bleed': Nikolas Cruz Threatened Ex's New Boyfriend, Report Says," *Miami Herald*, February 17, 2017, https://www.miamiherald.com/news/local/community/broward/article200735914.html.

11 Brittany Wallman and Megan O'Matz, "Broken Relationship Haunts Brothers Nikolas and Zachary Cruz," *Sun Sentinel,* April 16, 2018, https://www.sun-sentinel.com/local/broward/parkland/florida-school-shooting/fl-sb-florida-school-shooter-brothers-20180404-story.html.

12 Monique O. Madan, "Before Massacre, Nikolas Cruz Threatened to Shoot His Brother over a Jar of Nutella," *Miami Herald,* May 17, 2018, https://www.miamiherald.com/news/local/community/broward/article211203119.html.

13 Chris Lyons, "Summary of Social Media Posts and Witness Interviews Showing Prior Unreported Knowledge of Cruz's Behavior," Presentation at the MSD Public Safety Commission, Tuesday, November 13, 2018, http://www.fdle.state.fl.us/MSDHS/Meetings/November-Meeting-Documents/MSDHS-Meeting-Agenda-Nov-13-16-FINAL-(1).aspx.

14 Monique O. Madan, "Before Massacre, Nikolas Cruz Threatened to Shoot His Brother over a Jar of Nutella," *Miami Herald,* May 17, 2018, https://www.miamiherald.com/news/local/community/broward/article211203119.html.

15 Ibid.

16 Statement of Mary Hamel to the police.

17 *Washington Post* Staff, "Red Flags: The Troubled Path of Accused Parkland Shooter Nikolas Cruz," *Washington Post,* March 10, 2018, https://www.washingtonpost.com/graphics/2018/national/timeline-parkland-shooter-nikolas-cruz/?utm_term=.ffa7f61d4296.

18 Megan O'Matz, David Fleshler and Stephen Hobbs, "Deputies Faulted over Parkland Shooter Tips, But Neither One Is Fired," *Sun Sentinel,* September 7, 2018, https://www.sun-sentinel.com/local/broward/parkland/florida-school-shooting/fl-school-shooter-broward-deputies-disciplined-20180907-story.html.

19 FBI Deputy Director David Bowdich later testified to the U.S. Senate that if Cruz had had an arrest record, then, at least in theory, the FBI would have linked the threat to an individual and taken some action.

20 Senate Judiciary Committee, "See Something, Say Something: Oversight of the Parkland Shooting and Legislative Proposals to Improve School Safety," March 14, 2018, https://www.judiciary.senate.gov/meetings/see-something-say-something-oversight-of-the-parkland-shooting-and-legislative-proposals-to-improve-school-safety.

21 E-mail from James Snead to Jeff Morford, "Nikolas Jacob Cruz," December 4, 2017. On file with authors.

22 Scott Travis, "Scathing Report Paints Unfair Picture of Stoneman Douglas Assistant Principals, Lawyer Says," *Sun Sentinel,* February 19, 2019, https://www.sun-sentinel.com/local/broward/parkland/florida-school-shooting/fl-ne-stoneman-douglas-assistant-principals-letter-20190219-story.html.

Chapter 8

1 This chapter draws heavily upon witness statements given to the Broward County Sheriff's Office and the Florida Department of Law Enforcement which have been acquired via public records requests. It also draws upon presentations

by investigators from the MSD Public Safety Commission on November 13–15, 2018, as well as the final report published on January 2, 2019. Full report can be accessed online here: http://www.fdle.state.fl.us/MSDHS/Meetings/2019/January/Documents/MSD-Report-Public-Version.aspx?fbclid=IwAR12x-a8k9YycpSfAoZsoXzt2wxvsUFpEnw2_hj04lAa0F-KMGTirJ1KG-ns.

2   Andrew Medina, first statement to the Broward sheriff's office the day of the shooting. All statements by Andrew Medina are taken from his comments to the police the day of the shooting.

3   Full video of Andrew Medina's sworn statement to the Broward Sheriff's Office can be viewed online. Amy Rock, "2 Stoneman Douglas Security Monitors Reassigned, Criticized for Response," Campus Safety, June 7, 2018, https://www.campussafetymagazine.com/safety/stoneman-douglas-security-monitors/.

4   Lisa J. Huriash, "Retired Secret Service Agent had Warned Stoneman Douglas About Security Failures," *Sun Sentinel*, June 8, 2018, https://www.sun-sentinel.com/local/broward/parkland/florida-school-shooting/fl-sb-douglas-secret-service-steve-wexler-20180605-story.html. Later training indicated that anyone could call a Code Red, but staff evinced confusion on this count when interviewed by the Florida Department of Law Enforcement. Andrew Medina recalls being told that it should only be called if you see a gun; David Taylor recalled something similar though less categorical. It is astonishing that multiple campus security monitors who either knew or suspected that there was an active shooting refused to call a Code Red. The MSD Commission report considered this a system failure, rooted in bad policy and training.

5   The details of the law enforcement response in this chapter come from the presentation made by Pinellas County Sheriff's Deputy John Suess at the November 14, 2018, meeting of the MSD Public Safety Commission, accessed November 29, 2018. http://www.fdle.state.fl.us/MSDHS/Meetings/November-Meeting-Documents/Nov-14-100pm-Law-Enforcement-Response-John-Suess.aspx.

6   Bob Norman, "Broward County Sheriff Scott Israel's Photo Taken Off Official Cars," News Channel 10, September 29, 2015, https://www.local10.com/news/florida/broward/broward-county-sheriff-scott-israels-photo-taken-off-official-cars-.

7   Charles Bethea, "The Troubled Tenure of Scott Israel, Sheriff of Broward County," *The New Yorker*, March 16, 2018, https://www.newyorker.com/news/news-desk/the-troubled-tenure-of-scott-israel-sheriff-of-broward-county.

8   Marjory Stoneman Douglas High School Public Safety Commission Meeting, Remarks by Sheriff Israel, November 15, 2018, http://www.fdle.state.fl.us/MSDHS/Meetings/2018/November-Meeting-Documents/11-15-18.aspx.

9   Later, Sunrise Police Officer Cardinale arrived on the scene and spotted several BSO deputies at the gate. "Don't go in," one told him, "the shooter's in that building right there," Carindale's son was in the building. "Fuck you," Cardinale responded, "I'm going in." He entered and helped triage the wounded for medical attention. His son was unharmed.

10 Nicholas Nehamas et al., "'The Cavalry Is Here, I Can Let Go': Inside the Long Wait for Help at Parkland Massacre," *Miami Herald,* December 19, 2018, https://www.miamiherald.com/news/local/community/broward/article223332970.html.

11 The MSD Public Safety Commission noted that "The Broward County Public School's decision not to allow law enforcement live and real-time direct access to the school camera systems in Broward County, including the system at MSDHS, severely affected law enforcement efforts to locate Cruz and delayed victim rescue efforts." The commission recommended that all school districts in Florida should allow police real-time direct access and provide them with training on how to use it. At the beginning of the next school year, Broward County School District's Chief of School Performance and Accountability Valerie Wanza, wrote a memo to clarify that it would not change its policy position. In cases of "eminent [*sic*] threat," Wanza wrote, "law enforcement is permitted to view school video surveillance in the presence of school employees.... Requests for copies of video footage must be made through the subpoena process."

12 Megan O'Matz and Lisa Huriash, "More Medics Kept Asking to Go in and Rescue Wounded at Stoneman Doulgas. They Kept Being Told No." *Sun Sentinel,* May 31, 2018, https://www.sun-sentinel.com/local/broward/parkland/florida-school-shooting/fl-school-shooting-paramedics-entry-20180531-story.html.

Chapter 9

1 "Superintendent Faces Criticism as Parkland Students Return to School," CBS News, August 17, 2018, https://www.cbsnews.com/news/marjory-stoneman-douglas-high-school-robert-runcie-broward-county-superintendent-faces-criticism/.

2 Ross Brenneman, "Revolutionizing School Discipline, With a Flowchart," Education Week, November 5, 2013, https://blogs.edweek.org/edweek/rulesforengagement/2013/11/a_flowchart_to_revolutionize_school_discipline_broward.html.

3 Ibid.

4 Greg Allen, "Fla. School District Trying to Curb School-to-Prison Pipeline," Code Switch, November 5, 2013, https://www.npr.org/sections/codeswitch/2013/11/05/243250817/fla-school-district-trying-to-curb-school-to-prison-pipeline.

5 Lizette Alvarez, "Seeing the Toll, Schools Revisit Zero Tolerance," *New York Times,* December 3, 2013, https://www.nytimes.com/2013/12/03/education/seeing-the-toll-schools-revisit-zero-tolerance.html.

6 Kim Greene, "Leadership Profile: Robert Runcie," Scholastic, Summer 2014, http://www.scholastic.com/browse/article.jsp?id=3758419.

7 The Broad Center, "Robert Runcie—An Unconventional Path," Leadership Lessons (blog), January 30, 2018, https://www.broadcenter.org/blog/leadership-lessons-robert-runcie/.

8   Arne Duncan, "Rethinking School Discipline," speech delivered at the Academies at Frederick Douglass High School, Baltimore, Jan. 8, 2014

9   Broward County Public Schools, "SBBC Workshop 6-19-18," accessed November 13, 2018, https://becon.eduvision.tv/Default.aspx?q=d0F7qPKKl cfzu2JffePz9A%3d%3d.

10 Caroline Glenn, "Blackburn Says He Did Not Seek Out CEO Job, Rebuts Speculation Behind His Resignation," *Florida Today*, May 15, 2018, https://www. floridatoday.com/story/news/2018/05/15/departing-brevard-superinten-dent-blackburn-says-he-did-not-seek-out-ceo-job-rebuts-speculation-be-hin/612424002/.

11 Mrs. Pangrace and Mr. Parks both spoke to the authors on condition of anonymity, for fear of professional retaliation. Interview with Mrs. Pangrace took place on May 2, 2018, and interview with Mr. Parks took place on May 16, 2018.

12 Discipline Matrix, Broward County school district, accessed February 2, 2019, https://www.browardschools.com/cms/lib/FL01803656/Centricity/Shared/ Discipline_Matrix_Secondary_2015.pdf

13 Alice B. Lloyd, "The Broward Blame-Game," *Weekly Standard*, April 13, 2018, https://www.weeklystandard.com/alice-b-lloyd/the-broward-blame-game.

14 "Policy 5006: Discipline Policy: Suspension and Expulsion, 2017–2020," Broward County Public Schools, accessed October 5, 2018, https://web01. browardschools.com/sbbcpolicies/docs/Policy%205006.pdf.

15 Ian Schwartz, "Ingraham: 'PROMISE Program' Hailed by Obama Admin Led to Florida Schools Ignoring Violent Students, RealClearPolitics, March 5, 2018, https://www.realclearpolitics.com/video/2018/03/05/ingraham_prom-ise_program_hailed_by_obama_admin_led_to_florida_schools_ignoring _violent_students.html.

16 Robert Runcie, "Schools Chief: Focusing on Safety and Security, and Toppling "Fake News" *Sun Sentinel*, March 23, 2018, https://www.sun-sentinel.com/ opinion/commentary/fl-op-viewpoint-broward-school-security-safety-mea-sures-20180323-story.html.

17 Broward County School Board et al., "Collaborative Agreement on School Discipline," October 5, 2016, https://www.scribd.com/document/372308388/ Broward-County-Promise-Program-Fully-Executed-Collaborative-Agree-ment-Final-Document.

18 Ibid.

19 Ian Schwartz, "Ingraham: 'PROMISE Program' Hailed by Obama Admin Led to Florida Schools Ignoring Violent Students," RealClearPolitics, March 5, 2018, https://www.realclearpolitics.com/video/2018/03/05/ingraham_promise _program_hailed_by_obama_admin_led_to_florida_schools_ignoring_violent_ students.html.

20 Broward County Public Schools, "PROMISE PSA," https://becon. eduvision.tv/default.aspx?q=CT1wecDsedAjQ95jhcPGOA%253d%253d&f-bclid=IwAR110PbOdScSnCdxXlZy_3tbRk2d60SgWK9PJHHRlC65FU-Osd-Mlftwgd5w.

21 Juvenile Justice Circuit Advisory Board, "Judicial Circuit 17 Juvenile Justice Circuit Advisory Board Meeting Minutes," January 10, 2018.

22 Juvenile Justice Circuit Advisory Board, "Judicial Circuit 17 Juvenile Justice Circuit Advisory Board Meeting Minutes," February 14, 2018.

23 Paul Sperry, "Broward County's Reverse Jail-to-School Pipeline," RealClear-Investigations, March 16, 2018, https://www.realclearinvestigations.com/articles/2018/03/16/broward_countys_jail-to-classroom_pipeline.html.

24 After this policy became the subject of controversy, the school district removed it from its website. A copy of the policy is on file with the authors.

25 "Behavior Management System, 2015–2016," Cypress Run Education Center, accessed October 5, 2018, http://www.broward.k12.fl.us/ospa/ospa-central2/_sip_plan_evidence/2017/2123_01272016_School-Behavior-Management-System.pdf.

26 Paul Sperry, "Broward County's Reverse Jail-to-School Pipeline," RealClear-Investigations, March 16, 2018, https://www.realclearinvestigations.com/articles/2018/03/16/broward_countys_jail-to-classroom_pipeline.html.

27 Broward County Public Schools, "SBBC Workshop 06-17-14," https://becon.eduvision.tv/Default.aspx?q=d0F7qPKKlcfzu2JffePz9A%3d%3d.

28 U.S. Department of Civil Rights and U.S. Department of Education, "Joint 'Dear Colleague' Letter," January 8, 2014, https://www2.ed.gov/about/offices/list/ocr/letters/colleague-201401-title-vi.pdf.

29 Max Eden, "Enforcing Classroom Disorder: Trump Has Not Called Off Obama's War on School Discipline," Manhattan Institute, August 13, 2018, https://www.manhattan-institute.org/html/enforcing-classroom-disorder-trump-has-not-called-obamas-war-school-discipline-11407.html.

30 American Association of School Administrators, "2018 AASA Discipline Survey: An Analysis of How the 2014 Dear Colleague Letter on Nondiscriminatory Administration of School Discipline Is Impacting District Policies and Practices," accessed October 5, 2018, http://aasa.org/uploadedFiles/AASA_Blog(1)/AASASurveyDisciplineGuidance2014.pdf.

31 Max Eden, "Enforcing Classroom Disorder: Trump Has Not Called Off Obama's War on School Discipline," Manhattan Institute, August 13, 2018, https://www.manhattan-institute.org/html/enforcing-classroom-disorder-trump-has-not-called-obamas-war-school-discipline-11407.html.

32 American Association of School Administrators, "2018 AASA Discipline Survey: An Analysis of How the 2014 Dear Colleague Letter on Nondiscriminatory Administration of School Discipline Is Impacting District Policies and Practices," accessed October 5, 2018, http://aasa.org/uploadedFiles/AASA_Blog(1)/AASASurveyDisciplineGuidance2014.pdf.

33 Annysa Johnson, "MPS Agrees to Settle U.S. Civil Rights Complaint over Discipline of Black Students," *Milwaukee Journal Sentinel*, January 17, 2018, https://www.jsonline.com/story/news/education/2018/01/17/mps-enters-into-agreement-feds-settle-civil-rights-complaint-over-alleged-discrimination-against-bla/1039370001/.

34 Elizabeth Doran, "DA: Syracuse Schools Must Drop Changes Made that Cut Suspensions, Get Tough on Discipline," Syracuse.com, May 26, 2017, https://www.syracuse.com/schools/index.ssf/2017/05/syracuse_school _district_needs_to_get_tougher_on_discipline_pledge_schools_will.html.

35 Katherine Kersten, "Undisciplined: Chaos May Be Coming to Minnesota Classrooms, By Decree," *Star Tribune*, March 19, 2018, http://www.startribune. com/undisciplined-chaos-may-be-coming-to-minnesota-classrooms-by-de-cree/477145923/.

36 Susan Berry, "Broward Superintendent Blasted over Cruz Shooting: 'We Hadn't Really Thought How We Would Plan for Something Like this," *Breitbart*, April 19, 2018, https://www.breitbart.com/politics/2018/04/19/broward-superin-tendent-blasted-cruz-shooting-hadnt-really-thought-plan-something-like/.

37 The Leadership Conference on Civil and Human Rights et al., "Letter to Secretary DeVos: Preserve the School Discipline Guidance," March 22, 2018, https://civilrights.org/letter-to-secretary-devos-preserve-the-school -discipline-guidance/.

38 Tim Willert, "Many Oklahoma City School District Teachers Criticize Disci-pline Policies in Survey," *The Oklahoman*, October 31, 2015, https://newsok. com/article/5457335/many-oklahoma-city-school-district-teachers-criti-cize-discipline-policies-in-survey.

39 Kiran Chawla, "I-Team: Classrooms of Fear," WAFB9, April 25, 2014, http:// www.wafb.com/story/25335469/i-team-classrooms-of-fear/.

40 Laura Frazier, "Portland Teachers Feel Classroom Environment Is Unsafe, According to Union Survey," *The Oregonian*, September 1, 2015, https://www. oregonlive.com/education/index.ssf/2015/09/some_portland_teachers _feel_cl.html.

41 Jackson Federation of Teachers, Paraprofessionals and School Related Personnel, "S.O.S.: Reclaiming the Promise of Great Public Schools in Jackson Through Common-Sense Student Discipline," accessed August 3, 2018, http:// www.jftpsrp.com/uploads/5/5/2/6/55262373/sos_discipline_report.pdf.

42 Denver Classroom Teachers Association, "DCTA Discipline Survey," Colorado Public Radio, accessed August 3, 2018, https://www.cpr.org/sites/default/files/ discipline_survey_results_3.15_-_all.pdf.

43 Julie McMahon, "Syracuse Schools Staff Feel Helpless in Face of Threats, Violence, Union Survey Says," Syracuse.com, December 10, 2015, https://www. syracuse.com/schools/index.ssf/2015/12/syracuse_teachers_asssociation_ survey_safety_violence.html.

44 Denver Classroom Teachers Association, "DCTA Discipline Survey," Colorado Public Radio, accessed August 3, 2018, https://www.cpr.org/sites/default/files/ discipline_survey_results_3.15_-_all.pdf.

45 Madison Teachers Inc., "Joint Committee on Safety and Discipline Survey," May 13, 2015, http://www.madisonteachers.org/wp-content/uploads/2015/05/ Joint-Committee-on-Safety-and-Discipline-Report-051315.pdf.

46 Charleston Teacher Alliance, "CTA Winter Survey 2017," accessed August 3, 2018, http://www.charlestonteacheralliance.com/uploads/3/0/5/9/30595451/ ctadata_all_170224.pdf.

47 Oklahoma City AFT Local 2309, "Survey Shows Educators Are Feeling Stressed Out," accessed August 3, 2018, http://okcaft.ok.aft.org/news/survey-shows-educators-are-feeling-stressed-out

48 Abigail Gray et al., "Discipline in Context: Suspension, Climate, and PBIS in the School District of Philadelphia," Consortium for Policy Research in Education, October 2017, http://www.cpre.org/sites/default/files/v2_cpre_disco_rr2017_4.pdf.

49 Oklahoma City AFT Local 2309, "Survey Shows Educators Are Feeling Stressed Out," accessed August 3, 2018, http://okcaft.ok.aft.org/.

50 Buffalo Teachers Federation, "Disruptive Behavior Results 2018," January 29, 2018, http://www.btfny.org/press/disruptive_behavior_results_2018.pdf.

51 Mackenzie Mays, "As Expulsions, Suspensions Decrease at Fresno Schools, Concerns about Out-of-Control Classrooms Grow," *Fresno Bee*, December 16, 2015, http://www.fresnobee.com/news/local/education/eye-on-education/article49482150.html.

52 Max Eden, "Investigation: In NYC School Where a Teenager Was Killed, Students & Educators Say Lax Discipline Led to Bullying, Chaos, and Death," *The 74*, June 11, 2018, https://www.the74million.org/article/investigation-in-new-york-city-school-where-a-teenager-was-killed-students-educators-say-lax-discipline-led-to-bullying-chaos-and-death/.

53 Erica L. Green, "Why Are Black Students Punished So Often? Minnesota Confronts a National Quandary," *New York Times*, March 18, 2018, https://www.nytimes.com/2018/03/18/us/politics/school-discipline-disparities-white-black-students.html.

54 Broward County Public Schools, "SBBC Meeting 10-5-16," https://becon.eduvision.tv/Default.aspx?q=d0F7qPKKlcfmtjfULqo9AQ%253d%253d.

Chapter 10

1 Megan O'Matz and Scott Travis, "Schools' Culture of Tolerance Lets Students Like Nikolas Cruz Slide," *Sun Sentinel*, May 12, 2018, https://www.sun-sentinel.com/local/broward/parkland/florida-school-shooting/fl-florida-school-shooting-discipline-20180510-story.html.

2 Ibid.

3 Mike Clary, "Cops Doubt Story from 7th-Graders Found with Gun, Knives at School," *Sun Sentinel*, March 25, 2015, https://www.sun-sentinel.com/local/broward/fort-lauderdale/fl-sunrise-middle-search-warrant-20150325-story.html.

4 Carli Teproff, "17-year-old Arrested After Bringing Loaded Gun to Former High School," *Miami Herald*, October 20, 2016. https://www.miamiherald.com/news/local/community/broward/article107398377.html.

5 Broward County Public Schools, "SBBC Workshop 06-19-18," https://becon.eduvision.tv/Default.aspx?q=d0F7qPKKlcfmtjfULqo9AQ%253d%253d.

6 Gateway Pundit, "Did Broward County Sheriff Israel's Son Get Special Treatment after Brutal School Crime? Sure Looks That Way," *Tea Party*, May 11, 2018, https://www.teaparty.org/broward-county-sheriff-israels-son-get-special-treatment-brutal-school-crime-sure-looks-way-304314/.

7 Bob Norman, "Parents Call for Investigation into Stoneman Douglas Assault Involving Sheriff's Son," WPLG Local10.com, May 25, 2018, https://www.local10.com/news/local-10-investigates/parents-call-for-investigation-into-marjory-stoneman-douglas-high-assault-involving-sheriffs-son.

8 Scott Travis, Megan O'Matz, and John Maines, "Broward School District Failing to Report Many Campus Crimes to State as Required," *Sun Sentinel*, June 8, 2018, https://www.sun-sentinel.com/local/broward/parkland/florida-school-shooting/fl-florida-school-shooting-discipline-reporting-20180607-story.html.

9 Donald Campbell, cited in Jerry Z. Muller, *The Tyranny of Metrics* (Princeton: Princeton University Press, 2018), https://www.amazon.com/Tyranny-Metrics-Jerry-Z-Muller/dp/0691174954.

10 *The Wire*, "Dead Soldiers," Season Three, Episode Three, Directed by Rob Bailey, HBO, October 3, 2004.

11 Rowan Moore Gerety, "How Miami-Dade Schools Made Thousands of Fights Disappear," WLRN, June 14, 2017, http://www.wlrn.org/post/how-miami-dade-schools-made-thousands-fights-disappear.

12 "DCTA Discipline Survey," Colorado Public Radio.

13 "Disruptive Behavior Results 2018," Buffalo Teachers Federation.

14 Records provided to us by Kenny Preston.

15 Records provided to us by Alice Lloyd.

16 Scott Travis, "Principals Accuse Teachers Union of Harassment, Sue District for Not Stopping Them," *Sun Sentinel*, April 28, 2018, https://www.sun-sentinel.com/news/education/fl-broward-principals-btu-lawsuit-20180427-story.html.

Chapter 11

1 "SBBC Meeting 10-5-16," Broward County Public Schools, Broward County, Florida, October 5, 2016, https://becon.eduvision.tv/Default.aspx?q=d0F7qPKKlcfmtjfULqo9AQ%253d%253d.

2 Megan O'Matz and Scott Travis, "Schools' Culture of Tolerance Lets Students Like Nikolas Cruz Slide," *Sun Sentinel*, May 12, 2018, https://www.sun-sentinel.com/local/broward/parkland/florida-school-shooting/fl-florida-school-shooting-discipline-20180510-story.html.

3 According to the letter of the PROMISE agreement, the decision of whether marijuana possession constitutes a felony or a PROMISE-eligible misdemeanor is made in consultation between assistant principals and law enforcement. We received records of instances where students caught in possession of more than a dozen bags were sent to PROMISE rather than face any legal consequence.

4 Shelby Webb, "The PROMISE of a Better Way in Broward," *Herald-Tribune*, accessed October 6, 2018, http://expulsions.heraldtribune.com/Chapter/4.

5 Ibid.

6 Lizette Alvarez, "Seeing the Toll, Schools Revisit Zero Tolerance," *New York Times*, December 2, 2013, https://www.nytimes.com/2013/12/03/education/

seeing-the-toll-schools-revisit-zero-tolerance.html; Russell Simmons and Gabourey Sidibe, Prison Kids, A Crime Against America's Children, directed by Alissa Figueroa, October 2015.

7 Broward County Public Schools Special Investigation Unit, "Investigative Report Concerning Belinda Hope 16/17-123, Principal, Pine Ridge Education Center," June 6, 2017.

Chapter 12

1 "Superintendent Faces Criticism as Parkland Students Return to School," CBS News, August 17, 2018, https://www.cbsnews.com/news/marjory-stoneman-douglas-high-school-robert-runcie-broward-county-superintendent-faces-criticism/.

2 Jessica Bakeman, "Stoneman Douglas Shooter Was Assigned to Controversial Broward Discipline Program, Officials Now Say," WLRN, May 6, 2018, http://www.wlrn.org/post/stoneman-douglas-shooter-was-assigned-controversial-broward-discipline-program-officials-now.

3 Broward County School Board, "PROMISE Community Workshop," May 7, 2018, https://becon.eduvision.tv/directplayer.aspx?q=CT1wecDsedColHhAUa aS9J9jQS%252fNr2VIfXIssa7zFKbv7GppWB72gr%252b-JmZQlSHI%252b&fbclid=IwAR1dyVNiQoCpbeB18pUE42YWCHMyL_OQAjXf49VKft_DePVG3yVWQkpSZuQ.

4 Tom Lauder, "Black Elected Officials Accuse Broward School Chair Nora Rupert of Using Parkland Tragedy to Attack Fellow School Board Members," RedBroward.com, May 27, 2018, https://redbroward.com/2018/05/27/black-elected-officials-accuse-broward-school-chair-nora-rupert-of-using-parkland-tragedy-to-attack-fellow-school-board-members/.

5 Lois K. Solomon, "Broward Black Officials Voice Support for Runcie and Promise Program," *Sun Sentinel*, May 25, 2018, https://www.sun-sentinel.com/local/broward/parkland/florida-school-shooting/fl-florida-school-shooting-black-officials-20180525-story.html.

6 Chris Joseph, "Ann Murray, Former School Board Member Busted for Using N-Word, Running for Reelection," *New Times Broward-Palm Beach*, July 22, 2014, https://www.browardpalmbeach.com/news/ann-murray-former-school-board-member-busted-for-using-n-word-running-for-reelection-6468105.

7 Broward County Public Schools, "SBBC Workshop, 06-19-18," https://becon.eduvision.tv/Default.aspx?q=d0F7qPKKlcfmtjfULqo9AQ%253d%253d.

8 BBEO Inc.'s Brian C. Johnson felt comfortable calling Ryan Petty, who lost his daughter Alaina in the shooting and was running for the school board to address the district's safety problems, a "flagrant racist" on the basis of a handful of out-of-context tweets provided to the *Sun Sentinel* by Petty's political opponent. Ryan Petty is a great man with nothing but love in his heart, and the smear campaign launched against him reflects solely on the morally challenged character of the Broward political establishment.

9 Almost a year after the tragedy, Andy and other parents of the victims met with Broward County State Attorney Mike Satz to raise their concerns about the implementation of the PROMISE program. Satz told them that he was

aware that the school district encourages under-reporting and under-charging criminal offenses, that the school district was operating in breach of the official agreement and not in good faith and characterized the district's actions as "obstruction of justice." When the families asked him to do something about it, he said that the most he could possibly do is send a letter to Runcie with recommendations. Anything more than that, he said, was politically untenable for him because he'd run the risk of being falsely labeled a racist.

Chapter 13

1   *Today*, "Parkland Officer Scot Peterson: 'I Never Thought of Being Scared,'" NBC, June 5, 2018, https://www.today.com/video/parkland-officer-scot-peterson-i-never-thought-of-being-scared-1248443459562.

2   Scott Stump, "Parents of Parkland Victims React to School Officer: 'He Doesn't Get My Sympathy,'" *Today*, June 7, 2018, https://www.today.com/news/parents-parkland-victims-react-school-officer-he-doesn-t-get-t130417.

3   Lisa J. Huriash, "Retired Secret Service Agent Had Warned Stoneman Douglas About Security Failures," *Sun Sentinel*, June 8, 2018, https://www.sun-sentinel.com/local/broward/parkland/florida-school-shooting/fl-sb-douglas-secret-service-steve-wexler-20180605-story.html.

4   David Fleshler, "School District Shuts Down Information after Stoneman Douglas Shooting," *Sun Sentinel*, May 11, 2018, https://www.sun-sentinel.com/local/broward/parkland/florida-school-shooting/fl-florida-school-shooting-district-stonewalling-20180510-story.html.

5   Joan Murray, "Runcie Recommends Comprehensive Review of Nikolas Cruz's Education," CBS Miami, March 6, 2018, https://miami.cbslocal.com/2018/03/06/runcie-nikolas-cruzs-education-reviews/.

6   Carey Codd, "Redacted Educational Records of Parkland Shooter Released," CBS Miami, August 3, 2018, https://miami.cbslocal.com/2018/08/03/hearing-on-release-of-confessed-parkland-shooters-school-records/.

7   Brittany Wallman, Megan O'Matz, and Paula McMahon, "Hide, Spin, Deny, Threaten: How the School District Tried to Mask the Failures that Led to the Parkland Shooting," *Sun Sentinel*, November 30, 2018, https://www.sun-sentinel.com/local/broward/parkland/florida-school-shooting/fl-florida-school-shooting-district-secrecy-20181112-story.html.

8   Ibid.

9   If Travis had been allowed to attend the graduation, he could have reported that the families and friends of the slain booed when a video message recorded by Runcie was introduced.

10 Bernie Woodall, "Florida Shooting Suspect Qualifies for Public Defender, Judge Rules," *U.S. Legal News*, April 24, 2018, https://www.reuters.com/article/us-usa-guns-florida-cruz/florida-shooting-suspect-qualifies-for-public-defender-judge-rules-idUSKBN1HV2K4.

11 Robert Spence, "Investigative Report Concerning Andrew Medina, Campus Monitor Marjory Stoneman Douglas High School," Broward County School Board Special Investigative Unit, May 14, 2017.

12 Scott Travis, "Runcie: HR Director Made Call to Keep Coach Accused of Sexual Harassment," *Sun Sentinel*, June 19, 2018, https://www.sun-sentinel.com/local/broward/parkland/florida-school-shooting/fl-florida-school-shooting-medina-runcie-20180619-story.html.

13 Scott Travis, *Twitter*, https://twitter.com/smtravis/status/1085332798003654658.

14 Scott Travis, "Runcie: HR Director Made Call to Keep Coach Accused of Sexual Harassment," *Sun Sentinel*, June 19, 2018, https://www.sun-sentinel.com/local/broward/parkland/florida-school-shooting/fl-florida-school-shooting-medina-runcie-20180619-story.html.

15 Ryan Petty posted a letter from a Maryland mother on his Twitter account suggesting that students should "walk up, not out," i.e., reach out to socially isolated peers rather than walk out of school in a post-Parkland protest. It went viral and for a day or two appealed to almost everyone. But then came the torrent of Twitter hatred for trying to "distract from gun control." Disappointed but determined, Ryan created the WalkUp Foundation to encourage more kindness. His campaign was then attacked in many opinion articles. At times, it seemed like literally everything, from understanding what went wrong in Parkland to even promoting human compassion, was attacked by the media as a threat to the gun control agenda.

16 One additional story worth relating: 18-1958's brother Zachary gave the community a huge scare when he trespassed on MSD's campus six weeks after the shooting. When Runcie was asked how Zachary Cruz got on campus, he insisted that there had been no security breach. But it turned out that Zachary skateboarded through an open gate, past a sheriff's deputy, Moises Carotti, who was asleep in his car. According to the *Sun Sentinel*, the sheriff's official review of the incident found: "The Cruz incident ended about 4:50 p.m., the report says. At 5:15 p.m., the report says an unidentified student caught the attention of Sheriff's Office Sgt. Greg Lacerra, pointed at Carotti asleep in his patrol and shouted, "Is this how you guys do stuff here at BSO?"... A YouTube.com video had been playing on Carotti's laptop when he was found, but the report didn't say what he had been watching."

17 Anne Geggis, "Fired: Deputy Found Sleeping at Stoneman Douglas After Shooting," *Sun Sentinel*, September 7, 2018, https://www.sun-sentinel.com/local/broward/parkland/florida-school-shooting/fl-florida-school-shooting-sleeping-deputy-20180907-story.html.

18 In late November 2018, the MSD Public Safety Commission disclosed what they found about the actions of school administrators leading up to the tragedy. They found less than we did, but it was enough for the district to finally do *something:* temporarily reassign Assistant Principals Reed, Morford, and Porter as well as security specialist Kelvin Greenleaf, pending an investigation. his part, Ty Thompson helped to lead a student protest against this small sliver of accountability. During the protest, Thompson was asked whether he was familiar with the findings of the commission. He replied, "I've listened to some of it. I refuse to listen to all of it just because."

19 Carey Codd, "MSD Principal 'Outraged' At Reassignment of Assistant Principals, School Security Specialist," CBS Miami, November 27, 2018, https://miami.cbslocal.com/2018/11/27/msd-principal-outraged-at-reassignment/.

Chapter 14

1 Nancy Smith, "Democrat Nan Rich's Enduring, Families-First Rise in Florida Politics," *Sunshine State News*, November 26, 2013, http://sunshinestatenews.com/story/democrat-nan-richs-enduring-families-first-rise-florida-politics.

2 *Sun Sentinel* Editorial Board, "Put Laurie Rich Levinson, Who Supports the Schools Superintendent, Back on the School Board," *Sun Sentinel*, August 7, 2018, https://www.sun-sentinel.com/opinion/fl-op-editorial-laurie-rich-levinson-broward-school-board-20180807-story.html.

3 Martin Vassolo and Colleen Wright, "Parents of Slain Parkland Teens Want to Work with Runcie on School Board," *Miami Herald*, May 15, 2018, https://www.miamiherald.com/news/local/community/broward/article211119744.html.

4 Kyle Kashuv and Kenneth Preston, "Broward Superintendent Runcie: A Strong Case for His Dismissal," *Daily Wire*, May 31, 2018, https://www.dailywire.com/news/31318/kashuv-preston-broward-superintendent-runcie-kyle-kashuv.

5 Scott Travis, "Teachers Union Not Endorsing Any Candidate with Ties to Stoneman Douglas," *Sun Sentinel*, July 12, 2018, https://www.sun-sentinel.com/news/education/fl-reg-btu-endorsements-parkland-20180711-story.html.

6 Tom Lauder, "Broward Teachers Union gave $155k to Shadowy Group Tied to SEIU and Voter Registration Fraud," Red Broward, November 5, 2018, https://redbroward.com/2018/11/05/btupac/.

7 Reflecting on Runcie's strong political support from Keith Koenig, Broward education gadfly Buddy Nevins wrote in his "Broward Beat" blog two weeks before the school board election: "There is also an ugly subtext to this support for Runcie. The superintendent is black. The lily-white businessmen would never publicly attack a black superintendent. They don't want to be labeled racist. Runcie's weak liberal bosses on the School Board are cowed by him for the same reason. They fear they will be labeled bigoted if they fire him."

8 Buddy Nevins, "Broward Politics: Fight over Schools' Future Part of County's Changing Demographics," BrowardBeat.com, August 15, 2018, https://www.browardbeat.com/broward-politics-fight-over-schools-future-part-of-countys-changing-demographics/; Brittany Wallman, Megan O'Matz, and Paula McMahon, "Hide, Spin, Deny, Threaten: How the School District Tried to Mask the Failures that Led to the Parkland Shooting," November 30, 2018, https://www.sun-sentinel.com/local/broward/parkland/florida-school-shooting/fl-florida-school-shooting-district-secrecy-20181112-story.html.

Chapter 15

1 The *Sun Sentinel*'s coverage reminds us of what journalism can and should be, and also what is tragically being lost as local newspapers downsize and the news media is increasingly dominated by a clickbait competition tied to national flashpoint issues of the week. In particular, Sun Sentinel education

reporter Scott Travis must be singled out for commendation. Without his years of in-depth reporting on the inner workings of the Broward County school district, much of this book would not have been possible to write. And without his reporting after the shooting, the voters of Broward County would have been left in the dark.

2 Scott Travis, "School District Told to Level with Taxpayers about Bond Projects," *Sun Sentinel*, June 29, 2018, https://www.sun-sentinel.com/news/education/fl-broward-school-bond-delays-costs-20180629-story.html.

3 Ibid.

4 Scott Travis, "School Renovations at Risk as Broward Money Runs Low," *Sun Sentinel*, July 24, 2018, https://www.sun-sentinel.com/news/education/fl-broward-schools-bond-money-shortage-20180724-story.html.

5 Scott Travis, "Broward School Board Demands More Updates on $800M Bond Progress," *Sun Sentinel*, August 22, 2018, https://www.sun-sentinel.com/news/education/fl-sb-broward-school-board-bond-report-20180821-story.html.

6 Leo Nesmith was formerly the principal of Lauderhill Middle School, where he was named in a lawsuit against the district for being aware of and not stopping the serial statutory rape of a student. In his role as director of the office of Runcie's chief of staff, he helped manage the school district's safety, security, and facilities issues. In September 2018 he was promoted to director of administrative services.

7 Tonya Alanez, "Lauderhill Middle Staff Ignored Teacher-Student Sex, Lawsuit Claims," *Sun Sentinel*, May 16, 2013, https://www.sun-sentinel.com/news/fl-xpm-2013-05-16-fl-lauderhill-teacher-sex-lawsuit-20130516-story.html.

8 Scott Travis, "Broward School Board Demands More Updates on $800M Bond Progress," *Sun Sentinel*, August 22, 2018, https://www.sun-sentinel.com/news/education/fl-sb-broward-school-board-bond-report-20180821-story.html.

9 Hank Tester, "Broward School Board Votes Down Idea of Arming Teachers, Employees," CBSMiami.com, April 10, 2018, https://miami.cbslocal.com/2018/04/10/broward-school-board-votes-down-arming-teachers/.

10 The Marjory Stoneman Douglas High School Public Safety Act specifically says, "Excluded from participating in the Coach Aaron Feis Guardian Program are individuals who exclusively perform classroom duties as classroom teachers," https://www.flsenate.gov/Session/Bill/2018/7026/BillText/er/pdf.

11 Scott Travis, "Most Applying to Be Broward Armed Guardians Fail to Meet Qualifications," *Sun Sentinel*, July 13, 2018, https://www.sun-sentinel.com/local/broward/parkland/florida-school-shooting/fl-florida-school-shooting-broward-guardians-sros-20180712-story.html.

12 Brittany Wallman, Stephen Hobbs, and Scott Travis, "School District Came Up Short with School Guards, Needed Assist from Fort Lauderdale," *Sun Sentinel*, August 15, 2018, https://www.sun-sentinel.com/local/broward/parkland/florida-school-shooting/fl-sb-school-security-lauderdale-20180814-story.html.

13 Scott Travis, "District Suspends Retired Secret Service Agent's Stoneman Douglas Review," *Sun Sentinel*, August 1, 2018, https://www.sun-sentinel.com/local/broward/parkland/florida-school-shooting/fl-florida-school-shooting-review-suspended-20180801-story.html.

14　Scott Travis, "Metal Detector Plan Scrapped for Stoneman Douglas," *Sun Senti-nel*, August 3, 2018, https://www.sun-sentinel.com/local/broward/parkland /florida-school-shooting/fl-stoneman-douglas-metal-detectors-update-20180802-story.html.

15　Broward County Public Schools, "SBBC Meeting 8-7-18," accessed November 7, 2018, https://becon.eduvision.tv/Default.aspx?q=d0F7qPKKlcfmtjfULqo9AQ %253d%253d.

16　StreamVu Ed, Marjory Stoneman Douglas High, https://view.streamvued.com/ v2api/view/captionsTranscript/14969/84.

17　Broward County Public Schools, "District Statement Regarding Court Ruling to Release the Collaborate Educational Network's Report regarding Niko-las Cruz," August 3, 2018, https://www.browardschools.com/site/default. aspx?PageType=3&DomainID=14019&ModuleInstanceID=60855&ViewID =6446EE88-D30C-497E-9316-3F8874B3E108&RenderLoc=0&Flex DataID=92786&PageID=38282.

18　David Ovalle and Kyra Gurney, "School Probe Finds Little Fault with Handling of Nikolas Cruz; His Lawyers Call it 'Whitewash,'" *Miami Herald*, August 3, 2018, https://www.miamiherald.com/news/local/article216065060.html.

19　Brittany Wallman and Paula McMahon, "Here's What Broward Schools Knew about Parkland Shooter—Details Revealed by Mistake," *Sun Sentinel*, August 3, 2018, https://www.sun-sentinel.com/local/broward/parkland/ florida-school-shooting/fl-florida-school-shooting-consultant-report-full-20180803-story.html.

20　Patricia Mazzei, "Parkland Shooting Suspect Lost Special-Needs Help at School When He Needed It Most," *New York Times*, August 4, 2018, https:// www.nytimes.com/2018/08/04/us/parkland-florida-nikolas-cruz.html.

21　Marc Caputo, Twitter, https://twitter.com/MarcACaputo/status/102970545 1133435904.

22　Scott Travis, "School Board Filed for Contempt against Sun Sentinel—and Then Learned about It in Sun Sentinel," *Sun Sentinel*, August 7, 2018, https:// www.sun-sentinel.com/local/broward/parkland/florida-school-shooting/ fl-florida-school-shooting-school-board-contempt-20180807-story.html.

23　Broward County Public Schools, "SBBC Meeting 8-7-18," https://becon.eduvi-sion.tv/Default.aspx?q=d0F7qPKKlcfmtjfULqo9AQ%253d%253d.

24　"Superintendent Faces Criticism as Parkland Students Return to School," CBS News, August 17, 2018, https://www.cbsnews.com/news/marjory-stoneman -douglas-high-school-robert-runcie-broward-county-superintendent-fac-es-criticism/.

25　Lisa Miller, "David Hogg, After Parkland," *New York*, August 19, 2018, http:// nymag.com/intelligencer/2018/08/david-hogg-is-taking-his-gap-year-at-the-barricades.html.

26　A full recording of the press conference can be found on Cameron Kasky's Twitter account: https://twitter.com/cameron_kasky/status/1027593685691772928.

27　Ibid.

Chapter 16

1 Video on file with authors.

2 Facebook, https://www.facebook.com/MendelsonPhD/videos/217243921282
   9902/.

3 Scott Travis, "Cops Called as School Board Candidates Clash at Polling Sites,"
   Sun Sentinel, August 25, 2018, https://www.sun-sentinel.com/local/broward/
   parkland/florida-school-shooting/fl-broward-school-election-nasty-cam-
   paigns-20180824-story.html.

4 Tom Lauder, "Sister of Slain MSD Coach Aaron Feis Claims Verbally
   Attacked By Husband of Broward School Board Member Laurie Rich Levinson," Red Broward, August 21, 2018, https://redbroward.com/2018/08/21/
   sister-of-slain-msd-coach-aaron-feis-claims-verbally-attacked-by-husband-
   of-broward-school-board-member-laurie-rich-levinson/.

5 Ibid.

6 During the November 2018 election, the incompetence and potential corruption of Broward County Elections Supervisor Brenda Snipes became national
   news, as she continued to "find" Democrat votes for a week after the election.
   After the 2016 Democratic primary, a statistical analysis commissioned by
   progressive Democrat Tim Canova determined that his loss in a House primary
   in 2016 to the former Democratic National Committee chairwoman, Rep.
   Debbie Wasserman Schultz, contained "implausible statistical irregularities."
   Canova sued Snipes in 2017 for access to the ballots. But she illegally destroyed
   them. The Florida Republican Party sued her in 2018, alleging that she opened
   thousands of early voting and absentee ballots in secret and may have simply
   tossed out Republican votes. A judge issued an injunction ordering that she
   not open any ballots in secret. On August 28, the day of the school board election, she appealed that injunction and opened ballots in secret anyway. Months
   after the school board election, Andy received a call from deputies informing
   him that for the first time they'd ever seen, Sheriff Scott Israel let Snipes's elections officials into the prisons in order to register as many (Democrat) voters
   as possible. They even went into solitary to register 18-1958, who was not yet a
   convicted felon, to vote. (When Snipes was asked about the criticism she faced,
   she said it was "probably" motivated by racism. NBC News later ran a story
   suggesting that criticism of Snipes was racist.)

7 Sources for preceding footnote: Anthony Man and Tonya Alanez, "After
   a Bumpy Day of Missing Ballots, Troubled Broward Recount Put on
   Ice Until the Morning," *Sun Sentinel*, November 17, 2018, https://www.
   sun-sentinel.com/news/politics/fl-ne-broward-manual-recount-agri-
   culture-commissioner-20181117-story.html; Jerry Ianelli, "Tim Canova
   Spreads Study Claiming Election May Have Been 'Manipulated,'" *Miami
   New Times*, October 24, 2016, https://www.miaminewtimes.com/news/
   tim-canova-spreads-study-claiming-election-may-have-been-manip-
   ulated-8872979; Larry Barszweski, "Broward Elections Supervisor
   Illegally Destroyed Ballots in Wasserman Schultz Race, Judge Rules," *Sun
   Sentinel*, May 14, 2018, https://www.sun-sentinel.com/local/broward/

fl-sb-broward-elections-supervisor-broke-law-snipes-canova-20180514-story.html; Marc Caputo, "Judge Sides With Florida GOP in Absentee Ballot Dispute with Broward County," *Politico,* August 13, 2018, https://www.politico.com/states/florida/story/2018/08/13/judge-sides-with-florida-gop-in-absentee-ballot-dispute-with-broward-county-555553; Marc Caputo, "Florida GOP Chairman Accuses Broward Election Chief of 'Shenanigans' in Absentee Ballot Court Fight," *Politico,* August 28, 2018, https://www.politico.com/states/florida/story/2018/08/28/florida-gop-chairman-accuses-broward-election-chief-of-shenanigans-in-absentee-ballot-court-fight-582745; Robert Gearty, "Parkland School Shooter Registered to Vote While in Jail, Outraging Victim's Father," Fox News, November 10, 2018, https://www.foxnews.com/us/parkland-school-shooter-registered-to-vote-while-in-jail-outraging-victims-father; David Smith, "Florida Official Brenda Snipes: Racism 'Probably' A Factor in Attacks Against Me," *The Guardian,* November 17, 2018, https://www.theguardian.com/us-news/2018/nov/17/brenda-snipes-florida-election-recount-senate; Janell Ross, "How Brenda Snipes and Other Black Election Workers Got Falsely Targeted by Trump," NBC News, November 24, 2018, https://www.nbcnews.com/news/nbcblk/how-brenda-snipes-other-black-election-workers-got-falsely-targeted-n939661.

8   A copy of this e-mail can be viewed on Twitter: https://twitter.com/TimWSternberg/status/1039674852268011520.

Acknowledgments

Andy

I would like to thank everyone on our team. All of these people were totally new, and they became both family and fellow warriors in the common cause to try to make something good come out of it. Max Eden flew down here for a scoop and ended up becoming like a brother, devoting eight months of his life to the fight for answers and justice. Kenny Preston messaged me on Facebook and became almost like another son to me. Kimberly Krawczyk was one of the few teachers who wanted to learn and expose everything. Because she didn't give a shit whether she got fired for trying to do the right thing. Royer Borges and I almost share the same soul because of what happened to our children. Timothy Sternberg devoted his gentle and sensitive soul to trying to help expose these people. Richard Mendelson became almost a twin brother to me during the campaign. It's hard to imagine how anyone else could have worked harder. Without all of my new family, this story would not have been possible. I hope that even if what we did here couldn't fix things in Broward, the example set by all of you in this book can make something good come out of what happened for other places.

My lawyer, David Brill, has become another new brother. He isn't really featured much in the book, so I owe him an outsized acknowledgment. David is leading the wrongful death lawsuits against those responsible for Meadow's murder. I had always hated lawyers and didn't like how lawsuit-happy our country can be. I wanted to think that we could fix enough of our problems and have accountability through the democratic process. But after I realized that few people in Broward gave a shit, I also realized what an essential service lawyers like David provide to our country. David has also helped moderate me a bit politically. He's an old-fashioned moderate Democrat who gets it: these liberal, politically correct discipline policies prioritize a smug set of self-righteous and self-interested bureaucrats while screwing over our next generation. I hope that Democrats across America are still more like him and less like the morally challenged leadership of Broward County.

I also owe immense gratitude to everyone who helped out with the campaign, especially my core group of volunteers and supporters: Ray and Joanna Feis, Cathy and Candace Lerman, Joe and Lisa Valko, John Daly, Brandon Jeanneret, Mechelle Boyle, Bob Sutton, Sara Betzazel, Erin DeSantis Kneer, Nathalie Adams, Jeanne Kacprzak, Tom Jones, Alex Arreaza, Christian Rowell, Gurmeet Matharu, Steven Brown, Diana Taub. They were the core of my campaign—my extended family. For the two hundred others I don't have the space to name, please know how grateful I am.

Last but definitely most, my sons Huck and Hunter have been pillars of support. I can't express my feelings in words, so I won't even try. And my wife, Julie...you are a rock of kindness, warmth, and compassion, and I can't imagine how I could have done any of this without you.

Max

I also owe a deep debt of gratitude to all of the above whom Andy has named. And to Andy, who opened his home and his heart to me as we joined forces to achieve the mission of exposing everything so that the country could see it and understand.

I'd also like to thank our agent, Thomas Flannery Jr., whose diligence and patience helped shepherd this project from conception to publication, as well as Lee Habeeb, who helped connect me to Tom and the team at AGI Vigliano. David Bernstein at Post Hill Press was an invaluable thought partner on this project, which he has strengthened in so many ways.

ACKNOWLEDGMENTS

Most everything I know about education and much of what I know about writing I learned from my former boss and mentor, Frederick M. Hess, at the American Enterprise Institute, for whose steady support I am grateful. This book has been immeasurably improved by my eagle-eyed, crackerjack editor and close friend Jenn Hatfield.

My father and mother have both been extremely supportive and patient with me throughout this project (not to mention my life). And I do not know how I could have helped write this book without the shrewd editorial judgment and enduring patience of Amber Todoroff.